To

From

Originally Published in English in South Africa by
Struik Christian Media under the title: *All Things New Devotional*

Written by Cherie Hill
Designed by Struik Christian Media
Artwork by Annabelle Grobler
Scripture quotations are taken from the *Holy Bible*, New Living Translation, copyright © 1996, 2004,
2015 by Tyndale House Foundation. Used by permission of Tyndale House Publishers, Inc., Carol
Stream, Illinois 60188. All rights reserved.
Scripture taken from the New King James Version,® copyright © 1982 by Thomas Nelson, Inc.
Used by permission. All rights reserved.
Scripture taken from the Holy Bible, New International Version,® NIV.® Copyright © 1973, 1978,
1984, 2011 by Biblica, Inc.® Used by permission. All rights reserved worldwide.
ISBN 978-1-4964-1999-6
Printed in China

22	21	20	19	18	17	16
7	6	5	4	3	2	1

Inspire

All
things
New

Creative coloring & journaling
365 Day Devotional

Cherie Hill

Dear Reader

Life brings about circumstances that tempt our faith to doubt. But when we continually seek God, constantly rely on His promises, and trust Him no matter what, we're going to see God's miracles in our lives in more ways than we can count. And when today's troubles threaten tomorrow's hope, God tends to show up right when we need Him—not a moment too soon, but never too late.

The constant battle of faith is that we want to trust God, but we find ourselves in the midst of our struggles questioning God and feeling hopeless, even as we cling to His promises. And that's the place of surrender—when we have no other option, no other place to look except up. Our struggles drive us toward our faith, and that's the place God wants us to be continually—at His feet.

All Things New will take you not only into the presence of God but into the depths of your faith daily. And through each devotion you'll find new hope to trust God in every area of your life. With each new day, God has promises for you. Yes, for you. Be prepared to hear His voice and enter into His presence with an open heart that is ready to be transformed. Let each and every word sink deep within your soul, and be determined to trust God in every area of your life. And get ready to see God's glory as He will make "all things new" in every way you need Him to.

Blessings,
Cherie

Contents

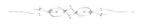

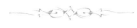

Confident Trust

God has promised that He will deliver you and that you will share in His glory.

In what ways are you struggling to trust God? The smaller issues may seem easy to trust Him on, but the bigger ones tend to leave room for doubt—doubt in His sovereignty, His love for you, even His very existence. Your life situations will call you to walk upon the water, but there is nothing to fear. God oversees every detail of your life, and He is God Almighty, the God of the impossible. Know that, even as your heart is breaking, as life appears to be unraveling, the Lord is with you to deliver you from all that threatens to overcome you. You can trust Him completely.

Psalm 24:1–10; Psalm 34:18, 19; Psalm 40:3;
Psalm 47:7–9; Psalm 48:1; Psalm 121:5–8;
John 6:37; Romans 8:16–18

Though fear threatens my faith,
I will trust in You, O Lord, completely.
I lift You up above my circumstances and
will confidently trust in You to deliver me,
giving me grace to share in Your glory.

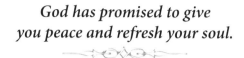

Resting in God's Peace

***God has promised to give
you peace and refresh your soul.***

God has promised you a constant peace, even in the midst of the chaos of life. It's a peace that goes beyond your circumstances and enables you to rest in Him as you continue to trust in His sovereign, victorious hand. The peace He offers is supernatural— His power at work in and through you to strengthen you when you are weary and give you hope when you are helpless. When you are struggling in faith, unsure of what the future holds, fearful and overwhelmed, know that you can cling to God's promises. Seek Him in all you say and do, allowing the Spirit to uphold you and God's grace to sustain you. Allow God to do what only He can do. All He wants is your faith, which opens His heart and moves His hand to work in the miraculous ways you need Him to.

Psalm 19:14; Psalm 27:5; Psalm 27:10, 13, 14;
Psalm 60:11, 12; Psalm 119:76, 77; Proverbs 12:25;
Isaiah 54:13, 14; Isaiah 58:11; Isaiah 61:1; Matthew 11:28

*Almighty God, I thank You for Your gift of peace.
I will rest in You and trust in Your faithfulness
at all times and in all ways.*

Standing Strong in Faith

If you will have faith,
God has promised to be faithful.

$\mathcal{I}$f your faith is depending on the faithfulness of God, there is no reason to doubt what you cannot see. He is always true to His Word. There will always be challenges and circumstances in your life that are beyond your control, but they are never beyond God's control. In moments when all hope seems gone, put your hope in God alone—waiting patiently, yet confidently. Choose to believe in His promises to you instead of relying on your feelings and emotions to determine the state of your faith. When you're weak and weary, turn immediately to God in prayer, and He will give you peace and strengthen you, guarding you in all your ways.

John 3:14, 15; Romans 5:1, 2; Galatians 2:20;
Philippians 4:6, 7; Colossians 3:16; 2 Thessalonians 3:3;
Hebrews 11:1–3; Hebrews 11:6; Titus 2:12, 13

Lord God, help me to stand strong
in my faith regardless of what lies before me—
relying on Your hope, guarded by Your peace.

Trusting in God's Power

***God has promised to protect you and
bless you with His presence, power, and peace.***

Often life's circumstances will take you into unknown territory. You have so many questions, and too few answers. But you can rest in the knowledge that you know the One who holds your future and who promises that it is full of hope. When you're fearful of what tomorrow might bring, remember that God has only given you enough grace for today. His grace will be sufficient in the moment you need it. He has promised He can do the impossible while assuring you that He will fill you with His peace, which surpasses all your understanding. Nothing is too difficult for God, and everything is possible if you'll continue to trust Him, walking by faith and never just by sight.

Psalm 3:1–8; Psalm 11:1–7; Psalm 18:28–30; Psalm 22:3, 4;
Psalm 56:3, 4; Psalm 56:11, 12; Psalm 62:8; Psalm 91:4; Psalm 125:1–5

*Heavenly Father, thank You for always being with me, for never
leaving me nor forsaking me. Help me to fully trust and rest in You.*

Hoping in God's Faithfulness

Put your hope in God because He is always
faithful and His compassion never fails.

It's easy to be consumed by the worries of life. When the relationship isn't working out, the diagnosis wasn't what you expected, and what you owe is far more than you earn, it's easy to become desperate. Yet it's in those moments that you can trust God the most. Be strong and take heart, let nothing move you, and stand firm in your faith. He will give you hope. He is the anchor for your soul to keep you at peace, even amid the chaos. Though you're in deep water, God's mighty hand can pull you out. Though He seems to be taking a long time to show up, keep waiting and praying, expecting Him to be faithful to His Word. Trust in His great love for you.

Psalm 27:13, 14; Psalm 130:5, 6; Lamentations 3:22–25;
Zephaniah 3:5; 2 Corinthians 4:8–11; 2 Corinthians 4:17, 18;
2 Corinthians 5:1; Hebrews 6:19; Hebrews 10:23;
Hebrews 10:35, 36

Lord God in You I will wait and put my trust.
I will not fear but will rely on Your love to
save me. You alone are my hope.

Joy in the Lord

***God promises to renew your spirit
as you look to Him for your source of joy.***

*J*oy won't come from what you have or through obtaining what you don't have; the joy that is everlasting can come only from peace with God. That is what refreshes and renews your soul. It's easy to get caught up in experiential faith. We tend to want the blessings and answered prayers so that we *feel* joyful. But that's not the way it works. We're to come before God with thanksgiving, with humble expectations that He is faithful and that we can find joy in Him regardless of our circumstances. When all hope seems gone, we must place our hope in God and leave the details to Him. Faith is what enables you to be satisfied completely with God's unfailing love and to sing for joy and be glad each and every day.

Psalm 51:10, 11; Psalm 62:3–5; Psalm 90:14; Psalm 95:2; Psalm 118:24;
Proverbs 15:13; Luke 15:7; John 15:11, 12; Romans 14:17

Heavenly Father, I will rejoice in You continually—for all that You are, all that You've done, and all that You have yet to do. You are my joy and my strength.

Firm in Faith

Stand firm in your faith,
for God is faithful and He is with you.

There will be days and long, long nights where all you have to hold on to is your faith. One day, everyone and everything may let you down, but God never will. Your hope is found in God's promises to you. Each promise will build your faith and give you strength to take one more step in trusting God, being courageous and not afraid. There's no need to be discouraged. You can stand firm in knowing that God has given you His Word. Hold on to the hope God gives you and do not be moved by your circumstances. In a moment, the faith you've walked by will suddenly gain sight.

Joshua 1:9; Luke 1:37; 1 Corinthians 15:58; 2 Corinthians 5:7;
Ephesians 6:15, 16; Hebrews 10:23; Jude 3; Jude 21, 22; Jude 24, 25

Lord, I will hold on to my faith in You, trusting You regardless
of my circumstances, knowing that You are with me always.

Rich in Mercy

God's love knows no bounds;
His grace trumps your sins.

Our failures can overtake us with such shame and sorrow that we allow them to define us instead of allowing God's grace to rescue us. We feel so undeserving, so unworthy of such a love that we hide from God instead of running to Him. We should rejoice that God's love does not treat us in the way we deserve to be treated according to our sins. He repays us with mercy and love. His grace is greater than any of our sins. There may be discipline, turning you back to the path of righteousness, but God's mercy always wins out. You are in God's hands. Simply praise Him, and He'll give you rest from your burdens and hope through your hurting.

Psalm 55:22; Psalm 103:10–12; John 12:25;
Colossians 3:2; 1 Timothy 6:17–19; 1 Peter 2:9

Heavenly Father, how great is Your love and mercy.
I praise You and thank You that Your grace is always sufficient for me.

Safe in the Shadow

**There is nothing to fear because God has
promised to be your refuge and strength.**

*G*od has promised "Here on earth you will have many trials and sorrows"—you can count on it. But just because the world is separated from God by sin doesn't mean we are; through His grace and mercy, we are saved by faith. And it's through faith that we are able to walk through circumstances with courage and strength that are given to us by His Spirit, enabling us to be at peace and have hope in the most dreadful situations. Don't allow fear to get the best of you. God's power and protection have no bounds. There is nothing that God cannot do, and if God is for you, who dare be against you? Simply rest in the shadow of the Almighty's wings, and never allow fear to stand between you and God's promises for you.

Psalm 17:8; Psalm 23:4; Psalm 27:5; Psalm 56:8, 11;
Psalm 62:5–7; Isaiah 43:2; Jeremiah 17:17

*Lord God, I will not fear.
I know You are with me to protect me,
to deliver me from evil.*

Growing in God

God has promised that if you rely on Him,
He will be all you need.

We tend to believe we need to do it on our own, that somehow God has enough to handle without tending to our petty problems, but we've got it all wrong. God's way of making us perfect and complete is bringing us to a place where we are utterly dependent upon Him. The more we need Him, the more we come to know Him and see His power, presence, protection, and provision in our lives in greater ways than we can possibly imagine. His Word daily feeds us if we meditate upon it day and night as we've been commanded. His promises give us what we need to grow in Him, building our faith and supplying us with all the grace we need.

Joshua 1:8; Psalm 32:8; Psalm 46:1–3;
Psalm 63:1, 2, 5–7; Psalm 107:5–7; Psalm 111:3, 4;
Isaiah 30:15; Isaiah 41:10; Isaiah 65:24; Matthew 11:28–30;
John 15:5; 2 Corinthians 1:9, 10; 2 Corinthians 5:6, 7;
2 Timothy 1:7, 9

Lord, help me to grow in You.
Thank You for Your boundless grace that is
always sufficient, giving me all I need.

33

Power in Prayer

When you pray, God has promised to hear you and answer you.

When we don't get immediate answers to our prayers, we're tempted to doubt that God cares, and we question if He's even there. But He's promised to hear every cry, bottle every tear, and answer us within His perfect love and perfect will. He has promised not only to hear you and answer you, but also to guard you and deliver you from the depths. He has promised to pour out His mercy onto you when you come to Him and to strengthen you in your weakness. Great is His faithfulness. Don't give up just because the circumstances of your life are pressuring you to give in. God's love and grace triumph over all your troubles, and He has promised to always be a ready help in times of trouble.

Job 22:27, 28; Psalm 55:17; Psalm 86:6, 7; Matthew 6:5, 6;
Luke 18:1; 1 Timothy 6:17–19; Hebrews 4:16; James 1:6

Thank you, Almighty God, for always hearing me when I pray to You. I will wait in patient expectation, knowing that Your answers are out of Your great love for me.

Don't Lose Heart

Do not lose heart; God is able to do
more than you can hope for or imagine.

*G*od has promised that in this world we will have trouble. But we don't have to go through it alone. And we can go through it with the hope, strength, and peace that God provides. When the whole world seems to be against you, when you're struggling to even have faith for the moment, draw close to God and He will draw near to you. In His presence, there is grace sufficient for all that you need. Don't give in to hopelessness, for hope is never gone when you're trusting God for the final outcome. And God has promised that He will deliver you, and you will gain the victory if you do not lose heart.

Psalm 57:7; Psalm 60:12; Psalm 128:6; 2 Corinthians 4:16; Ephesians 4:22–24

Heavenly Father, I am in awe of Your great love for me.
I will wait with patient expectation of Your deliverance
and find my strength in Your promises.

Continuous Joy

Praise God continuously, thank Him for all He has done and all He has yet to do . . . He has promised that His joy will be your strength.

There will be times when you will struggle to be thankful. Bills are due, relationships are broken, life will seem like it's falling apart, and hope will appear to be gone—but it is not. You need God's promises to give you the hope and strength to take one more step of faith . . . and He's always with you, giving you grace for the moments that you need it. Each promise is a testament to His great love for you. Be thankful for His love. At all times, God is faithful to His Word. So rely on it, trust fully in it, and rejoice in Him so that He might refresh your soul.

Joshua 1:8; Nehemiah 8:10; Psalm 19:7, 8, 10; Psalm 42:8; Psalm 119:15, 16; Psalm 119:103

Lord, I give thanks that You are faithful. I rejoice in knowing that You are with me always, and I am overjoyed that Your love and grace are always sufficient.

Your Helper

When you need help, you have the Holy Spirit to lead you, guide you, comfort you, and pray for you when you simply cannot.

When you've exhausted all your resources and grown weary, you suddenly realize that the only place you didn't look for help was God Himself. We so easily forget that He is our ready help in times of trouble. But more than that, we have the Holy Spirit within us, affording us direct access to all of God's wisdom and power. We often allow ourselves to be influenced in our decision making by our emotions and the opinions of others. But God has a plan that we are to follow so that we might experience His very best for our lives. Seek His will. Don't miss out on the blessings He has for you; instead, rely on the Spirit in your faith walk at all times and in all ways.

Luke 12:12; John 14:26; John 16:7–12; Acts 1:4, 5, 7, 8;
Romans 8:11, 16–18, 26, 27; 1 Corinthians 2:11–13;
2 Corinthians 3:5, 6, 17, 18; 2 Peter 1:20, 21; Jude 20, 21

Heavenly Father, thank You for never leaving me alone and for having given me the Holy Spirit to guide me into Your perfect will.

The Test of Faith

Put your hope in God regardless of your circumstances, and God will strengthen you so you are not shaken in the midst of them.

aith requires testing; there's just no way around it. Without trials and tribulations, we would have no need for faith, and we would find God unnecessary. In His great love for us, and to strengthen our relationship with Him, God often allows trials that will test us, causing us to draw near to Him and lean on Him completely. Faith is never easy, but it does make all things possible, and we should praise God for that. We are blessed, even in our trials, that we are able to approach the throne of grace, mercy, and love, and get glimpses of God's glory while here on earth. When life has got you down, just remember to look up!

Deuteronomy 30:16; Job 23:10, 11; Psalm 43:5; Psalm 55:22; Psalm 69:16–18; Psalm 119:2; Proverbs 28:13; James 1:12, 22–24; 1 Peter 4:12, 13, 16; 2 Peter 3:8, 9

Loving Father, I will not fear, for I know that You are with me. I will trust in Your Word and find my hope and strength in You alone.

Walking by Faith

God is true to His Word. You can count on Him to fulfill
His promises in your life . . . just have faith that He will.

At times, life will leave you feeling as though all hope is gone. But hope is never gone when you're trusting in God and relying upon His promises in your life. All it takes is faith that God is true to His Word. It's that simple. Trusting God may take us the long way to obtaining His promises, but, eventually, we will see His glory if we keep walking out our faith in patient expectation. God doesn't ask us to sit idly by in being patient, but to search for Him, to be active in our faith by living our lives according to His Word and all that He has commanded in it. If we seek God and have confidence in what we hope for, assured of what we cannot see, our faith will ultimately gain manifestation.

Exodus 15:26; Matthew 6:33; Luke 1:37; Hebrews 6:12;
Hebrews 10:23; Hebrews 11:1, 6, 11; 2 Peter 1:4–8; 1 John 5:14, 15

God, my Father, thank You for Your promises to me
that fill me with hope in the most hopeless of circumstances.
Help me to trust in You, walking by faith and not by sight.

Seek the Kingdom of God above all else AND live righteously and he will give you everything you need

MATTHEW 6:33

A Little Faith

Having faith in God makes all things possible, so there's no reason to give in to doubt . . . just keep believing in God's promises to you.

When life gets hard—and it will!—the truth will be tainted with your emotional distress. Your feelings and emotions will make you forget what God has promised. It's when you're overwhelmed that you should draw near to God so that He can draw near to you. In His presence, as you call for grace through prayer, you'll come to find that God is closer than you think. He's with you in each and every step of faith you take. He's leading you, guiding you, making a path for you through your brokenness to His blessings. In your moments of doubt, God will uphold you and give you the strength you need to take just one more step of faith. And that's all you need. Trust in His love for you; a little faith is all you need.

Psalm 23:1–4; Psalm 91:2–4; Psalm 121:2, 3;
Psalm 121:5, 7, 8; 2 Corinthians 3:4, 5;
1 John 4:1; Revelation 1:17, 18

*Lord, I thank You for always being
with Me, for never leaving nor forsaking me.
I will look to You always, seeking Your
face as I wait upon Your hand.*

Waiting on God

Trust that God's timing is better than yours,
and know that His miracles in your life will never come late.

God doesn't move according to our timing . . . and that can be frustrating when our demands are not immediately met. We become impatient with God because we feel that time is running out and He might just miss His opportunity to answer us and perform the miracle we so desperately need. As we wait, we begin to doubt. We question whether God is listening at all. We so easily forget His promises. We forget that it's in times of silence that God is working out all things for good, sustaining us, strengthening us as we wait. We can rest assured that if we continue to hope in God, He will fill us with His joy and a level of peace that surpasses all understanding. The question is: Will you trust God, rest in Him, and wait patiently for His amazing grace?

Psalm 27:13, 14; Psalm 37:34; Psalm 130:5, 6;
Proverbs 3:5, 6; Isaiah 30:18; Isaiah 40:31;
Lamentations 3:25; Micah 7:7; Acts 1:4

Heavenly Father, help me to rest as I trust in You.
Fill me with Your peace and joy, and strengthen
my spirit with abundant hope.

When You're Disappointed

God knows your sorrows. Trust that although things don't appear to be working out, God has promised to grant you the desires of your heart.

*L*ife is often disappointing. We have expectations for our lives that simply don't match up with God's. The problem is that our expectations fall short of God's . . . not the other way around. God has more blessings lined up for us than we can comprehend, yet we still question His ways. Although He could bless us in the here and now, in the moment we want and in the way we want, He's doing something more, something miraculous. He's taking you from glory to glory. He's transforming your heart, strengthening your spirit, and preparing you for greater blessings than the one you think you've lost. Take hold of your faith and put your hope in God.

Exodus 33:14; Psalm 3:4, 5; Psalm 27:14; Psalm 130:6;
Isaiah 40:31; Hebrews 6:15; James 1:2–4; James 5:7, 8

Lord, I need You. Overwhelm me with Your mercy and grace.
Help me to trust in You when life doesn't go according to my plans.
Strengthen my spirit to desire only that my life go according to Your plans.

Wait FOR THE LORD be STRONG

PSALM 27:14

The Price Was Paid

Live daily in the freedom of being saved by grace;
it's through faith alone that you have eternal life.

No one is perfect, so don't think you have to be in order to receive God's love and grace. All of us make mistakes, of varying scale and impact, yet God freely forgives through the sacrifice of Christ. Because of His great love for you, you are able to come boldly to His throne of grace and have a personal, intimate relationship with the One true God. There is no greater joy than knowing you can commune freely with God, talk to Him, know that He's heard you, and wait in expectation of His answer. The price has been paid for you; you are released from the burden of sin, and that alone is reason to rejoice in the Lord.

Matthew 10:32; John 1:12; John 3:16; John 3:17; John 3:36;
Romans 5:12; Romans 3:23, 24; Romans 5:8; Romans 6:23; Romans 10:8–10;
1 Corinthians 15:1–4; Ephesians 2:8, 9; 1 John 5:11–13; Revelation 3:20

Thank you, God, for the sacrifice, the innocent blood
shed on my behalf so that I can be free from the burden of sin.
Truly, there is no greater gift, no greater love, and I rejoice in You.

A Life of Praise

When you need strength, look to God; He is worthy to be praised for all He has done in your life and all He has yet to do.

All too often, we get busy in life and forget who keeps our world in motion and gives us the life we have. Yet praise opens the door of prayer; that's why we are told to "enter His gates with thanksgiving" and to "go into his courts with praise." No matter our circumstances, we are to praise God for the past, present, and future, assured of His great love and confident in His faithfulness. Don't allow the troubles of life to steal your joy . . . your joy is in the Lord, not in your circumstances. There will be good times and bad times, but through it all, God is there, He is fully aware, and He is working all things together for good. Praise Him for that alone, and watch your heart move His hand.

Psalm 29:1, 2; Psalm 63:4, 5; Psalm 95:6, 7;
Psalm 96:9; Psalm 119:2, 10; Jeremiah 29:12, 13;
John 4:23, 24; 1 Chronicles 16:11, 12

Heavenly Father, I praise You for all You've done and all You are going to do. Regardless of my feelings, no matter my circumstances, I will raise You up above all things.

Search for the Lord and for his STRENGTH
1 Chronicles 16:11

Above All Things

If you obey God, your faith will have a firm foundation, so when the troubles of life come crashing in, you will not be overcome.

*I*t's not enough to just know God and know His Word. You have to live your faith and breathe it, allowing it to become everything that you are. It's about standing upon the truth that God has given you and making His Word, the Bible, your instruction book for life. All too often, our faith is shaken because we're just not sure if we believe what God has promised. Doubt gets the best of us because fear comes flooding in and we fall into despair. But if we continually seek God first, His truth will prevail every time. We must believe what we know; we must do as God has commanded us to do, even when it doesn't make sense to us and we're not sure we're moving in the right direction. If we follow God's instructions in our lives, He has promised the blessings will follow.

Luke 6:47–49; Luke 16:10; John 14:15;
Acts 5:29; Hebrews 10:38; Hebrews 12:9, 10;
James 1:22; 1 John 2:17

Lord God, I pray that Your Word will permeate my soul and consume my spirit with Your love, mercy, and grace. Help me to live in obedience to Your Word in every area of my life.

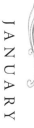

Seeking God

In all things, in all ways, seek God first.
He is the answer to every problem. He is all you need.

Why do we tend to seek God only after we've exhausted ourselves trying to solve our problems our own way, when we know that God's way is always the best way? It's because we try desperately to rely on our own understanding instead of trusting God with all our hearts. We so easily forget that God keeps the entire universe in motion . . . surely He can keep our lives from falling apart. We so quickly forget the miracles He's performed, the ways that He's answered our prayers in the past. Somehow we lose sight of God's sovereignty, and we search for help outside of God, as if He were not enough. God isn't playing hide-and-seek. If you need Him, He is there. He has promised that if you seek Him, you will find Him, and He will strengthen you and deliver you.

Psalm 27:10; Psalm 34:4; Psalm 63:1; Proverbs 8:17; Proverbs 14:12;
Romans 10:9; 1 Chronicles 16:11, 12; 1 Thessalonians 5:15; 1 Timothy 4:13

Lord God, I will earnestly seek You, looking to You alone for answers, pursuing Your peace, and resting in Your promises to strengthen and deliver me.

Simple Praise

When you're not sure what to do,
simply praise God . . . that changes everything.

We rarely remember to simply praise God. We wait to experience something and then we thank God for the blessing of our faith taking sight. But we might see God's hand more readily if we simply praise Him before He moves His hand. He simply wants our hearts; it's our relationship with Him that brings us closer to His blessings and nearer to Him in every way. There will be moments when you're simply not sure what to do. You don't know if God is listening, not sure if He cares. All you'll be able to do is simply praise Him . . . and that's the best thing to do when you don't know what to do.

Psalm 48:1; Psalm 57:7–9; Psalm 63:3–5;
Psalm 69:30; Psalm 106:1, 2; Psalm 113:1–3;
Psalm 146:1, 2; Psalm 149:1; James 1:17

Heavenly Father, awaken my soul
to praise You continually. Thank You for
every good and perfect gift in my life.

Praying for God's Will

***When you're lost and feeling down, look up, draw near
to God in prayer, and wait patiently and expectantly.***

There will be more times in life than you'd like where you feel lost, unsure of which direction to take, and you'll desperately want God to fulfill the desires of your heart. But either the lack of God's immediate answer or receiving the answer you weren't hoping for makes you realize that your faith is being tested. God needs us to pray from our hearts but fully trust in His. His ways might not make sense, but we're supposed to "not depend on [our] own understanding." Your faith will be tested, but know that God will enable your faith to go through the fire and come forth as gold. God hears you, and He'll answer in His perfect way, in His perfect time, and in a way that is best according to His perfect love for you.

Psalm 55:17; Psalm 119:15, 16; Psalm 119:105; Psalm 119:165;
Proverbs 15:29; Daniel 6:10; Mark 4:20; Romans 10:17

*Lord God, I will cry out to You in my distress, knowing that You hear me
and will answer my prayers out of Your great and perfect love for me.*

Trusting God's Power

***Remain steadfast in trusting God. He has promised
to be your strength and to give you perfect peace.***

*O*ur fears and worries can steal our joy if we let
them. When we're struggling with the present and
unsure of our future, we tend to give in to despair. We
fail to trust God when our circumstances overwhelm us
beyond our ability to endure. Yet even in those moments
where all hope seems lost, God is there, securing our
hearts and strengthening our spirits. Even when we
have no reason to be at peace, God gives us a peace that
surpasses all understanding. So don't fear bad news;
don't worry about tomorrow—or today. God's grace is
sufficient for all that you need. Keep focused on God
and His promises to you. His help is on the way.

Psalm 71:1, 5, 8; Psalm 112:7, 8; Psalm 118:6, 8;
Isaiah 12:2; Isaiah 26:3, 4; Jude 20, 21

*Lord God, help me to walk by faith and
trust You completely. In my weakness, be my
strength and help me to keep my eyes upon
You when I don't know what else to do.*

Living with Purpose

There is no greater joy than living your life for the purposes of God; pray continually to be used by Him.

We tend to experience conflict between what we want in our lives and what God wants for us. We have an agenda, and often we're not sure that we can fit God's calling for our lives into it. We're afraid we might miss out on the best things in life if we set our plans aside and embrace God's. But nothing could be further from the truth. God has created you to have a specific purpose, to accomplish things that have been designed for you alone. If you miss out on hearing His voice and embracing His plans for your life, you will miss out on the fullness of the joy He intends you to have. Don't be afraid to follow the path God has clearly laid out before you. He is leading you into His perfect blessings for your life.

Psalm 5:3; Psalm 34:4; Psalm 104:33, 34; Proverbs 3:5; Isaiah 41:11–13;
Romans 8:1, 2; 1 Peter 4:10, 11; 1 John 2:28; 1 John 4:8

Heavenly Father, thank You for always hearing me. I will pray for my desires and wait expectantly for Your will, embracing it fully and resting in Your joy.

Trust in the LORD with all your heart

Proverbs 3:5

Praying for One Another

God has called you to pray for others. It's in that act of faith that you'll most powerfully see God using your life and witness countless miracles.

It is undeniable that prayer changes things—this alone should be our greatest indication that God is with us, at work in our lives and completely sovereign. Knowing that the God of the universe hears our every cry for mercy, collects and bottles every tear, and accepts every entreaty we've ever prayed or will pray in the future should drive us to our knees continually and without reservation. Though answers might not come right away, we can trust in God's promises that He will answer us. And we should wait expectantly for God to do the impossible, never giving up until our faith takes sight. If you want blessings in your own life and to be a blessing to someone else . . . pray for them.

Psalm 6:8, 9; Psalm 86:6, 7; Jeremiah 32:27; Ephesians 6:17, 18; Philippians 2:5;
1 Thessalonians 5:16–18; 1 Peter 3:12, 13; 1 John 4:4; 1 John 5:14, 15

I will pray continually and expectantly to You, O God. I will enter Your gates with thanksgiving, praising You constantly for Your amazing grace.

Life Out of Control

Life is never out of control when
you're trusting in the God who is in control.

*L*ife may take you in many directions, but God is there to make a way and guide you into His will. Having control over your troubles starts with keeping your heart from being troubled. There is much that you cannot control in life, but you can control your heart. It's God's Word that will give you peace and strength to walk in the faith He's called you to . . . trusting in His sovereignty and love.

Psalm 46:1; John 14:1–3; John 16:33;
Romans 10:10; Philippians 4:6; 1 John 5:4

Lord God, I look to You for all things. Though life appears
to be out of control, I will trust that You are always sovereign,
a ready help in times of trouble, the One who gives victory.

In Brokenness

God is close to the brokenhearted; know that He has promised
He is with you and will turn your mourning into joy.

When our hearts are breaking, our emotions take over and we feel as though we're all alone in our sorrow and pain. But God is there. We might not feel Him, but we have the Spirit to give us the strength we need in our weakness so that we will have faith that He is always with us. God hears your cries for help, He feels your pain, and He has a plan to bind up your heart and heal you from the inside out. Though His mercy might not bring immediate healing, it is sure to come. Trust that God is holding on to you even when you feel like letting go of Him. Simply draw near to Him when you're hurting and know that His grace will be sufficient. Nothing can separate you from His love.

Psalm 9:9, 10; Psalm 34:18, 19; Psalm 147:3; Proverbs 16:9, 33;
Isaiah 33:10; Isaiah 58:11; Matthew 11:28, 29

Thank You, Lord, that You are with me to comfort me in my pain, to strengthen me in my weakness, and to love me unconditionally when my heart is breaking.

Serious Illness

There is nothing for you to fear, not even death. God is with you and will comfort you in sickness, healing you through His promises.

*T*here is a time to be well and a time for sickness. We live in a fallen world where illness can lead us to places in our faith that we never thought we'd have to experience. When we're weak and unable to see how anything but a miracle will do, God is our comfort. Not only that; He's also our healer, our Great Physician who is able to do the impossible. And that's where our faith and hope must lie . . . in God alone. In Him, we can find peace and rest for our souls so that He can do what only He can do. He can heal you; believe that He can and wait upon His healing touch so that you might be an encouragement to others.

Psalm 23:4; Psalm 48:14; Psalm 49:15; Psalm 77:10–14;
Psalm 146:2; Jeremiah 17:14; 2 Corinthians 5:1

*Heavenly Father, I come to You for comfort and peace in my affliction.
Have mercy upon me and heal me according to Your promises.*

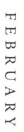

Financial Problems

When you're in need, God is all you need. He is with you to help you and is a ready help in times of trouble.

$\mathcal{S}$ometimes you might unexpectedly find yourself with little to survive on. Life has taken some turns you didn't anticipate, and the lack of finances overwhelms you in ways you're not sure you can get through. But even in these times, God is there. He cares and He can help you in supernatural ways that you do not expect. God knows every single one of your burdens and needs. Just lift your eyes up to Him, pray continually, and trust Him completely. Go ahead and give thanks to Him for His love for you, for His grace that will deliver you from your distress, and simply for who He is. Know that His goodness and mercy will follow you all the days of your life, and wait upon Him expectantly.

Psalm 57:7–9; Psalm 63:3, 4; Psalm 122:6; Psalm 136:1–4; Psalm 149:5, 6; Proverbs 11:28; Proverbs 13:18; Matthew 4:2–4

Lord God, I am overwhelmed. I am uncertain of the future, unable to know what today holds. Distress consumes me and I need Your deliverance. Please comfort me with Your peace and assurance that everything will work out for me.

Resting in God's Protection

You can have peace because God is with you. He has promised to protect you and give you rest, so there is nothing to fear.

All too often, your fear can overcome your faith. But you should know that whatever circumstances you're facing, God is with you and will either make a way through them or provide a way of escape. There is no reason to worry because there is nothing that God cannot do. If you truly believe this, if you're placing all of your trust in God, you can rest assured . . . you can sleep in peace, knowing that God has everything under control and that there's nothing to fear. You may be tempted to worry, things in life may be overwhelming and even frightening, but you can find comfort in God's promises to you as you dwell in the safety that He provides.

Psalm 4:8; Psalm 20:2; Psalm 27:1–5;
Psalm 121:5–8; Psalm 142:1; Proverbs 1:33;
Isaiah 43:2; Isaiah 54:17; 2 Thessalonians 3:3

*Lord, I thank You that I can lie down
and sleep, resting because of Your promise
to let me live in safety. I will not fear,
for I know that You are with me.*

Praising God's Goodness

God loves you with a boundless, unfailing love. Praise Him,
knowing that He is the One who rejoices over you.

We don't always feel like praising God. The circumstances of our lives may leave us empty, anxious, and even angry. We wish that faith protected us from the troubles of life, yet it seldom does. What faith does do is give us the assurance that God is with us through it all. There is no greater peace than knowing that the God of the universe is with you. Our deepest faith is displayed when we praise God even through the storms of life, declaring our trust in Him while holding fast to His promises. When you're not sure what lies ahead and are unable to feel God's presence, praise Him anyway, and you'll be powerfully drawn into His presence.

Psalm 34:1; Psalm 50:23; Psalm 56:10; Zephaniah 3:17

Thank You, Lord, for Your grace that consoles me.
I praise You for all that You are. Thank You for loving me without limits.

Offering Encouragement

*God has blessed you in ways that enable you to encourage
the faith of others. Let your light shine for those around you.*

Sometimes it seems as though the pain and sorrows we endure in life are in vain. It rarely feels like God is working all things together for good when we're facing the unthinkable and we're filled with loneliness and despair. But while God is working on your miracles behind the scenes, He's also giving you hope and strength through His promises so that you can be an encouragement to others. God will often ask you to meet the needs of others even when you are in need yourself. And although this doesn't make sense, obeying God without relying on your own understanding will bring about more blessings in your own life than you can count.

Psalm 32:7; Luke 12:32; Romans 12:15, 16; Romans 14:19; Colossians 3:1, 2;
1 Thessalonians 5:11; 2 Thessalonians 3:16; Hebrews 10:24, 25; 1 John 1:7; 1 John 4:9

*Heavenly Father, use my life to encourage others,
to bring hope to the hopeless and shine light in the darkness
as You purify and cleanse me for Your greater purposes.*

Being Confident in God

When you've lost all hope, you can hope in God alone.
He is faithful to His Word, and He will never fail you.

We can easily lose hope when we've placed our hopes in our own expectations for life or we're trusting in our ways instead of God's. And doubt tends to overcome our faith when we're struggling through the troubles of life. But we can find peace and strength in knowing that God is not merely almost sovereign—He's completely sovereign and has everything under control. When we're unsure of what the future holds and finding it difficult to hold on to faith, we can let go of all we're clinging to and just be held by the God who holds the whole world in His hands.

Psalm 71:1, 2, 5; Psalm 118:8; Psalm 121:7, 8;
Matthew 19:26; John 14:18; Philippians 1:3;
James 4:7; 2 Peter 1:2–4; 1 John 5:5

Lord, what great peace I have in knowing that
You are fully in control. I am so thankful that You
will never fail me and never forsake me. You are
my hope, my confident expectation.

Celebrating with Joy

Each and every day is a day the Lord has made, so celebrate with joy the amazing promises God has made to you.

Sometimes we don't feel like praising God. Life's circumstances can stand in the way of our worship as worries get the best of us. But each and every day God is blessing us in ways that we simply cannot see. You will have to step out in faith and worship Him even when things don't seem to be going your way. When life isn't going according to your plan, you can trust that it is always going according to God's. Faith will enable you to have peace in the storms of life and joy in the midst of them. Regardless of what you're facing in life, celebrate your joy in the Lord alone. He has made promises to you that lead to miracles beyond anything you could hope for or imagine.

Psalm 9:1, 2; Psalm 35:27, 28; Psalm 89:1; Psalm 89:15; Psalm 119:16, 27; Psalm 144:5; Proverbs 15:13; Isaiah 25:9; Jeremiah 33:10, 11; 2 Chronicles 29:30

Heavenly Father, I simply rejoice in Your love for me. Thank You for Your promises that give me hope and peace through all the circumstances of my life.

The Blessing of Friendship

God has blessed you with unique gifts
so that you might be a blessing to others.

There is no greater joy than being used by God. He has equipped you with a unique personality and countless spiritual gifts so that He might work in and through you to impact the world around you. If you have not experienced the great joy of being a blessing to others in their time of need, God readily and continually invites you to join Him in creating miracles in the lives of people around you. Come to Him daily in prayer, asking for the strength, wisdom, and ability to open your eyes to the needs around you. He's already got your need covered—trust in this and be willing to say, "Here I am, send me!"

Proverbs 17:17; Ecclesiastes 4:9; Matthew 12:50; John 15:12, 13; 1 Corinthians 12:12;
1 Corinthians 12:26; 1 Corinthians 16:14; Galatians 5:13; Hebrews 13:1, 2

Lord God, I pray that You will use my life mightily in the lives of others.
I want to be a friend, a blessing to those around me, giving all the glory to You.

Forgiven

There is peace and joy in knowing that the price has been paid for your sins. God's love for you is without limits.

God's love for you is the same forgiving love no matter who you are or what you've done. You can leave the past behind and look to a glorious future when you've placed your faith in God and accepted the sacrifice of Christ for the forgiveness of your sins. The price has been paid. There's no need for more sacrifice by living in guilt and shame. God wants you set free through the sacrifice, knowing that nothing can separate you from His love. It's up to you to receive the grace He is giving. And He gives it every day; His mercy is new each and every morning. Live in the joy of knowing that you are forgiven and can live free because Christ died for you.

Psalm 85:2; Romans 8:1, 2;
2 Corinthians 2:10, 11; 2 Thessalonians 3:3;
1 John 1:9; Jude 24, 25; Revelation 3:21

Heavenly Father, thank You for the gift of the Sacrifice. Your love amazes me and consumes me. Help me to live a life worthy of You.

Focusing on God's Love

Nothing can separate you from God's love, so live in that truth.
It's because of His love that you can live each day with joy and peace.

We tend to believe that God is constantly judging our thoughts and behavior and then handing down punishment accordingly. But His Word says something entirely different. His Word promises that nothing can separate us from His love. And we need to live in that truth, knowing that He is *always* our refuge and strength, not just when we're walking in His will. We will make mistakes, we will fail Him, but His love remains. It is unchanging and endures forever. What we must remember is that His grace is for everyone, just as it is for us, so His grace must flow through us into the lives of others. We are God's love in the flesh because we have been forgiven. Thank God for His love today and every day.

Psalm 46:1–3; Psalm 107:5–7; Psalm 111:3, 4;
Isaiah 30:15; Isaiah 41:10, Matthew 11:28–30;
2 Corinthians 5:6, 7; 2 Timothy 1:7, 9; Hebrews 13:5

Lord God, let me be an instrument of Your love.
May Your joy and peace be evident in all I say
and do. I want my life to glorify Your name.

Following God's Light

The world is filled with darkness, but when you live in the Spirit, you are consumed by light and your steps will be certain and sure.

God's Word is your light in a dark world. He promised that you will have trouble in this world. At times it will be hard to see which way to turn, and fear will tempt you to walk away from your faith. But the Spirit within you will give you the strength to keep taking each step, fully trusting God's Word, knowing that His purpose for you is for good. Seek the Lord each and every day. His Word is your lamp, and the Spirit will fill you with light as you believe in God's promises. You will have direction at every turn, peace amid the uncertainty, and God's protection through the darkest valley. Live in the light that God gives, and know that when you follow Him, everything is possible.

Psalm 119:11, 12; Proverbs 6:23;
Mark 9:23; Acts 17:28; Galatians 5:24, 25;
2 Timothy 2:15; James 4:8; 2 John 9

*Lord, I pray that I will always walk
in Your light, illuminating Your love, mercy,
and grace to the world around me.*

Being a Blessing

You are gifted to bring heaven to earth.
Pray that God will make you a blessing to others.

*E*ach day presents countless opportunities for us to give to others and bring glory to God. He has promised to meet each of our needs according to His riches in Christ. In return, we are to allow His grace to flow through us and into the lives of others. Often we are tempted to doubt our ability to give what God is asking of us, but in those moments, we can be certain that God is inviting us to trust Him more and to believe with confidence that He will meet all our needs while we focus on the needs of others. Make sure not to miss out on the opportunities to give that God places before you each day. He is sure to bless you if you serve as His hands and feet.

Psalm 82:3, 4; Proverbs 28:27; Proverbs 31:20; Micah 6:8;
Matthew 10:42; Luke 6:38; Galatians 6:9; 1 Peter 3:9; 1 John 3:16, 17

Heavenly Father, use my life to be a blessing to others, to give freely and unselfishly, knowing that You will bless all that concerns me and my life.

Serving Others

First seek God and His purpose for you, listening carefully for His voice and being determined to walk in His will.

Sometimes it's difficult to see beyond our own needs. The pressures of life can overwhelm and overcome us in an instant. We plead with God to help us, only to find Him asking us to help others. We're forced to trust Him, because we simply don't understand. It's in the moments where we have nothing to give that God works mightily in and through us, and then we witness His power and glory in greater ways than we ever thought possible. God's grace is not only enough; it's more than enough. And it's enough for you and your needs as well as the needs of others. In your weakest moments, let God be your strength, and work to meet the needs of others . . . trusting God to handle yours.

Psalm 138:8; Proverbs 29:25; Luke 16:10–13;
John 13:34, 35; Galatians 5:13; 2 Corinthians 2:14;
2 Corinthians 12:9; Colossians 3:23–25; 1 Peter 4:12, 13

*Lord God, make me an instrument of Your love.
Bring opportunities into my life to serve others,
leading lost lives to Your throne of grace.*

The Lord will work out His plans for my life

PSALM 138:8

Showing God to Others

Jesus is all you need for a godly life; simply surrender each and every day, and others will see Him in you.

You don't need to try to be like Jesus, you don't need to try to impress God . . . you just need to trust Him as you surrender your life to Him. Then His Spirit will do a mighty work in and through you. You were created to bring glory to God. When you live the life God intended for you to live, one of surrender and obedience to Him, you will find true joy and happiness. Don't try harder; just trust more. The Spirit moves and breathes within you, enabling you to do all that you think you can't do. You'll be filled with strength and peace to encourage others, compassion to comfort the brokenhearted, and the resources and wisdom to help others in their desperate times of need. Just let Him live through you. Rest, and let God do the work.

Isaiah 30:1; Mark 4:18–20; Romans 5:1–4;
Ephesians 6:10, 11; 1 Thessalonians 2:4; James 1:19–21, 27;
James 2:18, 22; 1 Peter 1:18; 1 John 1:3; 1 John 2:3, 5

Heavenly Father, I long for Your Spirit to shine in me, giving hope to the hopeless and displaying Your great love to the world around me.

Serving God

There is no greater joy than serving God Almighty.
Faithfully seek Him, and observe the miracles that He will perform.

Each and every day, you must choose whom you will serve—yourself and the world, or God. The temptations to meet our own needs and trust in ourselves and others for provision are countless. It's a daily struggle of faith, but the Spirit will give you the strength you need in your weakness. Pray fervently that God will empower you to faithfully follow Him in all you say and do. Don't hesitate to be obedient. Hold steadfastly to God, conforming to Jesus' example in living and suffering to serve God. If you make serving God your first priority, He promises to honor you and bless you in more ways than you can imagine.

Joshua 24:15; Joshua 24:24; Matthew 4:10;
Luke 3:10, 11; John 12:26; John 13:35;
Galatians 6:4–6, 9; 1 Timothy 6:17–19

Lord, use my life for Your purposes alone.
Let no temptation overcome me, and help me to
be faithful to You in every area of my life.

Facing the Years Ahead

You cannot always know what the future holds, but God does. And He's promised to send you good, so you can live a life filled with hope.

Worry about the future can consume us to the point that we're paralyzed and unable to daily live out our faith. How easily we forget that God has assured us of our future and that there's truly nothing to worry about. If He can secure our lives through salvation for eternity, certainly He can handle the day-to-day issues we face. We can find comfort and peace in the promises God has made to us, assuring us that we have a future and a hope. God has never and will never fail you. He knows the big picture and He will orchestrate every one of your circumstances for good. You simply need to trust that He will. Cling to hope through His promises to you, and then rest in Him completely.

Job 19:25, 26; Psalm 31:14, 15; Psalm 90:10, 12, 14;
Psalm 92:12–15; Proverbs 10:27; Romans 14:7, 8; 1 Corinthians 13:12

Heavenly Father, thank You for the joy in knowing that there is hope for the future. Quiet my heart to live full of peace and contentment.

God's Divine Protection

There is nothing to fear; God has promised to protect you.
Fear only Him, and He will keep you safe.

The world is filled with tragedy, and we can easily be overcome with fear. We reason that if we can't see God, how can He truly protect us in this physical world? But His power reaches beyond the physical world. His power is supernatural, and He reaches into our world in unseen ways until the miracle happens. He works mightily in our circumstances, behind the curtain of our lives. Faith enables us to trust Him, even in the most fearful situations. In the darkest places, He shines light. When you're filled with fear, fall upon your knees . . . God hears your cry for help, and He will be your refuge and your strength. His angels will encamp around you. You are safe in His arms.

Deuteronomy 33:27; Psalm 4:8; Psalm 27:1, 5; Psalm 34:7;
Psalm 91:1, 2; Proverbs 1:33; Isaiah 59:19; Matthew 10:29–31

Lord, thank You for protecting me in every way. I will lie down
and rest, dwelling in Your safety as I confidently trust in You.

Being Content

*God is all you need. Everything required for living out
His perfect will for your life, He will readily provide to you.*

We strive endlessly for those things that we imagine will bring us happiness. We desperately seek out what we believe is best, not realizing we may be passing up the opportunity to receive God's best. His best is what will bring everlasting joy, peace, and happiness that cannot be taken from us. If we surrender our will to His, we will find that in difficult times we can still enjoy life and be filled with contentment. The secret lies in trusting that God will provide all that we need and being thankful for what He gives. If we trust in Him completely, He will make sure we lack nothing.

Psalm 23:1; Psalm 121:5, 8; Isaiah 54:10, 13, 17; Isaiah 58:11; Romans 8:1, 2, 5, 6; 1 Corinthians 2:9;
2 Corinthians 3:5; Philippians 4:11, 12; Colossians 2:10; 1 Timothy 6:6–8

*Heavenly Father, thank You for Your great love. I am content because
You provide me with all I need to live a life of peace and trust in You.*

Discernment

God hears you. Be diligent in seeking Him and listening carefully for His voice. He will always lead and guide you.

Oftentimes we do all the talking to God, questioning if He hears us but seldom giving Him the chance to speak. Our prayers should be filled with thanksgiving and encompassed by a quiet heart. God will always lead and guide us, giving us His wisdom, but we must listen carefully in the quietness, waiting until we hear His voice. We can grow impatient, wanting to move ahead of God simply because He seems not to be listening or is taking too long about answering. But we must trust that God will speak and give us direction if only we wait upon Him. Trust Him. Don't try to understand His ways; just walk in them.

Psalm 119:105; Proverbs 14:12;
Matthew 7:15, 16; 1 Corinthians 14:33; 2 Timothy 1:7;
Titus 1:16; 1 John 4:2, 3; 2 John 7, 9–11; Jude 4

Lord, speak to me and open my heart to listen. Help me to trust You completely, even when I don't understand, and to walk firmly in my faith.

Understanding God's Ways

You can't depend on your own understanding. Faith in God requires you to trust without proof and believe in His promises.

We want to understand, we want things to make sense, but often they just don't. And it's in those moments, when we're forced to walk closely with God, that He takes our faith further than we thought it could go. The key lies in not giving up or giving in to doubt. Faith keeps going, trusting God fully without knowing all the answers, without needing to "see to believe." God just doesn't work that way. If He did, we wouldn't need faith, and we'd have no reason to believe in Him. His desire is that we fully experience His supernatural presence, power, and boundless grace. And in order for us to do that, we have to trust Him even when our questions are not answered. God always gives us the strength to take one more step forward in faith.

Job 32:8; Psalm 25:5; Psalm 119:27, 34, 73, 98, 104, 105, 125; Psalm 147:5; Proverbs 2:6, 7; Proverbs 9:6, 10; Proverbs 16:16, 17; Ecclesiastes 7:25; Isaiah 55:6, 8, 9; James 1:5

Heavenly Father, help me to trust You more. When my faith falters, strengthen me through Your Spirit to believe in all the promises You have made to me.

Seeking God's Sovereignty

God is always in control. There's no such thing as Him being "almost" sovereign. You can trust Him . . . completely.

*O*ften we're tempted to rule over our own lives, leaving God out and then wondering where He is. It's through our faith that we can fully trust that He is always in control, even when it seems as though He's not. Faith doesn't demand to "see" anything, but just trusts that regardless of what we see, God is at work, and nothing can separate us from His love. Faith isn't easy, but it makes all things possible, and that's what we're truly hoping for. We need God to show up, to make Himself known. And if we take one more step in patient expectation, He will!

Genesis 1:1–3; Exodus 3:13, 14; Psalm 19:1; Psalm 73:25;
Psalm 145:3, 4, 13; Isaiah 33:22; Isaiah 57:15; Jeremiah 23:23, 24;
Jeremiah 32:27; Luke 1:37; Romans 11:36

Lord God, help me to trust in You alone. Help me to wait with patient expectation, knowing that all You do is for my good and Your glory.

God's Love

Nothing can separate you from God's love, so rest in His grace and praise Him for the joy you have in Him.

We get so caught up in the day-to-day demands of life that we forget to stop and praise God for His love. Nothing is greater than being loved by God. His grace is boundless, giving us all that we need and more. When we're feeling alone, fearful, and uncertain about the future, we can find comfort in God's promises to us and rest in His peace that He so freely gives. We may not always feel like God loves us, but as we trust Him, in faith, we'll gain insight through hindsight and realize that He has loved us all along and always will.

Psalm 42:8; Proverbs 8:17; Jeremiah 31:3;
Hosea 2:19; John 3:16; John 14:21; John 15:9–13, 17;
Romans 5:8; Romans 8:38, 39; 1 Corinthians 13:13;
Ephesians 3:17–19; 1 John 4:7–12; 1 John 4:16, 19

*Heavenly Father, thank You
for Your unconditional love. I am so
thankful that Your love consumes me
and frees me to live in Your joy.*

God's Peace

*Even when life seems to be falling apart,
you can have peace because God is with you.*

Life can fall apart without warning, and it's in those moments, when your faith is tested beyond its breaking point, that you'll find yourself on your knees with nowhere to look but upward. That is right where you need to be to receive the peace you lack and the strength to walk forward in faith. The peace that God gives is not a feeling but a consuming blessing of complete contentment. It is being unsure what the future holds, yet simply trusting in the One who holds it. When you're feeling overwhelmed and restless in your faith, pray immediately and wait for God's still small voice. Know that His Word never fails and that all that He's promised you will be fulfilled. Rest in His peace and find strength in Him alone.

Psalm 4:8; Psalm 29:11; Isaiah 9:6–7;
Isaiah 26:3; Isaiah 26:12; John 14:27; Romans 5:1;
Romans 16:20; Ephesians 2:13, 14; Philippians 4:6, 7;
Philippians 4:9; Colossians 3:15

*Lord, I am in awe of Your grace
and so thankful for the peace You give
in the chaos of life. Help me to
trust You more and more.*

Discouragement

Though life will bring troubles, there is nothing for you to fear.
God has promised to give you the desires of your heart.

We have expectations for our lives, but often life falls short of them. Our faith is tested and we begin to question God through our discouragement. When life seems to be falling apart, we tend to walk by sight instead of by faith. And when God doesn't answer our prayers in *the way* we think He should and *when* we think He should, we tend to draw closer to giving up instead of drawing closer to Him. It's in moments of disappointment and discouragement that we should cling to the promises God has made to us and trust in them, even when we don't feel like it.

Psalm 27; Psalm 31:24; Psalm 138:7; Isaiah 51:11; John 14:1;
John 14:27; 2 Corinthians 4:8–9; Galatians 6:9; Philippians 1:6;
Philippians 4:6–8; Hebrews 10:35, 36; 1 Peter 1:6–9

Heavenly Father, I thank You for always hearing me when
I call to You. Prepare my heart to hear You and live in the confident
faith You have called me to, knowing that You are with me always.

Worry

If God can do the impossible, why worry? If you truly believe God is sovereign, trust that He will handle all that concerns you.

We worry because we want to be in control. We want to know our future, what lies ahead. But if we knew the future, we would have no need for faith and no desire to draw near to God. So God makes faith a requirement in knowing Him and mandatory in receiving His blessings. His desire is that you will develop a more intimate relationship with Him so that you have an unshakable faith for the rest of your life. So when worry finds you, seek God. Allow His promises to assure you that He is your refuge and strength and always a ready help in times of trouble.

Psalm 4:8; Psalm 91:1, 2; Psalm 119:165; Proverbs 3:24; Isaiah 26:3;
Matthew 6:25–34; John 14:1; John 14:27; Romans 6:8; Romans 8:6; Philippians 4:6, 7;
Philippians 4:19; Colossians 3:15; Hebrews 4:3, 9; 1 Peter 5:7

Lord, fill me with Your peace. Let nothing move me; keep my faith strong, even through the doubt . . . draw me nearer to You.

Confusion

Life might be confusing, but God is not.
His Word is clear, saying, "This is the way you should go."

*W*hen we're struggling to walk by faith, our sight can be clouded by doubt, and our hearts can be filled with confusion due to the troubles and trials we face. But if we seek God's Word, the light for our path, God brings a clear vision of our next step of faith. It's when we're trying to figure things out on our own, relying on our own wisdom and insight instead of God's, that we get lost in the darkness. When you're feeling confused, seek God's Word and wait patiently for Him to speak to you. He will give you insight, wisdom, direction, and clarity on all that troubles you. He has promised He will.

Psalm 32:8; Psalm 55:22; Psalm 119:165;
Proverbs 3:5, 6; Isaiah 30:21; Isaiah 40:29;
Isaiah 43:2; Isaiah 50:7; 1 Corinthians 14:33;
Philippians 4:6, 7; 2 Timothy 1:7; James 1:5;
James 3:16–18; 1 Peter 4:12, 13

*Heavenly Father, I need You to lead and guide
me, giving me clear vision of Your will for my life.
I will wait patiently for Your direction.*

I will Guide you along the BEST the pathway for your LIFE

Psalm 32:8

Patience

God's greatest miracles can never be rushed; His timing is always perfect. Trust Him, and He will give you strength to wait in faith.

We question God when He doesn't work in *the way* we thought He would and *when* we thought He should. Doubt so easily overcomes our faith in moments when we're desperate for God to answer our prayers. When His ways just don't make sense, we question His presence and love, and we become impatient for His response to our cry for help. God hears. Every tear cried is bottled; every heart that is broken is held in His hands to be healed. Use the times of waiting on God to know Him better and trust Him more. When you do, you'll find yourself with more blessings than any of your prayers could ever request.

Psalm 27:14; Psalm 37:7, 8, 16; Psalm 40:1;
Ecclesiastes 7:8, 9; Isaiah 40:31; Lamentations 3:25, 26;
Romans 5:3–5; Romans 8:25, 26; Romans 12:12;
Romans 15:4, 5; Galatians 5:22, 23; Ephesians 4:2;
1 Thessalonians 5:14; Hebrews 6:12; Hebrews 10:35, 36;
Hebrews 12:1; James 1:2–4; James 5:7, 8

Lord God, please give me the faith to wait upon Your very best in my life. Draw me nearer to You and help me to know You better, trusting in You completely and relying on You continually.

Doubt

God has promised you that He will fulfill His Word to you.
Draw near to Him and allow Him to strengthen you in your faith.

We encounter doubt more than we want to. We truly want to live in faith, but life sometimes makes it hard to. God has made so many promises to us, yet we often fail to know them, much less believe them. God invites us, through our trials and troubles, to know Him better, to witness miracles in our lives by simply having faith that He is God alone. When you're filled with doubt, uncertain of the future, you can be assured that God is stepping out of His silence and calling you closer to Himself. Embrace the doubt upon your knees and not only will you be consumed with God's presence, but you will also find unspeakable peace in the embrace of God's grace.

Psalm 18:30–32, 36; Isaiah 46:10, 11; Isaiah 54:10; Isaiah 55:3, 6, 10, 11; Isaiah 59:1; Mark 11:22–25; Luke 12:29–31; Romans 4:19–21; Romans 10:17; 1 Thessalonians 5:23, 24; 1 Peter 4:12–14; 2 Peter 3:9

Lord, in my doubt, help me in my unbelief.
I long to know You more, to trust You, and to have complete peace.

God will make this happen for you who He calls is faithful
1 Thessalonians 5:24

Troubles

God knows what you're going through. He is your ready
help in times of trouble; you need only call upon Him.

W hen we're down, we often fail to look upward, to God—the only One who can truly help us. In the midst of our struggles, we need nothing short of a miracle. We wrestle with our faith in God because we're always trying to do things ourselves, relying on our limited human power instead of counting on God's infinite, Divine power. If you're facing situations that are beyond your ability to understand or deal with, go with confidence to God's throne of grace. All that you need, He is able to give you, and it's through your faith that God will give you more than you can dare to hope for or imagine. So pray confidently and wait expectantly upon God.

Psalm 31:7; Psalm 121:1, 2; Psalm 138:7;
Isaiah 42:16; Isaiah 43:2; Isaiah 51:11; Nahum 1:7; Matthew 6:34;
John 14:1; Romans 8:28; 2 Corinthians 1:3, 4; 2 Corinthians 4:8, 9;
Philippians 4:6, 7; Hebrews 4:15, 16; 1 Peter 5:7

Lord, though troubles surround me, I know that You
are my strength and my song . . . my Deliverer.

Faith

God has promised that if you have faith in Him, nothing will be impossible.

*W*e struggle through the daily pressures of life, not fully walking in faith and doubting that God can really do what we need Him to. We read His Word, we seek Him, but we're just not sure we can believe what we cannot see. We pray, but nothing seems to be getting better . . . only worse. What we're asking God for is the impossible, and although we want to believe He can do miracles, we're just not sure He'll do them for us. So we struggle in our troubles, but what we really need is the childlike faith that God requires of us. Simple, unquestioning, without understanding, just trusting in His grace and knowing that He is with us, loving us with His sovereign love. Just have a little faith and watch what God will do.

Matthew 9:20–22; Matthew 9:28, 29; Matthew 17:20;
Mark 9:23, 24; Mark 11:22–24; Romans 1:17; Romans 10:17;
Romans 12:3; 2 Corinthians 5:7; Hebrews 11:1; Hebrews 11:3;
Hebrews 11:6; Hebrews 12:1, 2; James 5:14, 15;
1 Peter 1:7–9; 1 John 5:3–5

*Heavenly Father, strengthen my faith.
Help me to trust You completely with every
detail of my life, knowing that You are
always sovereign and forever loving.*

Speaking God's Word

There is power in God's Word.
Let your heart believe it and your mouth speak it.

The power we need to be at work in our lives is always available to us. Are you seeking God's Word and His promises? His Word breathes life into us and fills us with the strength and power that comes from Him. But we cannot just *read* His Word; we must allow the Spirit to drive it deep into our souls so that it will lead and guide us in all that we say and do. His Word is where we get our faith. It is our hope and our salvation. Pray that God will fill you to the full with His promises, and then be ready to speak the hope you receive into the lives of others.

Deuteronomy 18:17–19; Psalm 103:20–22; Proverbs 12:18, 22; Proverbs 13:2, 3;
Proverbs 16:21, 23, 24, 27; Proverbs 18:4, 7, 20, 21; Matthew 12:34b, 36, 37; Mark 4:39;
Mark 11:23; Luke 17:6; John 12:49, 50; Romans 10:8–10; 2 Corinthians 4:13, 14;
Hebrews 10:23; Hebrews 11:3; James 1:26

Lord God, turn my eyes from worthless things and give me
life through Your Word. Fill me with the hope that is found in
Your promises, and help me radiate Your light to those around me.

Answers to Prayer

*God promises that He hears you when you pray. Trust that
He will answer you in His perfect way and perfect time.*

It's often difficult to believe that God has heard us, but we can trust His Word that says He does. Sometimes we don't want to have to walk by faith, but God requires that we do. So when we're crying out to God, calling upon His mercy, we must rely on His promise to us that He hears us and will answer us—and that if we believe, guided by the Spirit, He will give us what we ask for. But it's the "what-if-He-doesn't" that drives us into doubt. And it is in those moments that we must go deeper in our faith, believing that God knows and wants what is best for us in every area of our lives. And then we must walk forward in faith, trusting continually, no matter what.

Psalm 37:4, 5; Psalm 91:15, 16; Psalm 145:18–20; Proverbs 15:29; Isaiah 65:24;
Jeremiah 33:2, 3; Matthew 6:6; Matthew 7:7, 8; Matthew 18:19, 20; Matthew 21:22;
Mark 11:24, 25; John 14:13, 14; John 15:7; John 16:23; Hebrews 4:16; 1 John 3:22–24

*Heavenly Father, I thank You that You hear my prayers. I will seek You,
assured that I will find You, relying on Your promises for hope and peace.*

Take Delight in the LORD and he will GIVE you your Heart's desires

Psalm 37:4

Count Your Blessings

God's blessings are countless. Take a moment to think of all He's done for you and thank Him for all He will do.

God's Word is filled with the promise of blessings in your life, but do you know what they are? There is a fullness of grace that is yours through faith, but are you receiving it? God's love for you is greater than you can comprehend, and the ways in which He wants to bless you are countless. But when life is falling apart, we begin to doubt what we know to be true, and it is then that we must seek God with all that we are so that He might strengthen us and fill us with hope. Pray that He will give you eyes to see all the ways in which you are blessed, and ask Him to help you be a blessing to others so that they might experience the love of God as you do.

Deuteronomy 8:10; Joshua 4:19–24;
1 Chronicles 29:12, 13; Psalm 118:19–21;
Psalm 136:1; Mark 10:13–16; John 1:16, 17;
Acts 3:25; Romans 10:11–13

Lord, I am so thankful for who You are and Your love for me. Give me the strength to believe all that You have promised me and to simply live in the peace and joy of just knowing You.

Comfort

***In your distress, cry out to God. He hears you,
and He's promised to strengthen and comfort you.***

In the moments when the sorrows of life are troubling and the tears that fall aren't containable, know that God is there with you . . . even when you feel so very alone. Through the deepest of waters, and when your faith is tested in the fire, God is there to not only hold your heart but heal it. Come to Him when you're in need of help in need of a friend, in need of a God who does the impossible . . . including turning your pain into joy. More than anything, know that you are not alone. God's arms are not so short, nor His ears so deaf, that He cannot save. Trust His love for you and find comfort and peace under the shadow of His wings.

2 Samuel 22:5–7; Psalm 103:17; Isaiah 40:1, 8;
Isaiah 40:11; Isaiah 41:10, 15, 16; Isaiah 49:13–16;
Isaiah 53:4, 5; Isaiah 56:8; Jeremiah 31:25;
Matthew 10:29–31; 2 Corinthians 1:3–5

*Loving Father, comfort me with Your great love.
I feel so alone. Give me faith to believe that You
are with me always. Embrace me with Your grace
and strengthen me through Your promises.*

Anger

There's no reason to let anger destroy you. Allow God to handle all that comes against you. His justice prevails.

*A*nger can get the best of us. We may have justification for being angry, but it's what it does to our souls that is detrimental, and ultimately we are the ones who end up suffering. When we're consumed with anger, we must immediately take it to God and seek His wisdom. Reacting according to our emotions instead of responding in God's way and in God's timing can be detrimental to the situation we're dealing with. Go to God in prayer, asking for Him to calm your heart and fill your soul with peace, and then wait upon His direction and surrender to His will.

Psalm 102:1–4; Psalm 102:12; Psalm 120:7; Psalm 121:1–3;
Psalm 133:1, 2; Proverbs 14:29; Proverbs 15:17, 18; Proverbs 16:24, 32;
Proverbs 17:14; Proverbs 21:23; 1 Corinthians 1:10;
1 Corinthians 14:33; Ephesians 4:26; Colossians 4:6; James 1:19, 20

Lord God, help me to remain calm when faced with feelings of anger. I need help from the Spirit to quiet my soul and rely on Your justice.

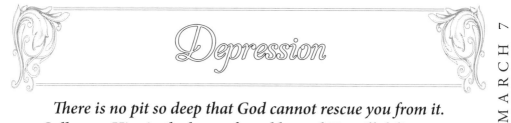

Depression

There is no pit so deep that God cannot rescue you from it.
Call upon Him in the hour of trouble, and He will deliver you.

Life can take us to very dark places where we feel there's no way out. But God always provides a way out if we trust Him completely. There will be times when the sorrow and disappointment in life may tempt us to doubt God's love, but through His Word, we can know for sure that He still loves us and will never abandon us. He is there to comfort us, to heal our hearts, and to fill us with peace during the shadows of doubt.

Psalm 106:8; Luke 17:33; Hebrews 10:36, 37;
Hebrews 11:1–3, 13; Hebrews 12:4–6; Hebrews 13:6;
James 1:12–16; James 4:7–10; 1 Peter 3:16–18;
1 Peter 4:16, 19; 2 Peter 2:9; 1 John 2:1, 2

Heavenly Father, from the pit of despair, I call out to You.
Comfort me with Your love and fill me with Your joy.

Resist the DEVIL AND HE will FLEE FROM YOU — James 4:7

Adversity

There's one question your faith demands you answer in the face of adversity: "If God is for us, who can ever be against us?"

We live in a fallen world, where evil exists and often threatens our faith, bringing us quickly into a state of fear. But with all God's promises of protection and security, why is it so difficult to trust that He will be our fortress and stronghold? It's because we tend to let our physical world overrule the spiritual one, and we find it easier to walk by sight instead of by faith. But it is by faith that the angels of God's army present themselves strongly on our behalf, taking on the battle for us, defending us, and keeping us from harm. If you're facing the enemy and obstacles threaten to overcome you, stand behind God's Word and stand firmly in your faith; help is on the way, and the battle belongs to the Lord. You need only be still; the Lord will fight for you.

Exodus 23:22; Deuteronomy 33:27; Psalm 10:12–18;
Psalm 18:1–3; Psalm 83:1–3; Psalm 105:14, 15;
Daniel 3:16–19, 23–25; Daniel 6:19–22; James 4:7

Lord God, fill me with Your peace. Help me to stand firm in my faith, trusting in Your protection and allowing You to fight the battle for me.

Job Change

God has promised to be with you always. When you feel overwhelmed, know that He can give you the strength and peace you need.

Change can bring about feelings of inadequacy and overwhelming uncertainty. But God is with you. Don't think that He doesn't know what you're going through, that He doesn't know the fear in your heart. He is aware of all you're going through and all that is required of you in daily life. And He is your help. He will give you all the wisdom you need to make the right decisions and to fulfill all that you must do. Don't lose sight of the big picture—His purposes in your life. In every situation in your life, God gives you opportunities to live out your faith in the midst of fear and uncertainty. And He'll give you all that you need to live victoriously in His will.

Psalm 146:3–5; Proverbs 18:10; Proverbs 23:4, 5;
Ecclesiastes 2:18–20, 26; Ecclesiastes 3:9–13;
Ecclesiastes 4:4–6; Matthew 6:25–34;
1 Corinthians 3:11–15; 1 Timothy 5:18

Heavenly Father, when I feel overwhelmed, assure me through Your Word that You are my help and there is nothing to fear. Strengthen me so that I might bring glory to You in all I say and do.

Give Your Problems to God

Whatever it is you need, God can give you. Whatever burdens you carry, God can carry them for you. Give it ALL to God.

Troubles will come. We know that—God has promised it. But with Him, all things are possible, and He is a ready help in times of trouble. So give all your cares and worries to Him immediately, because He cares about you and is looking after all that concerns you. If there is nothing He cannot do, we should quickly be approaching His throne of grace with everything in our lives, big or small. And we must trust the way in which He handles the problems in our lives, the answers He gives to our prayers, because He is sovereign and loving and has promised to give us a future and a hope.

1 Samuel 12:22; 1 Kings 8:56–59; Job 11:13–18; Isaiah 61:1–3;
Matthew 19:26; 2 Corinthians 1:9, 10; 2 Corinthians 2:14–17; 2 Corinthians 4:8–10, 15–18;
2 Thessalonians 1:7–12; 2 Timothy 2:7, 11, 12; 1 Peter 3:12–15

Lord, thank You for Your endless love. Help me to come to You with all that concerns my life, knowing that You alone are my future and my hope.

Christ's Return

In the end is glory. You can rejoice today because you have been promised that Christ is coming again.

We tend to get caught up in day-to-day life, consumed with our trials and troubles, struggling to make it through the day with any strength or joy. But we have a promise to hold on to that should continually fill us with a consuming peace, namely the joys that are to come and which will last forever. We know the end of the story, we know all about the coming glory. So take a moment to breathe in God's promise and realize that whatever you're facing, it is irrelevant and insignificant compared to the joys of eternity that await you through your faith in Christ.

Psalm 103:17, 19; Isaiah 51:11; Isaiah 65:17–19; Lamentations 3:26; Matthew 24:27–31; Luke 21:25–28; Acts 1:11; Titus 2:13; 2 Peter 3:10–12; 1 John 3:1–3; 1 John 5:10–13; Revelation 21:4

Heavenly Father, thank You for the peace I have in knowing that Christ is coming again and that I will spend eternity with You and that I can rest in Your promises to me.

Compassion

**God has continual compassion for you, loving you without limits,
so that His love and compassion might flow through you into others.**

*T*he Lord's compassion never fails. There is always enough for you and all those around you who are in need of His love through times of trouble. Often all that we need, and all that others need, is to know that someone cares, that they're there, even when they can't fix the problem or resolve a broken heart. It is God's love and compassion flowing through us, and others, that brings hope to the hurting. When the weight of the world is upon your shoulders, reach out to someone else who is carrying burdens even heavier than yours, seek God's strength, and receive His grace that is always sufficient.

Genesis 24:67; Exodus 2:6–10;
Proverbs 31:20; Isaiah 49:15; Isaiah 66:13;
1 Peter 4:8

*Lord, I am so grateful that Your
compassion never fails. Thank You for Your
love that is all-embracing and comforting so
that I might share Your compassion with
others and draw them near to You.*

Filled with Faith

It is impossible to please God without faith. Cling to His promises to you and you will find yourself filled with faith.

Life will take you into doubtful places where you'd rather not have your faith tested, but there's no such thing as faith without a test. God allows the situations in our lives to be the fire that our faith must go through in order that we might draw near to Him and know Him better. It is in the midst of our trials, when our faith is shaken to its core, that we learn that our faith cannot come from ourselves, but by trusting in God's promises and relying fully on His faithfulness. Faith comes by the Word of God, so we must read it and believe it, and then we'll be filled with faith.

Exodus 2:3; Ruth 2:12; Matthew 15:28

Heavenly Father, turn my eyes and heart from worthless things and give me faith and life through Your Word.

Guidance

God is not just with you; He's with you to lead and guide you,
to protect you, to provide for you, and to help you in every way.

You can have hope today and every day because God is with you to help you in all the ways that you need Him to. His sovereignty and provision enable you to walk confidently in faith every moment of your life. There is nothing He cannot do. We shouldn't hesitate to run to God when we're filled with uncertainty, not knowing which direction to take and which decision to make. If we call upon Him, He will answer us and lay out the path before us, one step at a time . . . so that we have to rely on His presence and power continually. Seek Him and you will find Him, and He will show you the things that you don't know.

Psalm 91:11–16; Psalm 143:10, 11; Romans 8:31, 32; 1 Corinthians 2:10–16;
2 Corinthians 3:17, 18; Galatians 5:5; Galatians 5:16–26; 1 John 4:13

Lord, I need You with every step of faith I take.
Please lead and guide me through Your Word and help me
to trust confidently in You at all times and in all ways.

Trusting God

When you're impatient, ask God for His strength and grace so that you might wait expectantly for His promises to be fulfilled in your life.

God knows what you need before you yourself know it. But still He wants you drawing near to Him, praying continually, so that you might know Him better. And it's all the uncertainty in your life that will be the testing ground for your faith, requiring that you trust God a little more in ways that maybe you never have before. Don't become doubtful just because you can't see what God is doing or if He's there at all; just trust, have a little faith, and when you're not sure you can, believe Him anyway. Trust Him to do the impossible in your life because that's what He does. And then wait patiently, confidently, and expectantly for Him to prove Himself strong on your behalf.

Ruth 1:12, 13, 16–18; Psalm 40:1; Psalm 62:5–8; Psalm 129:5–8;
Proverbs 30:5; Isaiah 40:31; Isaiah 45:5, 6; Isaiah 64:4; Joel 2:26; Zephaniah 3:17;
Matthew 5:18–20; 2 Corinthians 6:9, 10; Hebrews 6:12; Hebrews 13:8; James 1:16, 17

Heavenly Father, help me to trust You more. When I'm filled with doubt, strengthen my soul. Thank You for Your love and mercy that give me peace for the moment.

Provision

God will provide all you need,
so trust Him when you're fearful of the future.

*W*e get caught up in worrying about tomorrow and forget that God has that covered. We're so easily overcome by the uncertainties of life that we struggle with our faith much more than we should. We know that God has promised to supply our needs according to His glorious riches in Christ Jesus, but we're just not sure we believe it. We wish He'd give us more than our "daily" bread, but God insists on keeping us near to Him, safe and secure within the promises of His grace. So accept His love for you; know that He is aware of all that concerns you and will care for you in every way you need Him to.

Exodus 2:3, 4; 1 Samuel 2:19;
Proverbs 31:16; Luke 2:7

Lord, fill me with peace in knowing that You hold my life in the palms of Your hands. Help me to trust You more and more and to rely on Your grace each and every moment of my life.

Abundance

God's love for you will never run out. He will supply you with all you need, including his love, in abundance.

God's miracles don't run out. Whatever you need, He'll supply to you; and, more than that, He will give you all you need and more so that you might be a blessing in the lives of others. In your prayers and supplications, trust Him for more. Believe that He'll do more than you could dare to ask for or imagine, and then wait expectantly for Him to provide you with all you need to walk in His will for your life. Never doubt what God can do and what He can give. When you're uncertain of whether or not God can provide you with enough, find the assurance of hope in His promises and know that His grace is always sufficient.

Genesis 24:60; Genesis 30:20;
1 Kings 17:16; Matthew 2:11; Colossians 1:11, 12

Lord God, help me to rest in all that You give. Help me to be content, knowing that whatever I need, You will give me. Give me the faith to stand firm in the face of doubt.

Be FILLED with Joy always THANKING THE Father

Colossians 1:11, 12

Grace

God promises you grace for today—there will be more than enough for tomorrow. So rest in the peace of knowing that you have His favor.

We try to grab God's grace for tomorrow when what He really wants us to do is live in this moment. We want to get ahead of life, to reap blessings before they're ready, and we miss out on the *now* by striving for what is meant to be *later*. God's timing is always perfect. If you haven't seen answers to your prayers, trust that He's giving you grace for the moment, enough to sustain you and give you strength to take another step of faith. Rely on Him at all times, and trust in Him completely. His love for you will never fail.

Genesis 29:31, 32; Luke 1:50; Luke 7:13; Galatians 1:15

Heavenly Father, thank You for Your amazing grace.
Help me to rest in Your peace and know that You are God.
It's Your love for me and Your promises that give me hope.

Miracles

The Power of the Word

You can trust God; He's given you His Word. If you'll have faith in His promises, countless blessings will come to you.

*T*he greatest miracle in your life is that you can draw near to God and receive His grace, enveloped in the faithfulness of His Word. Out of His great love for you, He has made you countless promises, which you can rely on and receive the fullness of His glory. When you're struggling through the troubles of life, stop to gain God's perspective on it all through His Word. It brings clarity and hope to all the trials that you must face in life.

Psalm 12:6, 7; Psalm 107:20; Psalm 119:89, 90;
Isaiah 40:8; Luke 21:33; John 1:1–4; 2 Timothy 1:13;
2 Timothy 3:15, 16; Hebrews 4:12

Heavenly Father, I thank You for Your Word that gives me hope and strength to live the life of faith You've called me to. Fill me with Your truth so that my life will glorify You.

When You Face Trials

Don't give up when life gets hard. God has promised that if you stand firm in your faith, you'll be richly rewarded.

*L*ife is hard. Yet walking in faith gives you the hope to face your trials and troubles with the confidence that Almighty God is with you and able to do the impossible. When you're overwhelmed with uncertainty, drowning in despair, you can find strength in God's promises to wait upon His mercy. When you're facing the unthinkable, you must build up your faith and pray. Pray continually—never ceasing. Take God at His Word that He will never fail you, and obey His command not to worry. If God is in control, there's nothing that isn't under His control. Stand firm, hold fast—God's help is on the way.

Job 23:10, 11; Psalm 23:1–4; Psalm 34:17–19; Psalm 55:22;
Psalm 56:11–13; Psalm 69:14–18; Psalm 77:10–14;
Isaiah 43:2, 3; Micah 7:8; Matthew 6:31–34;
2 Corinthians 12:9; Philippians 4:13

Lord, overcome my doubt with Your promises to me. Help me to stand firm in my faith and resist walking by sight. Fill me with Your Word so that I might live according to it.

Stress

*There's no reason to worry; God has promised to help you—
to strengthen you, to deliver you, to guard your heart.*

It's easy to give in to worry. Life can be overwhelming when your faith is tested. But God has commanded us not to worry. And there's a reason: He's in control. We need to find our strength in Him and fully realize, through our faith and through His Word, that He is in control of our lives, so there's no need to worry. No matter what happens, God is in control of it. His sovereignty is never interrupted. So when you are consumed with despair, struggling to make it through the next moment, seek God, and keep seeking Him until you have His peace. He's promised to give you peace that will not only surpass all understanding but surpass all stress that tries to overcome you.

Psalm 46:1–3; Isaiah 41:10; Matthew 11:28–30; Mark 4:38–40;
John 8:36; John 14:27; Philippians 4:6–8; 2 Timothy 1:7, 9

*Heavenly Father, I need Your peace. I am overwhelmed,
uncertain of what to do, but I will keep my eyes upon You.*

Building a Life of Prayer

When you don't know what to do . . . pray. God is listening and ready to help you whenever you need Him, in whatever way you need Him.

*G*od has declared prayer to be the way in which we speak to Him and the way in which He speaks to us. We are to live a life of prayer, bringing all of our hearts to Him because He cares for us. Whatever you're facing in life, moment to moment, bring it to God. Ask for His wisdom and rely on His grace. If you are unable to sense His presence, know that He's still with you. If you cannot yet hear His voice, know that He will answer you . . . He has promised to. So keep praying and wait expectantly for God to answer, resting in His peace, knowing that He is always with you.

Job 22:27–28; Psalm 5:3; Psalm 55:16, 17; Psalm 95:2;
Matthew 6:5, 6; Matthew 18:18, 19; Romans 8:26; Philippians 4:6;
Hebrews 4:16; Hebrews 11:6; 1 John 5:14, 15

Heavenly Father, I thank You that You always hear me when I call to You. Prepare my heart to hear You and live in the confident faith You've called me to, knowing that You are with me always.

Obtaining God's Promises

*You might know God's promises to you,
but the key is believing them. Ask the Spirit to help you.*

When we've lost all hope and our faith is failing, our spirit can be revived through the promises of God. We get caught up in the moment, overwhelmed by life and consumed by worry, and we forget what we've been promised by God Almighty. Don't ever doubt God's love for you; don't for one second believe He'll renege on His promises—His Word stands forever. And there's nothing you can do to earn His promises; they're yours to receive through faith alone. Each and every moment of your life there's a promise of God that applies to your situation, so pray that God will speak His Word continually into your heart.

Exodus 15:26; Isaiah 1:19, 20; Isaiah 59:1, 2;
Matthew 6:33; Mark 11:23; Hebrews 6:12; Hebrews 10:23;
Hebrews 10:35–37; Hebrews 11:1, 6, 11;
2 Peter 1:4–8; 1 John 5:14, 15

*Lord, Your promises are my hope;
they breathe life into me and help me to
have faith even through my doubts.*

Peace

Come to God when your heart is troubled.
He will give you His peace to strengthen your doubting faith.

Many times in life we're searching for peace but failing to seek God. His peace is what we need because the peace we seek, and often temporarily find, is fleeting, changing according to our circumstances . . . and that's not peace at all. The peace that God gives helps us to rest, assured that God is with us, that He's in control, and that there is nothing to fear. When you're overwhelmed and uncertain of the future, struggling to have faith and doubting that there's any hope, pray and wait upon God to give you what He's promised to give—His peace.

Psalm 19:1; Psalm 19:14;
Psalm 27:1, 2 , 5, 10, 13, 14; Proverbs 3:26;
Isaiah 54:13–17; Isaiah 58:11; Isaiah 61:1–4

Heavenly Father, I need Your peace.
I want to rest in simply who You are and
find my hope within Your promises.

God's Power

***Don't forget that there is
NOTHING that God cannot do.***

$\mathcal{D}$on't give in to the lie that you can live this life on your own and that it's better lived your way. You might not always understand God's ways, and at times they may be difficult to trust, but His ways are always best. You may need a miracle in your finances, in your relationships, or in your health that goes far beyond your resources to deal with, but there is nothing that is beyond God's power. He is able to do the impossible, and you can trust Him to work miracles in your life in the right way and at the right time. Just have a little faith, and God's power will far surpass all of your expectations. He delights in giving your faith sight.

Job 38:4–27; Psalm 8:1–9; Psalm 18:1–19; Matthew 11:25–30;
Revelation 1:18; Revelation 2:25–28; Revelation 3:21; Revelation 21:1–7

*Lord, help me to come to You quickly and wait upon You patiently.
I trust in Your Word, the power to save me.*

Fear

Know that God is with you when your fear and faith collide. God is with you—always.

*F*aith seems to work until it's faced with our fear. Then we begin to doubt and find ourselves cast into a state of despair that we're certain we'll never get out of. But God has assured us there is nothing to fear. If He is with us, nothing can come against us. God has the victory. It's when you're faced with the troubles of life and the odds are stacked against you that you wonder if God is even there. But He's promised you He is; it's up to you to trust Him. Fear is nothing but a feeling, but faith is the trust in God's promises to you, so don't allow your emotions to keep you from the peace God gives you. Declare within your spirit, "I trust God, no matter what . . . and I will not fear!"

Matthew 28:20; Philippians 4:13; 2 Timothy 1:7; Revelation 1:17, 18

Heavenly Father, help me to trust You more. Fill me with Your peace and give me strength to stand firm in my faith in the face of my fears.

Assurance

You can take God at His Word. Stand firm
in your faith by holding fast to His promises.

*G*od has made known to us from the beginning that His purposes will stand and that His Word will accomplish all that He desires . . . which is why we should never give in to doubt. When we take our eyes off God and focus on our circumstances, we become full of doubt instead of full of faith. When you're uncertain of the future, unable to have hope in tomorrow, seek God, cling to His promises, and you'll find confident hope— not in what tomorrow brings, but in the One who holds it in His hands. God is sovereign, all the time, and He is not a lesser God according to your circumstances. Trust Him always.

Psalm 18:30; Isaiah 46:10; Isaiah 55:10, 11; Isaiah 59:1;
Mark 11:22–24; Luke 12:29–31; Romans 4:20, 21;
1 Thessalonians 5:24; 1 Peter 4.12, 13; 2 Peter 3:9

Lord God, fill me with Your Word. Give me
faith that is confident, assured not in just
what You do, but who You are.

When You're Dissatisfied

*Though life will leave you dissatisfied at times,
you can be completely satisfied in the joy you have in the Lord.*

We don't always get what we want in life. But whether we accept it or not, it's what's best for us. God's love for us goes further than our temporary pleasures. Still, even if we have faith, we struggle when we have expectations for our lives and reality falls far short of them. We want to be satisfied, but we find it difficult to see beyond this moment. We have a hard time looking at the big picture, what God is focused upon. When you're feeling disappointed or let down by life, come to God in prayer and ask Him to give you peace as you trust in His promise that if you believe in Him, you'll never be disappointed.

Psalm 18:30; Isaiah 46:10;
Isaiah 55:10, 11; Isaiah 59:1; Mark 11:22–24;
Luke 12:29–31; Romans 4:20, 21;
1 Thessalonians 5:24; 1 Peter 4:12, 13; 2 Peter 3:9

*Heavenly Father, help me to be
content. Strengthen me to have faith
that You will never fail me.*

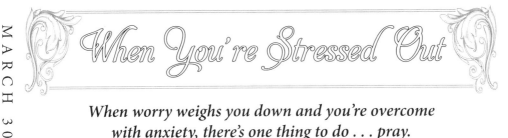

When You're Stressed Out

When worry weighs you down and you're overcome with anxiety, there's one thing to do . . . pray.

We tend to use prayer as a last resort. When we can't figure it out . . . maybe, just maybe, we'll give God a shot at it. Our faith, at times, seems to be far smaller than a mustard seed, and life's problems seem too big for even God. But nothing is too big for God. Your circumstances are well within God's control even if they're not in yours. Look upon those things that cause you to worry as drawstrings that pull you closer to God. Come to Him more often and ask Him to give you greater faith and deeper peace through it all. What are you to do when you don't know what to do? Simply pray.

Psalm 23:2–4; Psalm 46:1–3; Psalm 56:3, 4; Isaiah 41:10;
Mark 4:38–40; John 14:27; Ephesians 4:26, 27; Philippians 4:6–8; 1 Peter 5:7–10

Lord God, I come to You, overwhelmed and in need of help. I rely upon Your promises to save me and Your love to comfort me and fill me with peace.

Jesus Your Deliverer

*When you need to be delivered, faith in the power
of Jesus can bring about the victory you need.*

You may find yourself in a pit so deep that long days and dark nights seem to be all there is in life, but God's grace is able to deliver you. Regardless of the loneliness you feel, God is with you. No matter how overwhelming your circumstances, God is able to overcome them all. Know that God's glory trumps any tragedy and His love for you is boundless and ever reaching. In your moments of despair, come to Jesus; His resurrection power will meet you where you are, delivering you in whatever ways you need Him to.

Psalm 31:7; Isaiah 9:4; Isaiah 61:1; Luke 10:19; John 8:32, 36;
Romans 6:22; Romans 8:2; 2 Corinthians 3:17; Revelation 12:11

*I need You, Jesus. Every moment of my life,
awaken me with Your Spirit. Deliver me from anything
that is not of You. I rejoice in Your boundless love.*

The Eyes of the Lord
watch over those
who do right,
and his ears are open to
their prayers.

1 PETER 3:12

APRIL

Praying Effectively

*There's only one way to pray the right way:
with an open and surrendered heart.*

You can't hide anything from God. He is all-knowing . . . especially when it comes to your heart. But God still asks you to draw nearer to Him in prayer, opening your heart and coming to a place of surrender, realizing that He is your God and loves you beyond measure. In order for God to hear you and you to hear Him, it's vital that you be willing to empty yourself before Him, relying on Him to fill you to the full with His love, mercy, and grace. And when you pray, fully believe that God hears you; He will answer you because He's promised you He will.

Psalm 55:17; Psalm 141:1, 2; Proverbs 15:29;
Isaiah 55:11; Lamentations 3:26; Matthew 18:18, 19;
Mark 1:35; Luke 6:12; Luke 11:9; Luke 18:1;
Philippians 4:6, 7; 1 Thessalonians 5:17; Hebrews 4:16;
Hebrews 11:6; James 5:16, 17; 1 Peter 3:12

*Lord God, I bring my heart before You,
surrendered in every way. Fill me with Your hope
and give me the faith to believe that You always
hear me and will answer my prayers.*

Understanding God's Will

God's will for your life is far better than your own. Trust Him to give you your heart's desires, as He promised to do.

aith comes down to simply trusting that God knows best and that His promises are all you'll ever need. He alone is your hope. You may be uncertain of what your future holds, but God knows and He's assured you that He is with you every step of the way—providing for you, protecting you, and loving you with His amazing grace. At times, God will give you vision, the ability to see what lies ahead, but more often, He'll only give you the faith to take the very next step in front of you. In your struggle of faith, remember to surrender and let God be God in every area of your life.

Deuteronomy 32:10–12; Psalm 78:72; Proverbs 16:9, 33;
Proverbs 20:27; Isaiah 52:12; Isaiah 55:8, 9; Isaiah 58:11;
Luke 15:7; 2 Timothy 1:7; 2 Peter 3:9; 1 John 4:1; 1 John 5:7, 8

*Heavenly Father, help me to trust that Your ways
are always best. Bring my heart to a place of surrender, and
fill me with Your peace as I trust You more and more.*

Building Your Faith

With God, everything is by faith. And faith comes by trusting in His Word—that's how all things are possible.

There will be more times in life than you can count that you will need God to do the impossible. Yet miracles of God require faith, and we tend to doubt. So even on the days when our faith is not demanded, we must continually build a foundation of faith through reading and believing God's Word. If we are living and breathing His Word, His power is able to work in and through us. His Word supernaturally works within us to bring us into His will and helps us walk in it. Don't wait until you're faced with the impossible; make all things possible by reading and believing God's promises to you each and every moment of every day.

Joshua 1:9; Isaiah 40:8; Luke 1:37; Romans 1:17; Romans 4:20, 21;
Romans 8:31; Romans 10:17; 2 Corinthians 4:8–10; 2 Corinthians 5:7;
Hebrews 11:1, 3, 6, 27; James 1:5–8; 1 Peter 1:7–9; Jude 20, 21

Lord God, give me faith through Your Word. Help me to trust in it and walk in it. Strengthen me to believe that with You, ALL things are possible.

The GRASS withers and the flowers fade, but the WORD of our GOD stands forever. *Isaiah 40:8*

Jesus Your Answer

*There is one answer to
every question you have: Jesus.*

*C*ountless questions beg answers when we're struggling with the issues of life. But we tend to overlook the obvious truth that the answer to every situation is Jesus. In Him, we have the power and wisdom to walk in God's will, resulting in the blessings of His glory. When you're unsure of what to do, go to Jesus. When you don't know what to say, ask Jesus. And when your heart is heavy, let Jesus carry it. His resurrecting power can transform your life in any way you need it to. He can do anything when He is your everything.

1 Chronicles 28:9; Mark 11:24; John 15:7;
2 Corinthians 9:8; 2 Corinthians 12:9; Ephesians 1:3;
Ephesians 1:19, 20; Ephesians 6:10; Philippians 4:12, 13

*Jesus, I need You. In every area of my life,
You are my hope. Help me to rest in the
truth that You have risen!*

Ask the Lord to Fill You

When you're empty and thirsty,
Living Water will fill you to the full.

*L*ife will, at times, leave you feeling empty and alone. But Jesus is at the well, waiting for you. Through His life and resurrection, you can be filled with hope and joy, even when life tries to take those things away from you. In Him, you have everything. It's in your weakness that He is your strength and when you're empty and alone that He is closer to you than He's ever been. Nothing changes His love for you and nothing thwarts His power. Come to Him whenever you're feeling thirsty, and in His love, you will never thirst again.

Psalm 37:4, 5; Psalm 103:5; Psalm 107:9;
Isaiah 55:2; Isaiah 58:10, 11; Matthew 5:6;
John 6:35; John 15:16; Romans 8:32

Lord, life often leaves me feeling empty.
I need You to fill me, to give me hope
when all hope seems gone. Keep my eyes
and heart focused upon You.

When Trouble Hits You

God is your ready help in times of trouble. So when troubles come,
come to Him—He will give you the victory.

We so easily get overwhelmed when we can't control the uncontrollable. Life happens, and we feel that we're merely able to react to it. But we know that while God has promised that troubles will come, we can have peace in knowing that God already knows before they come . . . and that He already holds the victory to our problems in His hand. Don't allow yourself to be anxious and full of worry; simply approach God's throne of grace so that He might handle what you cannot. Trust in His promises and walk confidently in the faith that God will work all things together for good.

Psalm 31:7; Psalm 121:1, 2; Nahum 1:7; John 14:1;
Romans 8:28; 2 Corinthians 1:3, 4; Philippians 4:6, 7; James 1:2, 3, 12

Heavenly Father, I come to You in times of trouble for help,
comfort, peace, and the assurance of victory. I will find strength
in You alone and walk by faith instead of by sight.

He comforts US in ALL our Troubles 2 Corinthians 1:4

Remorse

You'll make mistakes, but God forgives—
continually and completely.

God's love focuses on forgiveness, and there's a reason for this . . . we're human and we make mistakes. But God doesn't want us living within our guilt, shame, and regrets. He wants His love to cover our sins and free us to live in joy. So come to Him when you feel remorse, when you know you've made mistakes and you're in need of your soul being set free from the chains of sin. He is always waiting with loving, open arms, so confess, repent, and then live in the peace He gives. Don't hesitate to run to Him; His mercy and grace will be all you need.

2 Chronicles 30:9; Psalm 32:1, 5; Psalm 103:10, 12; Isaiah 43:25;
Isaiah 55:7; Jeremiah 31:34; John 3:17, 18; John 5:24; John 8:10, 11; Romans 8:1;
2 Corinthians 5:17; Hebrews 8:12; Hebrews 10:22; 1 John 1:9; Revelation 12:10, 11

Lord, I come to You, confessing my sins, asking for Your grace
to forgive me. Cleanse my heart and make me new.

When You're All Alone

**God has PROMISED you that you
are never alone . . . He is with you ALWAYS.**

*W*e continually struggle with walking by faith. What we see seems far more believable than what we don't. And indeed, God can seem unbelievably distant when life's troubles come crashing in on us. When we're struggling, we wonder why life is so hard. Shouldn't God be with us to protect us, to provide for us, to keep us from the troubles of life? But the answer is simple: God allows trouble because greater purposes are at hand. Long-term, eternal purposes. And those are the things we can't see or understand. Faith thus takes us into the presence of God, assuring us of His power. We don't have to have life all figured out, because God has made us countless promises to assure us that He is there and always will be. And we must rest in that truth.

Deuteronomy 4:31; Deuteronomy 31:6; 1 Samuel 12:22;
Psalm 9:10; Psalm 27:10; Psalm 37:25; Psalm 43:5; Psalm 91:14, 15;
Psalm 94:14; Isaiah 41:17; Isaiah 49:15, 16; Isaiah 62:4;
Matthew 28:20; 2 Corinthians 4:9; 1 Peter 5:7

*Heavenly Father, often I feel so alone.
Assure me that You are with me always.
Speak to me through Your promises.*

Receive God's Grace

God's grace is boundless, and it's available to everyone who will receive it. Don't miss out on the blessings and favor that God longs to give you.

You can't earn God's grace. He freely gives it out of His great love for you, through your faith. Whatever you think God can do, He can do more. But don't get too focused on the giving. Keep your eyes and heart on the Giver. God's greatest desire is that you will know Him better, that you will trust Him more, and that you will fully experience the wonders of His presence, power, and peace. When you find yourself struggling with your faith, find strength in His promises to you. Sit quietly in His presence and just be with Him. Pray through each and every moment of your life and allow God's favor to find you right where you are.

Exodus 33:17–19; Job 10:12; Psalm 5:12;
Psalm 84:11; Psalm 115:12, 13; Proverbs 3:3–6;
Proverbs 8:35; Proverbs 10:6, 22, 24;
Acts 4:33; 2 Corinthians 4:15; Hebrews 4:16

*Lord, embrace me with Your grace.
Help me to find peace within Your promises
and grant me faith for this very moment.*

Spiritual Warfare

Don't forget that the battle belongs to the Lord.
Stand firm in your faith and trust in God for the victory.

It's easy to believe that you are fighting your battles on your own. And sometimes it seems doubtful that God is a ready help in times of trouble when we feel utterly alone. But God promises not only to be with you at all times and in all ways, but also to fight your battles for you. When we are struggling through the issues of life, we tend only to see them for what they are on the surface. Yet they go far beyond that; the battle is truly spiritual, and the battle can be won only in a spiritual way . . . through faith. All battles are won upon your knees, in prayer, calling on the power of God that always brings victory.

Deuteronomy 18:10–14; Isaiah 53:11, 12; Romans 16:20; 2 Corinthians 10:3, 4;
Ephesians 6:10–12; Ephesians 6:13–18; 1 Thessalonians 5:8; 2 Thessalonians 1:6, 7;
2 Timothy 2:3, 4; 2 Timothy 4:18; Hebrews 2:14, 15; James 4:7; 1 Peter 5:8

Heavenly Father, I come to You, surrendering my life, entrusting my battles to You. Give me the strength to stand firm in my faith, letting nothing move me.

God hears you. Never doubt that He does.
He's told you to pray and expect answers.

$\mathcal{O}$ften it seems like God is not listening, but He is. Your circumstances may lead you to believe that He will never answer you, but He will. One day, in some way, your faith will take sight. Don't set boundaries on God's miracles in your life. Be open to His omniscience. Be trusting of His love for you and be steadfast in your faith. Don't allow the worries of life to drown out His voice. Trust in His Word and stand firmly upon His promises to you, and you'll never be disappointed.

Psalm 37:4, 5; Psalm 91:15, 16; Psalm 145:18–20; Proverbs 15:29; Isaiah 65:24;
Jeremiah 33:2, 3; Matthew 6:6; Matthew 7:7, 8; Matthew 18:19, 20; Matthew 21:22;
Mark 11:24, 25; John 14:13, 14; John 15:7; John 16:23; Hebrews 4:16; 1 John 3:22–24

Lord, my hope comes from You alone. I will trust in You completely,
knowing that Your love for me will bring Your very best answers to my prayers.

Loving the Lost

*We have all been lost and led astray. Allow God's light
to shine through you and lead others to Him.*

When God takes hold of us and fills us with His light, our greatest desires become His own. And at the apex of these is the desire for others to know Him and to be saved through faith. We want those we love—and even those who are hard to love— to experience God's grace, to be set free as we have been. But it's not always easy to lead them. Their path to salvation may be very different from our own. So we must pray for God's wisdom and patience to help us live out our faith before others, enabling them to find God for themselves. God didn't force Himself upon us, and neither should we force ourselves upon others. Pray, be willing for God to use you when He wants and in the ways He wants, and wait expectantly for the lost to be found.

Psalm 55:23; Psalm 98:2, 3; Proverbs 22:6;
Isaiah 44:3–6; Isaiah 50:10; Isaiah 56:1; Matthew 18:12–14;
John 16:7–9; Acts 11:14; Acts 16:31; 1 Thessalonians 5:21, 22;
1 Thessalonians 5:23, 24; 2 Peter 3:9

*Heavenly Father, use my life to lead others to You.
Help me to be patient and trust in Your timing.
Let all that I do and say be representative of You.*

Time Management

Our daily joy will come in prioritizing God's will above our own.
Each day, find God first . . . He'll lead you the rest of the way.

Each and every day is a gift from God. Some days may not seem like it when we're consumed with troubles and filled with anxiety because of them. But there is purpose in all that God does and all that God allows. We can rejoice that today is a day that God has made simply because He has given us hope through His promises. Walking with God can bring pain and sorrow, but with Him, we know that the joys to come will last forever. Don't miss a moment with God in your daily life. Make the most of each breath He's given you. Cling to His hope and remain in step with Him, fully embracing His presence, power, and peace in all that you say and do.

Psalm 90:12; Proverbs 4:20–26; Proverbs 5:21;
Proverbs 10:4, 5; Proverbs 12:2; Proverbs 12:24; Proverbs 13:20;
Proverbs 17:17; Proverbs 23:4, 5; Proverbs 25:11; Ecclesiastes
3:9–14; Ecclesiastes 8:5–7; Ecclesiastes 10:18; Acts 1:7

Lord, thank You for this very moment.
Help me to make the most of the time You've
given me. Lead me and guide me into
Your perfect will for my life.

Pleasing God

You don't have to try to please God;
you just need to trust. He just wants your faith.

Our hearts long to please God, but there's only one thing that pleases Him: our faith. We don't have to be perfect—He gives us grace. We don't have to try to be like Him—He fills us with Himself. God just wants us to draw near to Him, get to know Him better, surrender our hearts, and bring ourselves humbly before Him. That's what pleases God. So cease your striving, enter into His rest and peace, and know that in trusting in His promises, you will be transformed from the inside out. You need only seek Him, and keep seeking Him; He will do the rest . . . transforming your life into His glory.

1 Samuel 16:7; 2 Chronicles 5:13, 14; Psalm 47:1; Psalm 109:30; Psalm 145:21;
Psalm 147:11; Psalm 149:1–6; Isaiah 43:7, 21; John 4:23, 24; Romans 8:8, 9; Romans 12:1, 2;
2 Corinthians 5:11, 12; Colossians 1:9, 10; 1 Timothy 2:1, 3, 8; Hebrews 11:6; Hebrews 13:15, 16;
1 Peter 2:5, 9; 1 Peter 3:3, 4; 1 John 1:9; 1 John 3:22; Revelation 4:11

Heavenly Father, I surrender my life to You. I long to be all that You've
created me to be. Take my heart and make it new. Make it wholly Yours.

His faithful love endures forever
2 Chronicles 5:13

Counting Your Blessings

**There's nothing good that God will withhold from you. Pray,
continually surrender your heart, and trust in His promises to you.**

There will be days when you're not at all sure you're being blessed. Everything seems to be going wrong, life has taken you in directions you never wanted to go, and you question God. Yet it is through our doubts, through the hard times where faith is a necessity instead of a convenience, that we realize we need God more than we thought. He opens our eyes and gives us glimpses of His glory when we get down on our knees. There are days when we won't *feel* God, but He's promised us that He is there. The God of the universe will never leave you nor forsake you. You are not alone, and that's a blessing.

Deuteronomy 8:10; Joshua 4:19–24; 1 Chronicles 29:12, 13; Psalm 118:19–21; Psalm 136:1;
Mark 10:13–16; John 1:16, 17; Acts 3:25; Romans 10:11–13; Romans 15:26, 27; 2 Corinthians 9:15;
Ephesians 1:3, 4; Ephesians 5:20; 1 Thessalonians 1:2, 3; Hebrews 6:7, 8; James 1:17, 18; 1 Peter 4:8

*Lord, Your love amazes me. Thank You for never leaving me,
for receiving me and calling me Your own. I find refuge
in You and will trust in Your faithfulness.*

Eternal Hope

You can have hope because Christ is risen.
Find your joy and strength in God's promise of eternal life.

THE Lord's delight IS IN those who fear Him

PSALM 147:11

Because of God's great love for us, we have hope that does not disappoint because God has promised that the joys to come will last forever. It's out of His great mercy that we are saved; it's His grace that has covered our sins and enabled us to live in the hope that He has given. And since His eyes of love see us without fault, we can share in His riches and experience His kindness and blessings through His sacrifice that covers our transgressions. Nothing can separate us from His love. Nothing.

Psalm 147:7–13; Romans 8:14–18, 24, 25;
Galatians 2:16, 20; Ephesians 2:4–7; Colossians 1:5, 6;
Colossians 3:1, 2; 1 Thessalonians 5:8–11;
2 Timothy 4:7, 8; 1 Peter 1:3–9

Heavenly Father, I am nothing without
Your love. I am hopeless without Your hope.
Thank You for Your grace that has captured
my soul and renewed the Holy Spirit
within me to live victoriously.

132

Ask God for Wisdom

Come to God when you need wisdom; He will lead and guide you through your fears and strengthen your faith to walk in His will.

God never meant you to live this life alone, depending upon yourself and others for guidance. You need Him every step of the way, with each decision you make and every word you say. There's nothing He doesn't know and there's nothing He cannot do. So come to Him each and every day for help. Whatever it is, He has unlimited resources to give you what you need, and He holds your future in His hands. His wisdom thus goes far beyond your own. God waits for you, so come to Him in prayer and wait expectantly and patiently for Him to direct your paths.

Psalm 90:10–12; Psalm 111:10; Proverbs 3:13–22;
Proverbs 4:5–11; Proverbs 5:1, 2; Proverbs 7:1–5;
Proverbs 9:10–12; Proverbs 14:16; Proverbs 16:16;
1 Corinthians 2:6–8; James 1:5, 6; James 3:17

*Lord, help me to know which direction to take,
and give me the faith to obey You readily.
You are my help; You are all I need.*

APRIL 18

Peace in Troubled Times

*In the midst of troubles, you can have peace—God's peace.
Find rest within God's promises. It's all you need.*

When troubles come—and they will!—it's often difficult to even find the words and strength to pray. We lose our peace when the chaos continues and causes us to endure more than our faith wishes to. We want quick resolutions, on-demand deliverance, and most of the time, that just doesn't happen. God makes us wait. But it's in the waiting times that we can know God better than ever before. If we draw near to Him, if we trust Him even when things don't appear to be moving in the direction we'd like them to, He will give us His peace. The peace that surpasses all our understanding brings about an inner strength and calm amid the raging storms of life. And that's all you need. If He is with you, you can rest.

Psalm 25:16–18; Psalm 31:7; Psalm 33:17–22;
Psalm 34:1–8; Psalm 147:2, 3, 5, 6, 13, 14; Proverbs 3:5, 6;
John 14:27; Romans 14:7; 1 Peter 5:7–11

Heavenly Father, I long for Your peace. Help me to rest in You and wait upon Your Divine hand. You are my strength and my song; You are all I need.

Defeated and Powerless

In times of despair, God's promises will fill you with hope.
Find your strength in His power and receive the fullness of His grace.

God knows your heart. He knows your fears and He holds your tears. He knows the things that bring you to your knees, and although they leave you weak, He will be your strength. He will help you to rise up again, to overcome in every way. You tend to want to fight the battle on your own, but the battle belongs to the Lord. Let Him fight while you rest. There is nothing for you to fear if God is with you and for you. You may feel hopeless and helpless, but you are not . . . the power of God lives within you. Come to the cross, surrender, and stand in awe. Let your faith fuel the fire within you. Declare that your God reigns.

Psalm 5:1–8, 11, 12; Psalm 9:10; Psalm 46:1–3; Psalm 86:1–6; Psalm 91:1–10;
Psalm 119:143, 144; Psalm 142:5–7; 1 Corinthians 2:1–5; 2 Corinthians 12:8–10

Lord God, in my weakness, be my strength according to
Your promises. Fill me with Your hope, and strengthen my faith
according to Your Word. You are my all in all.

Too Many Responsibilities

When you feel alone, you are not. God is always with you, and in your weakness, He will be your strength.

*L*ife brings with it moments of joy, but even more moments of feeling overwhelmed and out of control. And it is truly out of control—out of *our* control, at least. God is the one in control, and we desperately need to surrender to that truth. When we do that, we'll finally have peace. We wrestle with God when we should truly be resting. Resting in knowing that He will provide all that we need, in the moment we need it. When life becomes overwhelming we can bring our worries to God so that He can deal with them in ways that we cannot. We can leave all our troubles in His hands, knowing that He will help us and strengthen us in any way we need Him to. You can be at peace and rest in God; He's got everything under control. Trust Him.

Deuteronomy 31:6; Psalm 77:1, 3; Psalm 127:1–5; Isaiah 40:26–29; Isaiah 43:2, 5–7; Isaiah 54:10, Jeremiah 29:11–13; John 14:1; 2 Thessalonians 2:15–17

Heavenly Father, in You alone I trust.
Help me to rest in You, knowing that
You have everything under control.

Don't let your **HEARTS** BE troubled **TRUST** IN God AND trust also in me
❧ John 14:1 ☙

Always Worthy

God is always worthy to be praised; fall upon your knees and worship the God who gave you life.

There will be many moments in life when we simply don't feel like praising God. We wait for a feeling instead of simply obeying. God has blessed us in more ways than we can count, but we struggle daily to worship Him for even one simple blessing. It takes prayer and practice to put God first in your life, to lift Him up above all things . . . above all your worries, troubles, tragedies, and constant struggles. Instead of praising Him when His works are visible, we're to praise Him in faith, declaring His promises and assuring our hearts that God is in control and able to bring about the greatest miracles in our lives. In moments of doubt and in troubled times, we must simply praise Him, whether we feel like it or not.

2 Samuel 22:4; Psalm 89:1–4; Psalm 100:3–5;
Psalm 115:14–18; Psalm 145:1–4; Psalm 148:7–14;
Psalm 150:1–6; Isaiah 43:21; Daniel 2:23; 1 Peter 2:9

Lord God, You have been my God through every moment of my life. I praise You for who You are, regardless of my circumstances.

All You Need

***If you make God and His purposes your primary concern,
He has promised that you will have all you need.***

It is often difficult to believe that God can help us financially. Our greatest needs on earth can require finances that seem to go far beyond what is obtainable by us. But God is rich in mercy and grace and has promised to provide for us in every way. He knows what we want and what we need . . . He's promised not to withhold even one good thing. Our place is to trust in Him to do as He's promised, to provide resources supernaturally. In the process, He performs miracles in our lives and situations that go far beyond all we can dare to hope for or imagine. Whatever you need, God can supply. Pray and trust, and wait upon Him to do the impossible.

Deuteronomy 28:8; Psalm 34:10; Psalm 37:25–28; Psalm 69:32–34;
Isaiah 41:17; Isaiah 55:1–3; Jeremiah 31:14; Joel 2:26; Philippians 4:19; 1 Peter 5:7

*Lord, in You alone I trust for my every need. Though fear threatens
my faith, I will stand firm upon Your promises to me. Give me
the strength to have faith when my faith is failing.*

The Purpose of Problems

There is nothing that God can't do, so bring your problems to Him . . .
then wait and watch in faith; He's full of surprises.

We like to believe we've got life under control, that we've got things figured out, but then circumstances come by surprise and, within moments, we're left helpless and hopeless. We're brought to our knees with only one way to look: upward. Problems have purpose when we're trusting in God to use them. God's desire is to perfect your faith, to bring you to a place of peace and assurance in His power and constant presence. Problems have a way of drawing us near to Him, enabling us to view our lives through His eyes instead of our own. Lean on and trust in God when your circumstances overwhelm you with confusion, and let God handle your problems while you draw nearer to Him. There is nothing too difficult for God.

2 Samuel 22:33; 1 Kings 8:56–60; 1 Chronicles 29:12; Job 11:13–18; Isaiah 61:1–3;
Jeremiah 32:17; Matthew 19:26; 2 Corinthians 1:9, 10; 2 Corinthians 2:14–17; 2 Corinthians 4:8–10,
15–18; 2 Thessalonians 1:7–12; 2 Timothy 2:7, 11, 12; 1 Peter 3:12–15

Heavenly Father, I am overwhelmed, so I surrender my every care to You.
I know that You can do all things and that You are able to do the impossible,
so I will rest in Your truth and have hope in You alone.

Wisdom for Daily Living

God is always with you to lead, guide, and direct you in every area of your life. His ways are always best, so trust Him in all things.

We may not understand God's ways, but we must trust them. God's Word contains the instructions for life His way—the best way. More often than not, God instructs us to move in a certain direction, to make a particular decision, when it goes against all our human instincts . . . but we must obey. Obedience brings about God's power in and through our lives, and we should want nothing less. It isn't always easy to obey, but you have the Spirit to strengthen you in your weakness. Don't allow life to overwhelm your faith; continually come boldly to the throne of God and allow Him to pour His grace down upon you so that you might walk in His will.

Psalm 90:10–12; Psalm 111:10; Proverbs 3:13–22;
Proverbs 4:5–11; Proverbs 5:1, 2; Proverbs 7:1 5;
Proverbs 9:10–12; Proverbs 14:16;
Proverbs 16:16; James 1:5, 6; James 3:17

Lord, I need Your wisdom and grace. Help me to obey You quickly and trust You continually.

In Awe of the Lord

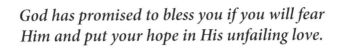

God has promised to bless you if you will fear Him and put your hope in His unfailing love.

We should daily be overwhelmed by God instead of by our problems. God has forgiven us and freed us, allowing us to live a life full of joy and peace, and that is enough to stand in awe of Him every moment of our lives. Life may not always go according to our plan, but we can rest assured it will always go according to God's. And He's promised that His plans for us are for good, to give us a future and a hope. There is no one more wonderful, more loving, and more amazing than the one and only God. He has loved you with an unfailing love; delight yourself in Him and the glory of His presence.

Job 28:28; Psalm 25:12–14; Psalm 112:1;
Psalm 147:10, 11; Proverbs 1:7; Proverbs 2:4, 5;
Proverbs 14:26, 27; Proverbs 16:6; Proverbs 19:23;
Ecclesiastes 12:13, 14; Malachi 3:16, 17

*Lord God, You alone are my peace and joy.
I stand in awe of You. Your love for me far
surpasses anything I can comprehend.
I will praise You more and more.*

Lacking Nothing

*Make Jesus your everything
and you will lack nothing.*

O ur faith tends to overlook the obvious. We pray for everything, but really we simply need to pray for more of Jesus in our lives. He is always the answer. When we're living our lives in Christ, depending upon all that He's done for us and the power that He holds, there is nothing we can't do. He is our impossible, the Savior who has overcome death. Surely He can help us to overcome our problems in life. He calls us to walk upon the water, having faith that He is there and He is all we need. The question is, will you get out of the boat? Will you make the decision in this moment, with whatever you're facing, to trust that Jesus is all you need? If you don't know what to do, keep your eyes on Jesus. That's when miracles happen.

Psalm 68:19; Matthew 21:22; Mark 11:24; John 15:3, 7; John 16:15, 23; Romans 8:37;
1 Corinthians 3:21–23; 2 Corinthians 5:17; 2 Corinthians 5:21; 2 Corinthians 9:8; Ephesians 1:3;
Ephesians 3:20, 21; Philippians 1:21; Philippians 4:13; Philippians 4:19; 1 John 3:22, 23

*Jesus, I need You continually, in every area of my life.
I need You to be my everything, at all times. Fill me with all that
You are and draw me nearer to You in every way.*

Right Where You Are

*There's one thing you need to remember no matter
what you're facing in life . . . God is always with you.*

You won't always feel like rejoicing and proclaiming, "Today is the day that the Lord has made." Sometimes we are just consumed with sadness—often for no particular reason. Life can get the best of us and cause us to struggle in our faith. But regardless of how we feel, we need to be assured that God is with us, even when it doesn't seem like He is. Our faith must overcome our feelings. When you're down, you're going to have to choose to go to the Bible, pray, and receive a Word from God. He'll meet you right where you are, but He won't leave you there. When you come to Him, He has promised to renew and refresh you.

Nehemiah 8:10; Psalm 30:5; Psalm 34:17; Proverbs 8:17; Isaiah 40:31; Isaiah 41:10; Isaiah 43:2; Isaiah 51:11; Isaiah 61:3; Luke 18:1; Romans 8:38, 39; 2 Corinthians 1:3, 4; Philippians 4:8; 1 Peter 4:12, 13; 1 Peter 5:6, 7

*Lord God, help me to always know that You are with me and that in
coming to You, I will have a renewed heart and refreshed spirit. Help me
to always pray and never give up, as You have commanded me.*

Those WHO Search WILL SURELY FIND me.

Proverbs 8:17

Peace That Rules

**God has promised that He will give you
perfect peace if you trust in Him.**

*L*ife can cause us to lose our peace . . . suddenly. But God's peace surpasses not only our understanding but our worries as well. You can have peace in every situation in life because of God's great love for you. You can have peace because God has promised to give you a future and a hope. You can have peace because God is always with you. You can have peace because through your faith, you have God's continual grace. Praise Him for the hope of His glory. Don't allow your feelings to mandate whether or not you have peace. Let the peace of God rule over your life and let nothing keep you from resting and trusting in Him.

Psalm 37:11; Psalm 37:17–19; Psalm 37:37;
Psalm 37:39, 40; Psalm 119:165–169; Isaiah 25:8, 9;
Isaiah 26:3, 4; Isaiah 26:12; Isaiah 55:8, 9, 12;
Isaiah 57:2, 19–21; John 14:27; Romans 5:1, 2; Romans 8:7–9;
Romans 14:17–19; Romans 15:13; 2 Corinthians 4:6, 8, 9;
2 Corinthians 13:11; Philippians 4:6, 7

*Heavenly Father, thank You for the peace
You give me, for Your love that never fails and for
Your mercy that is never-ending. I pray that You
will give me Your peace so that I might rest in
my faith, assured of Your glory in my life.*

Confident Faith

When you put your hope in God, miracles happen.
You can be confident in your faith because God is faithful.

We want desperately to be sure of things. We want to know what the future holds, but we just don't. And that uncertainty can bring with it a lack of joy and peace when we don't have the confidence that all will be well. Yet we can't allow our faith to waver because of our circumstances. We can't allow fear to get the best of us. We have a confidence that should be unshakable. If God is with us and for us, and He's made promises to us that address every issue in our lives, we can have faith because He is faithful. Our trust in Him changes everything. Because of Him, we can live in confident hope.

Psalm 103:2, 3; Proverbs 3:25, 26;
Isaiah 40:31; Isaiah 43:2; Habakkuk 3:19;
Zechariah 4:6; John 14:12; Romans 8:26, 27, 37;
2 Corinthians 7:16; Ephesians 3:12, 18–19; Ephesians 4:22–23;
Philippians 1:6; Philippians 4:13; Hebrews 10:35, 36;
Hebrews 13:6; 1 John 3:21; 1 John 5:14, 15

Lord, help me to stand firm in my faith, trusting
in You completely, being confident in the hope
You have given to me. Strengthen my soul and
help me to fully live in the joy You give.

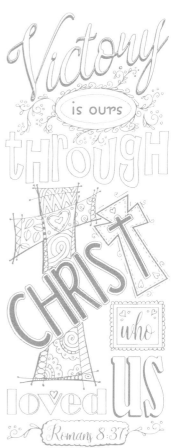

Victory is ours through CHRIST who loved us

Romans 8:37

When You Are Deserted

Though your feelings may disagree with the truth, you can strengthen yourself in the Lord, knowing that He is always with you.

We can find ourselves lonely, afraid, and unable to take another step of faith because we're certain God has abandoned us. It can seem as though He's led us astray because nothing is going right and everything is moving in the wrong direction. We tend to lose all hope when we walk by sight instead of by faith. But it's God's constant presence that we need to recognize clearly. He is with us always because He has given us His Word, His promises, for us to depend upon each and every moment of our lives. Trust God; He knows. He knows everything you're going through and He has promised never to leave you nor forsake you.

Deuteronomy 4:31; Deuteronomy 31:6; 1 Samuel 12:22; Psalm 9:10; Psalm 27:10; Psalm 37:25; Psalm 43:5; Psalm 91:14, 15; Psalm 94:14; Isaiah 41:17; Isaiah 49:15, 16; Isaiah 62:4; Matthew 28:20; 2 Corinthians 4:9; 1 Peter 5:7

Heavenly Father, I feel so alone and I need Your love, mercy, and grace to fully embrace me. In this moment, fill me with the assurance that You will never abandon me and that there is nothing to fear because You are with me.

God is a Merciful God
Deuteronomy 4:31

God, Our Source of Strength

When you're weak and feeble in your faith, find strength in God's Word. Be rooted and established in His promises to you and His great love.

God is our Refuge and Strength

Psalm 46:1

You may be out of strength, but God never is. His power is endless, and His grace is boundless. You can rely on Him to strengthen you in your weakness when you trust in His promises to you. We beg God to speak to us, but He already has; His voice is heard in reading the Bible—our hope, our confidence, our source of strength. In the Bible, God has declared who He is and all that He will do, and He is faithful. There's no reason to doubt. Your confident trust is in the One who holds the universe in His hands.

Nehemiah 8:10; Psalm 18:1–3; Psalm 27:1, 2;
Psalm 46:1; Psalm 119:28; Proverbs 8:14; Proverbs 18:10;
Isaiah 30:15; Isaiah 40:29–31; Isaiah 41:10; Daniel 10:17, 19;
Ephesians 3:16, 17; Ephesians 6:10; Ephesians 6:13, 14;
Philippians 4:13; Colossians 1:11, 12

*Lord God, help me to run to Your Word,
to refuse to focus upon what I see and walk by
faith alone. Strengthen me to trust You more
and depend upon You in every way.*

Within God's Grace

If you seek God, you'll find Him,
and His grace will follow you all the days of your life.

All that God gives us, we don't deserve. As sinners, we're lost—we all fall short. But God, so rich in mercy, has reached down, offering His grace continually without requiring anything other than our faith. And we don't need much faith. He's told us that faith just the size of a mustard seed will do. But we struggle, even within God's grace, to believe . . . to trust in what we cannot see. And we beg God to make our faith take sight, yet it rarely does. Within His grace, we are able to continue to trust, to lean on, and to rely upon Him, and that's right where God wants us—in His grace, drawing nearer to Him each and every moment of our lives.

Exodus 33:17–19; Job 10:12; Psalm 5:12;
Psalm 30:7, 8; Psalm 84:11; Psalm 115:12, 13;
Proverbs 3:3–6; Proverbs 8:35; Proverbs 10:6, 22, 24;
Proverbs 14:7–9; Isaiah 60:10; Acts 4:33;
2 Corinthians 4:15; Ephesians 1:5–7; Hebrews 4:16

Heavenly Father, Your grace amazes me. Thank You for Your love and mercy that have saved me and Your grace that is sufficient in every way.

The Fight of Faith

God will fight your battles for you; you need only stand in faith and watch Him bring about victory in your life.

We don't always see things for what they are. We live in a physical world, but we must fight spiritual battles. And the only way to win is to get upon our knees, pray, and trust God to do what only He can do. Our strength is found in Him alone. Trusting in His Word is the key to overcoming every obstacle and winning over worry. God's promises will break down walls of doubt and bring light into your darkness. God never intended for you to fight your battles, but to come to a place of surrender, trusting in Him and depending upon His presence and power in your life. That's the life of faith. That's the way battles are fought and wars are won. Trust God; that's all you need to do.

Deuteronomy 18:10–14; Isaiah 53:11, 12; Romans 16:20; 2 Corinthians 10:3, 4;
Ephesians 6:10–12, 13–18; 1 Thessalonians 5:8; 2 Thessalonians 1:6, 7;
2 Timothy 2:3, 4; 2 Timothy 4:18; Hebrews 2:14, 15; James 4:7; 1 Peter 5:8

Lord God, bring my heart to a place of surrender. Help me to always turn to Your Word for strength and use Your promises to overcome worry, fear, and doubt.

Transformed by Faith

Don't try to be something you're not; trust God to transform you so that you can fulfill His purposes. All He wants is your faith.

*A*ll too often, we struggle with religion instead of seeking after relationship. Our desire is to be pleasing to God, so we strive endlessly to become all that He wants us to be. And we fall short. The truth is that God doesn't expect us to change ourselves; we just need to come to Him with a surrendered, open heart. He wants us to allow Him into our spirit so that He might transform us into all that He's created us to be. We must be willing to have faith, even when we don't understand what God is doing. It's about relying on His Word to transform us from the inside out, fulfilling us in ways we have never imagined and finding peace that God loves us right where we are.

1 Samuel 16:7; 2 Chronicles 5:13, 14; Psalm 47:1; Psalm 109:30; Psalm 145:21;
Psalm 147:11; Psalm 149:1–6; Isaiah 43:7, 21; Luke 18:14; John 4:23, 24; Romans 8:8, 9; Romans 12:1, 2;
2 Corinthians 5:11, 12; Colossians 1:9b, 10; 1 Timothy 2:1, 3, 8; Hebrews 11:6; Hebrews 13:15, 16;
1 Peter 2:5, 9; 1 Peter 3:3, 4; 1 John 1:9; 1 John 3:22; Revelation 4:11

Heavenly Father, I come to You with an open heart. My greatest desire is to be transformed by You, able to fulfill all the purposes You have for my life.

In Your Weakness

God hears you. He knows all you're going through.
In your weakness, He will be your strength.

Hope is not gone. God hears you. He hears every prayer and collects every tear that is shed. It may seem like He has abandoned you, but He has promised that He never will. So pour out your heart; tell Him that you feel defeated and powerless against the problems that overwhelm you and threaten your faith . . . He will help you. He has promised to. Trust Him when you feel as though your faith is failing. Cry out to Him when you're just not sure you believe anymore. And then sit in His presence and wait for His power to strengthen you. It's all right to doubt when it brings you to His throne of grace. He is there, waiting to pour out His mercy upon you. He is with you to deliver you.

Job 5:6–9; Psalm 5:1–8, 11, 12; Psalm 9:10; Psalm 46:1–3; Psalm 86:1 6; Psalm 91:1–10; Psalm 108:12, 13; Psalm 118:28; Psalm 119:114; Psalm 119:143, 144; Psalm 142:5–7; 1 Corinthians 2:1–5; 2 Corinthians 12:8–10; Philippians 2:5–9

Lord God, hear my cry for help. I feel so alone,
defeated and powerless against the problems
of life. Strengthen me through your Word.
I wait upon You in faith.

Doubting God's Power

God is faithful. Whatever it is you need Him to do, He can do it. The question is, do you have faith to believe He will?

It's easy to doubt God when life's overwhelming obstacles are overcoming you. Life can take us into places where there's no way of escape, and even enduring seems impossible. But through it all, God is with us. He is our ready help in times of trouble. And we must trust Him when He says He will never leave us nor forsake us. It may seem as though He has, but we must never allow our feelings to dictate our faith. When your faith is in God alone, you're trusting in the power that raises the dead. In your doubt, declare your faith. Let nothing move you or deter you from trusting in the One who is above all. God is able to do more than you can ever hope for or imagine. So hope and keep hoping, ask and keep asking. God will answer.

Job 5:17–27; Matthew 8:23–27;
Luke 17:5, 6; Ephesians 1:15–23; Colossians 1:9–13;
1 Thessalonians 1:5; 1 Thessalonians 5:23, 24

Heavenly Father, help me to trust You completely, casting out my doubts and believing in every promise You've made to me. Increase my faith.

Trust, Wait, and Rest

Don't allow anything to make you doubt God and His timing. Allow Him to draw you nearer and increase your faith as you wait patiently.

Sometimes life doesn't allow us the luxury of patience. Our situation can often demand an instant miracle. But miracles are in God's timing, and they are miracles because they make the impossible possible. Just because the miracle doesn't happen when you think it should doesn't mean that God can't do what you need Him to do or show up when your life's circumstances require Him to. Remember that impossibilities require God's presence. You can count on that. He is faithful to His Word. So trust, wait, and rest in knowing that God is working all things for good.

Psalm 31:14, 15; Ecclesiastes 7:8; Daniel 12:12; Romans 5:3;
Romans 15:3–5; Philippians 2:1–4; Colossians 3:21; 1 Thessalonians 5:14;
2 Timothy 2:24; Hebrews 12:1; 1 John 4:13

*Lord, I struggle with waiting upon You.
I need You so desperately . . . if You don't appear,
my hope is gone. Help me to have patient faith.*

Run to God

God promises to be your strength, your rock, your fortress, your Deliverer, your stronghold. Victory is found in Him.

When you find yourself overcome by the adversities of life, run to God. Don't hesitate; don't wait to seek God, to seek His help, to call upon His power in your life. Don't struggle when there's no need to. Don't give in to doubt and despair. God is with you, and He is all you need. There will always be obstacles in life; don't allow them to diminish your hope. Your hope is in God, the One who does the impossible. Whatever you're facing, you are not facing it alone. God is with you, able to save you and determined to deliver you. Put your faith ahead of your fears and wait expectantly for God to manifest Himself in surprising ways.

Exodus 23:22; Deuteronomy 33:27; Psalm 10:12–18;
Psalm 18:1–3; Psalm 83:1–3; Psalm 105:14, 15;
Daniel 3:16–19, 23–25; Daniel 6:19–22; James 4:7

Heavenly Father, in my weakness, be my strength.
Help me to trust in You as I face impossibilities,
knowing that You make all things possible.

Fully Surrender

Either God is in control or He's not. His grace never runs out, so don't live as if it does—run to Him without hesitation.

We tend to forget all that God has done, only counting our blessings in the present moment. And so we fail to bring our problems to Him because we believe He's already somehow expended His grace . . . but that never happens. We must remember not to hold on to our problems but to fully surrender them along with our worries. Our faith decides the outcome of our situations. We either frame God according to our circumstances or frame our circumstances according to what we know to be true through God's promises to us. The decision is up to us. Trust that there is nothing too difficult for God . . . nothing.

1 Samuel 12:22; 1 Kings 8:56–59; Job 11:13–18;
Isaiah 61:1–3; Matthew 19:26; 2 Corinthians 1:9, 10;
2 Corinthians 2:14–17; 2 Corinthians 4:8–10, 15–18;
2 Thessalonians 1:7–12; 2 Timothy 2:7, 11, 12;
1 Peter 3:12–15

Lord God, help me to stand firm in my faith,
fully believing in Your promises, assured that
only You can do the impossible.

Generosity

Be eager to be a blessing to others and trust that God will bless you in the ways you need Him to.

The love that God pours into you was meant to be poured out. Often we find ourselves empty, but that's as it should be. We're supposed to be emptied so that we can be filled, and filled so that we can be a blessing to others. Our greatest desire should be to be used by God, to be the vessels by which He accomplishes His greatest purposes. There is no greater blessing than being a blessing to others . . . binding up the brokenhearted, setting lost souls free, and bringing light into the darkness. We're to comfort the mourning and embrace those who are alone, displaying God's glory through His grace. You have been chosen, but now you choose whether or not you want to be used by God and be blessed in more ways than you can count.

Deuteronomy 15:10, 11; 1 Samuel 2:7, 8;
Proverbs 14:31; Proverbs 17:5; Proverbs 22:9;
Proverbs 28:3; Matthew 19:21–24; Acts 4:32–35;
2 Corinthians 9:7; James 1:9–11; James 2:5, 14–17

Heavenly Father, open my eyes to see the opportunities You place before me to be a blessing to others. Use my life for Your glory.

Calling on God

Prayer is powerful because you're calling upon God.
He hears you, and He will answer. Just have faith that He will.

It often seems that God is distant, even absent, when we're praying but nothing's happening, nothing's changing. It's easier to walk by sight. But faith is what makes everything possible, so we've got to be determined not to trust only in what we see but in what we don't. We usually can't see what God is doing. We can't always know what lies ahead, but He does. And that's all we need to know. We need to trust in His Word and diligently seek Him in prayer, believing that He is faithful and resting in His grace that is always sufficient. Whatever you're praying for, know that God has heard you and will answer you in His perfect way. Be patient and trusting until He does. His love never fails.

Genesis 21:16; 1 Samuel 1:10–12; 1 Samuel 1:20;
1 Samuel 1:27, 28; Matthew 15:22–28

Lord God, I call upon You, resting in Your love and trusting
in Your ways, even when I don't understand them.

Paths of Righteousness

God's desire is that you come to Him in all things. He wants to lead and guide you into His perfect will and countless blessings.

The decisions we face in life are beyond number, yet each one has implications that go far beyond our understanding at the moment we must make them . . . which is why we need God in every area of our lives. Our greatest struggle in making wise choices is that we cannot see the future and don't know what lies ahead. But God does. So don't make hasty decisions based on your feelings and emotions. They can lead you astray. Come to God in prayer, laying your problems at His feet. And then seek His Word, listen, and trust that He will guide you into paths of righteousness, working all things for your good and His glory.

Job 31:18; Psalm 48:14; Isaiah 30:21;
Isaiah 49:10, 11; Isaiah 58:11;
Matthew 2:20, 21; Luke 12:12

Heavenly Father, thank You for always being there to lead and guide me. When I don't know what to do, I know I can turn to You and trust You for everything.

Understanding God

God is in control, so you don't have to be.
All that He requires is your faith in His great love for you.

*I*t can be difficult to trust God because His ways are so much higher than our own. There are some things we will simply never understand, but we can still trust. We can trust in God's character and His promises, knowing that He is with us, loving us with an all-encompassing grace that goes beyond all we can hope for or imagine. We don't need to always understand. God is full of surprises. He loves to draw us near to Him, teach us to trust and have patience, and then throw open the gates of heaven in ways that establish our faith into eternity.

Psalm 37:5, 6; Psalm 55:22; Proverbs 2:11, 12; Proverbs 24:3, 4;
Matthew 11:28–30; 1 Peter 3:5; 1 John 5:20

Lord God, help me to set aside my pride, my desire to always be in control and understand all that You are doing in my life. Fill me with Your hope and peace so that I might trust You more.

Happiness

*If you love God and rejoice in Him, He's promised
to surround you with favor as with a shield.*

Happiness is a feeling that can change with daily circumstances, but joy in the Lord fills you with a happiness that is unchanging. Life won't always satisfy you. In fact, mostly it won't. But when you're trusting God to handle the circumstances of your life—especially the ones that aren't meeting your expectations and are dragging you into hopelessness and despair—you can find a happiness that is long-lasting because your joy, hope, and peace are placed upon a firm foundation . . . God's promises to you. Nothing can bring you down when you're looking up.

Genesis 21:6; Genesis 30:13;
Psalm 5:11, 12; Luke 1:14; Luke 1:47

*Heavenly Father, in You alone I
find my joy and peace. Quiet my heart
and help me find happiness in trusting
in Your promises to me.*

Truth

There is no greater peace and joy than living in truth, and God's Word is the Truth that sets you free to live the life of faith.

*L*ife can come tumbling down within moments, without warning, taking with it every bit of hope we were holding on to. But when we place our trust in God, standing upon the firm foundation of faith—His promises to us—there are no miracles that are beyond Him. Whatever we regard as loss is gain in the hands of our loving Father. He picks up the pieces that have been broken and makes them new . . . better than before. Not only can God fix what's failed; He also recreates and redesigns within the realm of His perfection. So don't give up and don't give in to hopelessness. There is nothing that God cannot do. Pray that He will use His loving power in every area of your life where you are desperate for His help.

1 Chronicles 16:11; John 8:32, 36; John 16:13; 3 John 4

Lord, I need You to restore all that's been lost in my life. But more than that, I need You to transform all that I am into Your will and Your design, for Your purposes.

SEEK THE LORD and HIS STRENGTH
1 CHRONICLES 16:11

Restoration

It may seem like all is lost . . . but if you'll trust God,
you'll experience His promise to make all things new in your life.

We often find our lives in ruins. What we hoped would happen didn't, and when we needed God to be there, He wasn't . . . or so it seems. It's often when life is falling apart that it's really falling into place. But it's hard to trust God when we can't see anything happening, when all is lost and hope seems gone. But hope is never gone when your hope is in the God who does the impossible. There is nothing He cannot do, so trust Him to do what you think He can't.

Genesis 4:25; Ruth 4:15; Psalm 49:15; Luke 1:24, 25

Lord, I need to know that You are with me always,
ready to help in times of trouble and able to restore all that
is lost in my life. Renew my spirit to trust in You more
and to hope in You continually.

The Joy of the Lord

Your joy will be complete when you are trusting in God, believing in every promise He's made you, and finding peace in His grace.

*J*oy isn't about your feelings. It's about resting in God's promises and being assured that if God is holding your future, the joys to come will last forever. We tend to get caught up in the overwhelming finite problems of life instead of being captured by the infinite love, mercy, and grace of God. Instead of giving in to the doubt that so easily taints our thoughts, we must quickly run to God for strength to stand firm in our faith against all the odds. When we rest in the strength and peace He gives us, we are able to experience a joy that creates an inner calm and take continual steps of faith, knowing that God's power prevails and His grace always overcomes.

Genesis 4:25; Ruth 4:15; Nehemiah 8:10; Psalm 5:11, 12;
Psalm 49:15; Psalm 51:10–12; Psalm 57:7–9; Psalm 63:3–5;
Psalm 118:24; Psalm 149:5; Proverbs 15:13; Matthew 11:28–30;
Luke 1:24, 25; John 15:11, 12; Romans 14:17; Hebrews 13:5

Heavenly Father, in You alone I find my joy. No matter what I face in life, I will filter everything through Your love, mercy, and grace.

Despair

There will be moments when it seems that all hope is gone, but it is not. God does the impossible, so trust Him to do the impossible.

*L*ife will take you to unknown places where uncertainty overwhelms you. But God has assured you that although the world will shake you and troubles will come, He is your hope. And your hope in His Word will never return void. It will simply be a matter of holding on, trusting even though you're tempted to allow the light to be overcome by darkness, and knowing that even when everything is falling apart, there is nothing to fear. God is with you and for you, and He has already overcome every obstacle in your life. Place your hope in Him alone. He will strengthen you in your weakness. Have faith in the One who is holding you, and you will never be disappointed.

Genesis 3:15; Psalm 3:3–6; Psalm 27:13, 14; Psalm 71:5;
Psalm 119:114; Isaiah 40:31; Lamentations 3:22–24;
Romans 8:31; Romans 8:37–39; Romans 15:13;
2 Corinthians 12:9; Philippians 4:8

Lord God, at times my heart is filled with hopelessness. I need You to draw me nearer to Yourself and strengthen me to continue to have faith in Your faithfulness.

Encouragement

When life gets you down, look up.
Call to God, and He will answer you.

It's easy to give in to your thoughts; they can quickly take over when the circumstances of life consume you. It's not always easy to take steps of faith when life seems to be falling apart at the seams, but if you call upon God in prayer, He's promised not only to answer you but to encourage and strengthen you in your weakness. Don't try to figure it all out on your own; don't try to fight the fight of faith in your own strength—you were never meant to. God intends you to continually need Him. So don't be surprised by the trials you face; everything God allows in your life is with purpose. Just trust in Him, strengthen yourself by focusing upon His promises to you, and wait patiently and expectantly for His miracles.

Psalm 118:5–9, 14–17; Psalm 120:1, 2; Psalm 130:1–8; Isaiah 43:18, 19

Heavenly Father, I look to You. Increase my faith to believe
that with You, all things are possible. I will find encouragement in
knowing that You are my refuge and strength . . . my hope.

Courage

God has promised that there is nothing to fear. You can walk confidently in faith because He is with you and victory is His.

*G*od doesn't always move quickly. At times He may choose to move slowly, methodically, perfectly, causing you to trust Him continually. His purpose is not only to bring about victory in your life but also to perfect your faith. Yet perfecting your faith will include testing it. And testing your faith will cause you to fear because of the uncertainty and all the unknowns that you will face throughout your trial. So be determined to simply stand firm, to trust in all that God has promised you, and just hold fast to His love for you. He will protect you, provide for you, and bring about the victory your soul seeks. It's only a matter of time . . . His perfect time.

Deuteronomy 33:27; Psalm 27:14; Psalm 31:24; Psalm 118:17; Isaiah 40:31; Isaiah 41:10; Isaiah 51:11; Romans 8:38, 39; Philippians 4:13

Lord God, help me not to fear. Help me to know that You are with me always and that You will never leave me nor forsake me. Strengthen my faith to keep believing in Your promises.

MAY 21

Confidence

*You can be confident in God's promises. He is faithful to His Word.
Keep seeking, keep believing, and keep watching for God.*

At times when you are lacking the confidence to believe that God is there or that He cares, don't hesitate to come to Him with your disbelief. Life can take your faith into depths of despair, but don't allow your feelings to overcome you. You may not be able to change your circumstances, but God can. You can be confident in His wisdom and power when you've expended your own. If God does the impossible, and if you really believe that, you can live with an assurance that brings strength and peace in the most turbulent of times. If you're struggling with doubt, go to God's Word and wait upon His voice to speak strength to your faith.

Proverbs 3:26; Isaiah 40:31; Isaiah 43:2;
Habakkuk 3:19; Zechariah 4:6; John 14:12;
Romans 8:37; Philippians 1:6; Philippians 4:13;
Hebrews 10:35, 36; Hebrews 13:6; 1 John 5:14, 15

*Heavenly Father, help me to trust You when
doubt tries to overcome me. Fill my thoughts with
Your own and refresh my spirit with Your truth.*

Turn over Your Worries

Don't try to figure out what you simply cannot. Turn all of your worries over to God and allow Him to handle all that concerns you.

*W*e need to be clear on one thing: God is not a God of confusion. If we're confused, it's because we are under spiritual attack. God's promises take us from a state of confusion within our spiritual battles to a place of peace because it's His truth that sets us free from the lies of this world that bring about the confusion in our minds. When you're feeling restless and uncertain, find refuge in the Word of God, knowing that He is faithful and will do all that He's promised. Keep meditating on His promises to you, fill your mind with what is true, and God's love and mercy will fill you with unimaginable peace.

Psalm 32:8; Psalm 55:22; Psalm 119:165; Proverbs 3:5, 6; Isaiah 50:7;
1 Corinthians 14:33; 2 Timothy 1:7; James 1:5; James 3:16–18

*Lord, I need Your peace. In the uncertainties of my life,
I'm tempted to doubt. Fill me with Your truth so that I can
have faith and look for Your miracles in my life.*

Letting Go of Anger

Be quick to forgive and allow God's love to flow freely in and through you.
Let God handle the issues at hand so that your soul can remain in peace.

It's easy to allow our emotions to get in the way of God's commands to us. It's so vital to live our lives by faith instead of by our feelings. It's never easy, but obeying God's command to avoid anger is for our own good; anger does little to resolve issues and only drives our spirit into a desperate state of pride and bitterness. Whatever it is that makes you angry should immediately be brought to God. Ask Him to fill you with His love, and pray for His grace to flow in and through you so that your soul will be at peace and your spirit obedient to God.

Psalm 37:8; Proverbs 14:16, 17, 29; Proverbs 15:1; Proverbs 16:32; Proverbs 25:21, 22; Ecclesiastes 7:9; Matthew 5:22–24; Matthew 6:14; Romans 12:19; Ephesians 4:26; Ephesians 4:31, 32; Colossians 3:8; Hebrews 10:30; James 1:19–20

Heavenly Father, help me when I'm
filled with anger. I want to live in Your love,
experiencing peace at all times, so that I can
be a vessel of Your love, mercy, and grace.

Disillusioned by Life

It may be difficult to see what God is doing in your life, but you must continually trust that He's working all things together for good.

Y ou won't ever fully understand God and His ways, but you can trust in who He is. You may not be able to see His hand, but you can fully trust His heart. He's made promises to you that will encompass everything you encounter in life. So don't get caught up in trying to figure out what God is doing; just trust in what He's promised through His Word. God has commanded you not to depend on your own understanding because He wants you at peace—not wrestling to try to bring about miracles in your life that only He can bring. God wants you to enter into His rest, the place where you don't have to know all the answers because you are fully trusting in the One who does know.

Psalm 31:7; Psalm 121:1, 2; Psalm 138:7; Nahum 1:7; Matthew 6:34; John 14:1; Romans 8:28; 2 Corinthians 1:3, 4; 2 Corinthians 4:8, 9; Philippians 4:6, 7; Hebrews 4:15, 16; 1 Peter 5:7

Lord God, I struggle with wanting to understand every detail of my life, past, present, and future. Help me to trust in Your promises to me. I want to surrender my will to Yours, fully.

God's Powerful Word

There's one thing you can count on . . . God's Word. Trusting His promises will make all things possible in your life.

*I*f you want to know God better, to draw nearer to Him, to experience more of Him in your life, you must first diligently seek His voice in His Word. It is through His Word that everything in existence was created, and it is by believing and trusting in His Word that that same power is applied in your life. God's Word gives you peace among the storms of life, hope when all hope seems gone, joy when your life's circumstances consume you with sorrow, and strength when you are too weak to carry on. His truth will cast out the lies that try to defeat you and throw your soul into despair. So live it, breathe it, and trust completely in what God has said, and you will never be disappointed.

Psalm 33:6, 9; Psalm 119:89;
Isaiah 55:10, 11; Mark 13:31; John 5:39;
1 Corinthians 1:20; 2 Timothy 3:16; Hebrews 4:12;
1 Peter 1:23; 1 Peter 1:24, 25; 2 Peter 1:20, 21

*Heavenly Father, I trust in Your Word.
I pray that Your promises will work mighty
miracles in and through my life to
bring glory to Your name.*

Stay Centered in Christ

You don't have to try so hard to be what only Christ can be in and through you. Allow His Spirit to transform you.

PSALM 71:1

We often forget that we don't have to try to become like Christ. Our faith in Him allows His Spirit to dwell within us, transforming us into His likeness. All we have to do is focus on him, and He will give us all we need to live the godly lives we've been called to live. So stay grounded in Him through His Word. We must think as He thinks and live as He lived, not in our own strength but in His, trusting Him in every way to unleash His transforming power in and through us. Pray that He will continually transform your heart and bring glory to His name.

1 Chronicles 16:11, 12; Psalm 34:1–4;
Psalm 62:1, 2, 5–8; Psalm 71:1, 5, 8; Proverbs 8:17;
Jeremiah 23:23, 24; John 15:14–16; Romans 11:36;
Romans 13:14; Ephesians 5:19, 20;
Colossians 3:16, 17

Lord, I long to be transformed into the likeness of Christ. Help me to daily surrender my soul and use my life for Your perfect purposes.

173

A Future of Hope

When life gets you down, God will lift you up. He is with you to strengthen and encourage you, to give you a future and a hope.

There will be times in life when you'll feel as though hope is completely gone. It will be difficult to have any faith at all, and you'll wonder if God truly loves you. But those feelings don't determine what is true. God's Word is truth, and you must live your life based upon it. Don't allow your emotions to dictate how loving God is or isn't. He remains the same in every situation in your life. God is not a lesser God according to your circumstances. His love and power are able to overcome any obstacle in your life, so when your faith is wavering, hold fast to His promises to you and trust Him . . . no matter what.

Psalm 27:1–3; Psalm 31:24; Psalm 34:18; Psalm 138:7; Isaiah 51:11; John 14:1, 27; 2 Corinthians 4:8, 9; Galatians 6:9; Philippians 1:6; Hebrews 10:35, 36

Heavenly Father, I need You to encourage me, to give me hope in my hopelessness. Thank You for the promises You've made to me, giving me a future and a hope that do not depend on my circumstances.

Living in the Joy of Today

*Don't allow the worries of tomorrow
to rob you of the joy that is in today.*

The uncertainties in life bring our faith into desperate places, places where we're not sure we'll make it through. But our faith must rest on the promise that God is with us, that He is handling all that concerns us, and that He will never leave us, forsake us, or disappoint us. We simply have to believe Him even when we don't feel like it. Even when it seems as though God is not going to prevail, we have to trust that He will. We can't depend on our own understanding, or we'll end up consumed with worry instead of enjoying His joy and peace. Seek Him, pray, and then leave all your worries in His hands . . . that's where they belong anyway. Today is a day that the Lord has made; live in the now and rejoice that He is always with you.

Psalm 119:165; Isaiah 26:3; Isaiah 41:10; Matthew 6:27, 30–34; John 14:27;
Romans 8:6; 2 Corinthians 12:9; Philippians 4:6, 7; Colossians 3:15; 1 Peter 5:7

Lord, I need Your peace as the worries of life threaten to overcome my faith. Console me with Your presence and power and fill me with confident hope in You alone.

So don't WORRY ABOUT TOMORROW

Matthew 6:34

All That Concerns You

God has promised to give you all you need when you make Him your primary concern. Look to Him when you are in need.

No matter how great or how small your need, God wants you to come to Him. He has promised to supply all of your needs, but you must come to Him in faith, laying your burdens before Him and allowing Him to handle what only He can. God's desire is that you will trust Him with all things at all times and simply rest in His peace, walking in faith and living out the purposes He has for your life. When you don't know what to do, keep your eyes upon Him and know that He is watching over all that concerns you, while orchestrating miracles that go beyond anything you can imagine.

Deuteronomy 8:7–14; Psalm 23:1;
Psalm 34:10; Psalm 37:23–25; Proverbs 13:22;
Malachi 3:10, 11; Matthew 6:24, 31–33;
Luke 6:38; 1 Corinthians 16:2;
2 Corinthians 9:6–8; 1 Timothy 6:9–10

Heavenly Father, help me to overcome my doubt. I want to trust You for all of my needs, believing fully that You will fulfill all of my desires.

The Lord directs the steps of the Godly

Psalm 37:23

Losing a Loved One

God knows your sorrows . . . He holds your broken heart.
He promises to comfort you and turn your pain into joy.

*Y*ou may not see any way that God can heal your heart, much less turn your pain into joy in the midst of your great loss. And it may seem inconceivable that God could possibly comfort you in any way that will slow the tears that uncontrollably fall. But He can, and He will. He is always with you. And He is with you in this moment, as you mourn all that has been lost in this life. Though the pain seems inconsolable, God works miracles with His love that go far beyond our comprehension. Trust Him, keep crying out to Him, and He will soothe your aching soul. He will bottle each tear, He will record them in His book, and He will do what He has promised—give you beauty for your ashes.

Psalm 119:41, 50; Isaiah 41:10;
Isaiah 49:13; Matthew 5:4; 1 Corinthians 15:55–57;
2 Corinthians 1:4, 5; 2 Corinthians 5:8–10;
1 Thessalonians 4:13, 14; Revelation 21:4

Lord, my soul cries out to You.
The pain of my loss is so deep that it is beyond
my ability to endure. I pray that You will
strengthen my spirit through Your promises
and bind up my broken heart.

God's Will for Your Life

God has a purpose for your life. Seek Him in everything, and you will stand in awe at what He will do in and through you.

In the moments when life is confusing and overwhelming, when you're not sure why you're here or what you're supposed to be doing, seek God with all that you are. He created you on purpose to fulfill a specific part of His plan. Only you can live the life you've been created to live, but you must surrender . . . and surrender everything. You must surrender your will and embrace God's will, no matter what that means. He may ask you to travel roads you'd rather not travel and endure more than you want to, but His plans will be for your good and His glory. God has His hand on you; there's no reason to fear. Keep searching, keep trusting, keep walking in faith, and there's nothing He can't do in and through you.

Joshua 1:8; Psalm 31:3, 5; Psalm 32:8; Psalm 37:23, 24; Psalm 48:14; Psalm 119:105, 106; Psalm 143:10; Proverbs 3:1, 5, 6, 11, 12; Proverbs 6:20, 22, 23; Proverbs 16:3; Isaiah 30:21; Isaiah 48:17; Isaiah 58:11; Romans 8:14; Romans 12:2; Ephesians 5:17; James 1:5, 6

Heavenly Father, each and every moment of my life I surrender my will to Your will. Use my life for Your purposes, to bring glory to Your name, to draw others to You.

BE PATIENT in Trouble and KEEP on praying
Romans 12:12

JUNE

Let all that I Am

PRAISE
THE LORD

may I never forget the
good things he does for me.

PSALM 103:2

Growing in Your Faith

God doesn't leave you where He found you. His desire is to grow your faith and transform your life—He's writing your story.

We often think that when we find God, that's where the journey ends. But the truth is, that's where the journey begins. God meets us right where we are, and then, in our surrender, transforms our hearts, causing us to seek after Him in ways we never imagined. When we draw nearer to God, He will begin to grow our faith, which usually means going through challenges and pain and facing fears. But that's how faith grows. It must be stretched, sometimes to the point of breaking, for it to be strengthened and grow. So don't be surprised by the trials of your life. God will use them to increase your faith . . . enabling you to pray for more and expect God to move in more miraculous ways than you can dare to hope for or imagine.

Ephesians 4:14; Philippians 1:6, 9, 10;
Colossians 3:16; 1 Timothy 4:15; 2 Timothy 2:15;
Hebrews 6:1; 1 Peter 2:2, 3; 2 Peter 1:5–8; 2 Peter 3:18

*Lord, increase my faith. Strengthen me
for the tests that will grow my faith, and help
me to be at peace through it all.*

A Calm Assurance

You can have peace in every situation because God promises to give it to you. All He requires is your faith.

We rarely live in the peace God gives us. We allow our circumstances to dictate how much peace we do or don't have. And yet, our souls are desperate for peace . . . a peace that is unchanging and abundant. We want to live in the midst of difficulties with a calm assurance that we have nothing to fear and that God holds our tomorrows full of hope and joy. But we can only have that peace through our faith—our faith in who God is and all that He has promised. When we need peace, we only need God. So, in your restlessness, stay in God's presence, seeking Him continually, relying on Him completely, and He will give you the peace your soul is desperate for.

Psalm 4:8; Psalm 29:11; Isaiah 9:6, 7;
Isaiah 26:3, 12; John 14:27; Romans 5:1; Romans 16:20;
Ephesians 2:13, 14; Philippians 4:6, 7, 9;
Colossians 3:15

Heavenly Father, I need YOUR peace. Fill me with the calm assurance that You are with me always. Help me to rest in You and continually trust You, even in the face of doubt and fear.

Philippians 4:6

Forgiveness

God has forgiven you so that you might forgive others . . .
setting them free from guilt and shame, just as you have been.

*G*od has made forgiveness not a request but a command. God wants nothing to stand in the way of our faith and His blessings in our lives, and it all flows through His love for us. If His love isn't flowing through us, there is a hindrance to His presence and power in our lives . . . and it's not supposed to be that way. If you struggle to forgive, know that you can't do it in your own strength and willpower. True forgiveness can come only from God. So don't become discouraged if you find it nearly impossible to "let go and let God." Keep asking God for help. Keep leaning on Him for strength, and pray that His Spirit will work in and through you to enable you to forgive what only He can.

Psalm 32:1, 2; Psalm 85:2; Psalm 103:2; Isaiah 1:18;
Isaiah 43:25; Isaiah 56:7; Jeremiah 33:8; Mark 11:25;
2 Corinthians 5:17; Ephesians 1:5–7; Colossians 2:13;
Colossians 3:13; Hebrews 8:12; 1 John 1:9; 1 John 2:1

Lord God, I want to forgive,
but my soul yearns for justice. Help me
to trust in Your love to cover a multitude
of sins and heal my heart.

Contentment

When your soul is restless, find contentment in God's promises to you.
Your greatest hopes and desires are only fulfilled by your faith in Him.

We strive daily for all that we think will fulfill our lofty expectations of life, but we often end up feeling empty and alone. We forget all that God has promised us, and we depend on the world to satisfy what only God can. When we're feeling as though all that we long for requires nothing less than a miracle, we must set our worldly desires aside and seek God with all that we are . . . relentlessly. Our pursuit of Him will enable us to have His vision, to see that in whatever state we are, we can be content as we rely on His love, mercy, and grace to settle our souls and give us more and more faith in all that He has promised.

Psalm 68:19; Matthew 21:22; Mark 11:24; John 15:3, 7; John 16:15, 23; Romans 8:37;
1 Corinthians 3:21–23; 2 Corinthians 5:17, 21; 2 Corinthians 9:8; Ephesians 1:3;
Ephesians 3:20, 21; Philippians 1:21; Philippians 4:13, 19; 1 John 3:22, 23

Heavenly Father, help me to let go of my desires for my life and
embrace Yours. Fill me with peace and contentment and bring my soul
to a place of being settled on the foundation of Your promises.

Frantic and Stressed

*Don't allow life to get the best of you. Trust,
and keep trusting, regardless of your circumstances.*

It's easy to get overwhelmed in life. More often than not, our lives seem to serve up circumstances that require a miracle that seems highly unlikely. We tend to panic and allow the odds against us to overrule our faith . . . allowing fear to get the best of us. We can never allow our helplessness to make us think that things are hopeless. It's our helplessness that reminds us that God is God and we are not. So even our difficult times, all the uncertainty and stress, can be used by God to draw us nearer to Him—thereby strengthening our faith as we wait upon Him and pray patiently to have our faith take sight. Find solitude in God's sovereignty and allow Him to quiet your soul.

Psalm 27:14; Psalm 37:7, 8, 16;
Psalm 40:1; Ecclesiastes 7:8, 9; Lamentations 3:25, 26;
Romans 5:3–5; Romans 8:25, 26; Romans 12:12;
Romans 15:4, 5; Galatians 5:22, 23; Ephesians 4:2;
1 Thessalonians 5:14; Hebrews 6:12; Hebrews 10:35, 36;
Hebrews 12:1; James 1:2–4; James 5:7, 8

*Lord, I get so overwhelmed, trusting in
what I see instead of having faith in You alone.
Help me to find peace in Your sovereignty
over all that concerns me.*

Far from God

*There is nowhere you can go that God cannot find you—
no place where His grace cannot save you.*

We all are driven by human desires to go our own way, to seek things to satisfy our thirsty souls, when deep down we know that only God can. Those temporary pleasures in life seem to be far more appealing and thirst-quenching than what seems to be acquired through faith. Faith tends to take too long. It demands our patience, and we feel as though we just don't have that much time. But God's Word tells us something very different . . . the truth. The truth is that all we need is God. And although we may go our own way, He is always there, waiting, ready to embrace us with His love and grace. Wherever you are in life, turn to Him . . . no matter who you are or what you have done. God's love for you is unchanging and all-consuming.

Deuteronomy 4:2, 6, 9; Deuteronomy 8:5, 6, 11, 19;
Psalm 44:20, 21; Proverbs 10:9, 11; Job 41:11; Jeremiah 6:16;
Hosea 14:2, 4, 9; Malachi 3:7; Romans 12:2; Hebrews 3:12, 13;
Hebrews 4:11, 12; Hebrews 11:15; 2 Peter 2:20, 21; 1 John 1:9, 10;
Revelation 2:4, 5, 7; Revelation 3:2, 15, 16, 19

*Heavenly Father, I come to You,
desperate for Your love, mercy, and grace.
Hold me and never let me go.*

When Things Go Wrong

No matter how things appear, trust God.
His promises will overcome every obstacle in your life.

*L*ife won't always go according to your plan, but you can rest assured it will always go according to God's. You may not understand His ways, but you must trust them. He will allow your faith to be tested in order that it can be strengthened. So ask Him to strengthen you in your weakness; that's what He has promised to do. Don't allow your emotions of despair brought on by troubles to discourage your faith. Keep your eyes upon Him and stand firm in your faith. Hold fast and encourage yourself in God's promises to you. Don't allow what you see to determine what you know— namely, that God loves you. He's with you, and He will bless your faithfulness when you trust in His.

Psalm 27:14; Psalm 33:20; Psalm 62:5; Psalm 130:5; Psalm 145:15, 16;
Isaiah 25:9; Isaiah 40:31; Habakkuk 2:3; Romans 13:13, 14; Ephesians 5:8–11;
Ephesians 5:15; Hebrews 3:14; Hebrews 10:23; 1 John 2:28

Lord, I am so tempted to give in to doubt and despair. I need You to help me
have hope not in what I see but in what I can't—Your consuming grace.

The Life of Faith

The life of faith is about one thing: surrender.

We get caught up in living a life that is worthy of Christ without realizing that only He can accomplish that in and through us. It's through our surrender that His Spirit takes its place within us, enabling us to live the lives we're called to. There's only one thing you need to do on a daily basis to please God: surrender your will to His and allow Him to transform your life in the ways that He desires. He doesn't want you trying so hard, but simply trusting in Him to do all that you need Him to do to transform your heart into the likeness of Christ.

Psalm 15:1–5; John 15:1–4; Romans 16:3–5;
2 Corinthians 5:7; Galatians 6:9, 10; Ephesians 5:1;
Colossians 3:12–17; 2 Timothy 2:3; Acts 5:25–29

Heavenly Father, I surrender my heart to You.
Do with it what You will, enabling my life to
bring glory to Your name.

Power in the Word

In order to walk the walk, you must talk the talk.
Let your words be God's.

Proverbs 16:24

Our mind is a battlefield. We struggle against what we see, desperately wanting to trust in what we don't. Faith isn't easy. But faith only comes by hearing God's Word and believing it. So if you need more faith, you need more of God's Word, and your thoughts must be filtered through it. Once you are thinking as God does, your words will soon follow. And when they do, His power will be unleashed in ways that you can't imagine. His Word holds the power to do whatever it is you need Him to do. So trust Him, have faith in what He's promised, and then wait expectantly for His faithfulness.

Deuteronomy 18:17–19; Psalm 103:20–22;
Proverbs 12:18, 22; Proverbs 13:2, 3; Proverbs 16:21, 23, 24, 27;
Proverbs 18:4, 7, 20, 21; Matthew 12:34b, 36, 37; Mark 4:39;
Mark 11:23; Luke 17:6; John 12:49, 50; Romans 10:8–10;
2 Corinthians 4:13, 14; Hebrews 10:23;
Hebrews 11:3; James 1:26

Lord God, fill my heart and mind with
all that is of You. I need You to strengthen my
faith and help me to think as You would and
to speak truth in every circumstance.

Influencing Your World

Your life is meant to draw others to God, allowing Him to work in and through you so that the lost are found.

*T*t's easy to simply stay focused upon our own lives, instead of on the lives of others. Our natural self-centeredness prevents us from living a Christ-centered life. And that's why our daily surrender to God and His will for our lives is so vital. We will often feel as though our lives are meaningless, but whenever our lives are lived for God, our influence in the world around us reaches into eternity in ways we will not see in this life. Though sometimes we may not get an indication that we are having an impact, we can be certain that we are if we're seeking God's will for our lives and being obedient to whatever He asks us to do. And we can't question Him or choose a slightly different route . . . His way is the best way and leads to blessings that are beyond number.

Daniel 12:3; Matthew 5:14–16; Mark 16:15–20;
Luke 4:18; John 3:16; John 4:6, 16, 17, 28–30; John 4:13, 14;
John 6:44; John 13:34, 35; John 14:12; John 15:12, 13;
Acts 1:8; Acts 4:31; Acts 17:30; Romans 10:14;
Romans 12:2; Galatians 5:14, 22, 23; Colossians 3:23, 24;
Hebrews 11:1–3, 32–34; 1 Peter 2:9–12; 1 John 5:3–5

*Heavenly Father, use my life to draw
others to You. Help me to turn my eyes
from worthless things and to be consumed
with living my life for You alone.*

Listening to the Holy Spirit

***You can and will hear God speak to you if you seek Him
in His Word and trust Him with all your heart.***

There are times when we need to hear from God. Not just in a simple way, but in a way that is unmistakable and undeniable. Sometimes we can rest in His quiet presence, and at other times our faith demands more. Yet we are often desperate for His voice, failing to continually be desperate for Him. And our worries seem to interfere with our faith, preventing us from believing what He has said to us through His Word. God has spoken loud and clear, but we allow our despair to drown out His voice. Know that He longs to speak to you in more ways than you can imagine. Seek Him, pray, and then quiet your heart to hear what He says.

Isaiah 30:21; Isaiah 40:31; Luke 11:10–13; John 14:14, 15–18, 26; John 16:7, 13;
Acts 1:4, 5, 8; Romans 8:11, 16–18, 26, 27; 1 Corinthians 2:9–14; 2 Corinthians 3:6, 17, 18;
Galatians 5:22–25; Philippians 2:13; 2 Peter 1:3, 4

*Lord, quiet my soul so that I might hear Your voice in the ways
that I need to. Open my heart to whatever it is You have to say, and help
me to trust in Your ways even when I don't understand them.*

Defeat Your Deepest Fears

God is with you to fight your battles for you. He is with you always
. . . your faith in Him will overcome your fears.

ear can get the best of our faith. In the face of our dire circumstances, we tend to allow the unknowns to overcome what we know to be truth. We know God is with us, we know He has the power to do anything, but much as we try, fear tempts us to doubt. When our situations in life seem insurmountable, we tend to believe that they are too big even for God. But nothing is too difficult for Him. So when fear tries to overcome you, be determined to simply live each moment trusting who God is and what He has promised He will do—protect and deliver you.

Psalm 18:1–3; Psalm 18:28–30; Psalm 27:1–5; Psalm 37:4–6;
Proverbs 3:25, 26; Isaiah 60:19, 20; John 8:12; Romans 8:37–39

Heavenly Father, the circumstances of my life fill me with fear,
and my faith wavers in the face of it all. Help me to believe what I know
to be true . . . You are with me always and there is NOTHING to fear.

The Lord is my light and my salvation

Psalm 27:1

Honesty

*There is no way to live in faith
without living in truth.*

*A*bove all things, our hearts are deceitful, causing us to travel down wrong paths and reap consequences we were never meant to receive. So we must remain in God's truth, His Word. Remaining in His Word means not only being honest with others but also with ourselves . . . because it's easy to taint the truth when our earthly desires demand our attention. But the long-term consequences of this kind of dishonesty bring about more pain and sorrow than we can imagine. So ask God to search your heart each day and show you truth so that you might live in it.

2 Samuel 12:1–7; Psalm 86:11; Psalm 119:43–45;
Proverbs 3:27; Proverbs 12:22; Matthew 7:1–5;
Ephesians 4:21–23; Colossians 3:9, 10

*Lord God, help me to live in Your truth.
Search my heart and know me, show me if
there is any wicked way within me, and lead
me into the way that is everlasting.*

Waiting for God's Answers

God will always answer you. Keep seeking Him,
keep praying, and wait upon Him expectantly and confidently.

We tend to give up on God. He seems to take too long, longer than we think He should, and so we easily surrender to doubt. But it's in the waiting that God grows our faith in greater ways than we can imagine—provided we draw near to Him, even when He doesn't seem to be listening or answering. Our faith wants to see what we believe, and it will, in due time. But in the moments of waiting upon God to answer, we must dig deep into His Word, relying on His promises to help us take just one more step of faith. The very next step of faith could lead to the answer we've been waiting for . . . the miracle we've prayed for. So trust and keep trusting; don't allow your faith to waver until God answers.

Psalm 40:1; Psalm 62:5–8; Psalm 129:5–8;
Proverbs 30:5; Isaiah 45:5, 6; Zephaniah 3:17;
Matthew 5:18–20; James 1:16, 17

Heavenly Father, give me the faith to wait
upon You to answer my prayers. Make my spirit
steadfast in trusting in Your promises.

Praise at All Times

When everything in your life is going right,
praise God; and when everything isn't, praise God.

Our praise seems to hinge upon our circumstances . . . when life is falling apart, and when God seems to have abandoned us, we shout at Him, but not in praise. It's not easy to continue to have faith when troubles consume us and we're struggling with the difficulties that life brings. But we fail to realize that it's praise that beckons God's power. No matter what we're facing, however trying and hopeless, our first response must always be praise—whether we feel like it or not. In times of fear, praise God; in times of great loss and despair, praise God; in times when you want to walk away from your faith, praise God. And keep praising Him, regardless of your circumstances.

2 Samuel 22:4; Psalm 89:11; Psalm 100:3–5; Psalm 102:18; Psalm 115:14–18; Psalm 145:1–4;
Psalm 148:12–14; Psalm 150:1–6; Isaiah 43:21; Daniel 2:23; Daniel 4:1–3; Zechariah 2:10; 1 Peter 2:9

Lord God, I praise You for who You are, for Your love and boundless grace.
Though troubles come, I will praise You and trust in Your promises to me.

Lead Your Children to God

You are the path that leads your children to God.
Love them just as He has loved you.

The stress of raising your children can easily be lifted when you realize that they are ultimately God's children. It's in your example of loving God and living out your faith that they will come to love God as well. There's no reason to put pressure on yourself; God's light will shine in and through you as your children witness all that you do and say as a representative of the Lord. And when you make mistakes—and you will—you have the opportunity to show your children forgiveness by confessing your sins to God and helping your children to see that not only is God loving and forgiving, but you are as well. Allow God's love to flow through you so that they, too, might know the amazing grace of God.

Matthew 19:13–15; John 1:11, 12; John 3:3–7; 1 John 2:12–17; 1 John 4:7–21

Heavenly Father, I long for my children to love You. I want them
to be consumed by Your mercy and grace. Help me surrender my soul
more and more to You so that they might know You through my faith.

Decisions

Don't make a move without God.
Pray, and then wait for as long as it takes for His direction.

We tend to react without seeking God and waiting upon Him to lead and guide us. Each and every day we're faced with decisions about what direction to take when it comes to our jobs, relationships, health emergencies, and responsibilities of life, but often we fail to call upon the One who is fully aware and in control of our past, present, and future. Instead of immediately reacting to the decisions you are faced with, trust God enough to go to Him first. Pray continually until He gives you peace about a particular answer or direction you are to take. If you follow His path, His blessings are sure to follow you.

Joshua 24:14–16; Nehemiah 9:20;
Psalm 37:23, 24; Psalm 73:22–26; Psalm 119:65, 66;
Proverbs 3:5, 6; Proverbs 22:17, 18; Isaiah 30:20, 21;
Isaiah 48:12, 13, 16, 17; Isaiah 54:13;
Isaiah 58:11, 12; Philippians 2:14–16

Lord God, move my spirit to seek You
in all ways and at all times. Calm my soul
as I face unknowns, and help me to remember
that I must rely on Your wisdom to
help me walk in Your will.

Spiritual Growth

God's desire is to make you holy as He is holy, so know that any growth which takes place may be painful, but it is for a purpose.

We forget that our ways and our thinking are far below God's. He sees the big picture. He knows where our faith is at all times; and at a moment's notice, He may choose to test it in order to grow it. When things don't go our way and life seems to be falling apart, we quickly become filled with fear instead of with faith . . . that's our human nature. But our trials are what He uses to drive us to Him, to our knees, where we realize that we have nowhere to look but up. And that's where He grows us spiritually. He wants us depending upon Him in EVERY way. So don't be surprised if you're on your knees more often than you'd like . . . it means that God is close to you and He is growing you, caring for you in every way through the process.

Psalm 86:11, 12; Psalm 119:33–35; Psalm 121:2;
Proverbs 23:12; Luke 18:10–14; Romans 8:4–6; Romans 13:11–14;
1 Corinthians 10:21–23; 2 Corinthians 7:1; 1 Timothy 6:12;
1 Peter 1:16; 1 John 2:3–6; 1 John 5:1–3; 3 John 1–4

Heavenly Father, I am continually overwhelmed by Your love for me. Strengthen my spirit to persevere through all that You must do to increase my faith.

Psalm 121:2

When Children Disappoint

*We all fall short of God's glory, so pour out God's grace
upon your children when they fall short.*

God has promised never to abandon us, and neither should we abandon our children when they fall short of our expectations of them. Just as we need to know of God's love for us when we fail Him, so our children, too, need to fully feel our love for them—as well as God's—when they are feeling guilt and shame. It is in our love for them that they will see God. Help them to understand that an honest confession will set them free from the burden that weighs upon them for their shortcomings, and that it is your love and God's that will lift them up through forgiveness. Now is the time to forgive them and love them, just as God has forgiven and loved you.

Deuteronomy 4:31; 1 Samuel 2:12, 13, 15–17, 22–25; 2 Samuel 18:31–33; Psalm 92:13–15;
Psalm 94:14, 15; Psalm 147:3; Proverbs 17:2; Isaiah 44:10; Isaiah 49:4, 8–11; Isaiah 51:11;
Isaiah 53:6; Isaiah 54:7, 13; John 14:18; Romans 11:16; 1 Corinthians 4:4–5

Lord God, help me to love my children as You have loved me. Let Your grace and mercy overwhelm them through me, and strengthen us to move forward in faith.

Overwhelmed

*Life is hard, but God is with you
to carry your burdens . . . let Him.*

When you're carrying the burdens of life and the weight of the world is upon your shoulders, don't forget about God. He wants to help you, to carry what you cannot, to work miracles that you'll never be able to. If you come to Him, you'll be instantly aware that you are not in this alone. He'll never leave you nor forsake you . . . He's made that promise to you. So lay it all at his feet, pour your heart out to Him, and then rest in knowing that Almighty God is in sovereign control of your life and loves you with an unfailing love.

Deuteronomy 31:6; Joshua 1:9; Psalm 77:1, 3; Psalm 127:1–5;
Proverbs 3:5–7; Isaiah 40:26; Isaiah 40:29; Isaiah 43:2, 5–7;
Isaiah 54:10; 2 Thessalonians 2:15–17

Heavenly Father, my burdens are too much to bear. I need You to carry me. I cannot do this on my own. Assure me that I am not alone.

Changes in Life

God is with you through everything you go through in life.
Ask Him to give you the courage and strength you need.

*C*hange can be difficult and consume us with fear. We can get caught up in a comfort zone that we never want to set foot out of. But God can use changes in our lives to grow our faith and draw us nearer to Him. When you're encountering a change in your job, remember that God is with you and has promised to supply all your needs. Rely on Him for strength and wisdom. Let all that you do and say be representative of Him, and allow Him to work in and through you, thereby to be a light wherever you are and whatever you're doing. Do everything as if you are doing it for God, because you are.

Psalm 146:3–5; Proverbs 18:10; Proverbs 23:4, 5; Ecclesiastes 2:18–20, 26; Ecclesiastes 3:9–13; Ecclesiastes 4:4–6; Matthew 6:25–34; 1 Corinthians 3:11–15; 1 Timothy 5:18

Lord, I am so easily consumed with fear over all the changes in my life. Strengthen me and fill me with Your wisdom and love. Show me the way in every step of faith that I take.

God Will Guide and Protect

You can't always be with your children to watch over them and protect them, but God is. Trust Him to care for them . . . He is with them ALWAYS.

Depending upon God to care for our children in all the ways they need is difficult. We can hit a roadblock in our faith when we're concerned for our children as they journey out into a fallen world. But we must never forget that God is with them, even when we're not. Ultimately, they are His children, and there is no place where His love, mercy, grace, protection, and provision cannot go. It's our responsibility as parents to remain in constant prayer for them and keep our peace through trusting that God is always in control, always overseeing every detail of our lives and those of our children. We can rest through our trust and have peace in the assurance that God is fully sovereign.

Genesis 50:21; 1 Samuel 2:9; Psalm 119:63; Proverbs 6:22, 23; Proverbs 16:9; Isaiah 40:28–31; Isaiah 41:10; Isaiah 42:6; Isaiah 43:18, 19; Isaiah 45:2, 3, 12, 13; Isaiah 54:10; Isaiah 55:10, 11; Luke 19:10; 2 Corinthians 5:7; 1 John 2:1

Heavenly Father, I am tempted to worry about my children and the details of their lives. Help me to rest in knowing that You are in control and watching over their lives, loving them and protecting them.

Thankfulness

Thankfulness performs a miracle in your soul that unleashes the blessing of joy within your spirit.

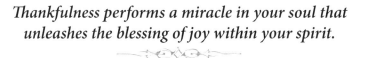

We forget to be thankful for the small things—and even the bigger things—in life. We have expectations for our lives, and when all is going according to plan, we tend to forget that every good and perfect thing comes from God. But when life falls short of our expectations, we tend to be filled with outrage and anger, confusion and fear, instead of thankfulness that God is with us regardless of our circumstances. Being thankful makes life's problems seem small. Our continued faith keeps fear from getting the best of us. So when you're overwhelmed with the ways in which life isn't going according to your plan, thank God that He is going to make sure it goes according to His. And trust that His plans are to give you a future and a hope.

Ruth 2:20; 1 Samuel 2:1; 1 Kings 1:31; 2 Kings 4:37; Luke 1:46–53

Lord, I am thankful for the simple truth that You are with me always. I may not always be fully aware of my blessings, so I pray that the Spirit will fill me with gratitude for all You have done, all You are doing, and all You are going to do.

My Heart rejoices in the Lord

1 Samuel 2:1

Whatever You Need

***God always finds a way to provide you with all you need.
Trust Him to supply your needs in ways you're not sure He can.***

*W*e're often tempted to believe that God can't truly meet our daily, detailed needs. We wrestle with our faith in trying to determine if He really can help us pay the bills and put food on the table. But His promises have assured us that He can and will. It's up to us to believe what He's promised. It's no use trying to set limits on God's resources and power, because there are none. God can use your desperate situations to draw you nearer to Him, to increase your faith, and to give you greater insight into His presence and power in your life. So when you're struggling with what you need, trust God in the ways you're not sure you can. Your faith beckons His mighty power and provision in your life in ways that will make you stand in awe.

Genesis 21:18, 19; 2 Kings 4:1–8; Proverbs 23:22; Matthew 2:12–15; John 19:25–27

*Heavenly Father, I am tempted to doubt Your power and
promise of provision in my life. Strengthen my spirit to pray and
wait upon You to bring about the miracles I so desperately need.*

Angels

God has commanded His angels to watch over you.
You can be at peace because God has you covered.

*Y*ou may be tempted to doubt the existence of angels. It may seem unlikely that there are such beings that would actually be watching over you. But God has said it is true in His Word, so you can be certain that they are not only real but active in watching over your life. We can't always understand how God works, but we must believe that He is working. Our faith unleashes God's power. When you're feeling alone, afraid, and unable to find peace in the now, you must trust in the promise that God's angels are watching over you, protecting you and constantly keeping you within God's love, mercy, and grace.

Genesis 16:7–11; Genesis 21:17;
Judges 13:1–5; Luke 1:13, 26, 27

Lord God, thank You for the angels that
You've commanded to watch over me. Help me
to be at peace, assured that I am protected
at all times and in all ways.

Overcoming the Enemy

In your fight of faith, the battle belongs to the Lord. Victory is found upon your knees—pray, trust, and wait upon God's deliverance.

Psalm 121:7

here are times when you may be fully aware that you're in a battle. Life is constantly coming against you, everything seems to be going wrong, and you're tempted to doubt God's goodness. Other times, you may be completely unaware that you're in a battle until you're struck unexpectedly and you suddenly lose all of your strength. Either way, you are not alone. God goes before you, He knows the battles you will face, and He will never leave you. You can find victory upon your knees. No matter how intense the battle, no matter what threatens to overcome you, the enemy is not greater than your God. There is nothing He cannot do, and because you are His, He is your refuge and your strength, your shelter, the One who saves you.

Psalm 95:2; Psalm 121:7–8;
Matthew 7:15–17, 20-23; Romans 12:2; Ephesians 4:26, 27;
Ephesians 5:11; Ephesians 6:11–14; Philippians 4:7, 8;
2 Thessalonians 3:3; 2 Timothy 4:18; Hebrews 2:18;
James 3:10, 11; James 4:4, 7, 8; 2 Peter 2:9

Heavenly Father, I will not fear in the fight of faith. I will remain upon my knees, assured of Your presence and power in my life to deliver me.

Suffering

***God knows of your suffering. Come to Him so that
He might comfort and strengthen you through it all.***

In our sufferings, we tend to believe we're all alone, and it seems unlikely to us that God is there or that He cares. Our human nature believes that if we are walking in faith, we should not suffer. But our suffering can grow our faith immeasurably, and sometimes God sees fit to allow us to go through sufferings so that we might not only draw nearer to Him but also experience His power in our lives in greater, undeniable ways—in ways we could not experience without suffering. The short-term pain is worth the long-term gain. As we walk through dark valleys, we gain a faith that cannot be shaken. Because when God manifests Himself—not only to help us but also to rescue us—our faith gains the strength to carry us through any doubt.

Romans 8:17–18; 2 Corinthians 4:8–10, 17, 18; Philippians 4:12, 13;
2 Timothy 2:3, 11, 12; Hebrews 2:9; Hebrews 2:10; Hebrews 5:8, 9;
Hebrews 12:11–13; 1 Peter 2:21; 1 Peter 4:1, 2, 12–17, 19; 1 Peter 5:10–11

Lord God, help me to know that You are with me through my suffering. Please comfort and strengthen me to walk in faith and not give in to fear and doubt.

Hope

Hope in God, and
you'll never be disappointed.

Situations in life can make us feel that all hope is lost. Trials and the troubles of life can send us into a tailspin of doubt, and the fight of faith can strip us of our strength. But when we're trusting in God's promises to us, believing in His faithfulness and resting in truth, we can have hope even when all hope seems lost. Don't allow your feelings to get in the way of your faith. You can face your fears and defeat your doubt through meditating on God's Word and continually trusting in what He says . . . no matter what. God will strengthen you to believe and to keep taking steps of faith. And He will be your strength when you are weak. When your hope is in Him alone, you will never be disappointed.

Psalm 25:6; Psalm 30:10, 11; Psalm 33:9, 10; Psalm 86:5–8; Psalm 92:12–14;
Psalm 126:5, 6; Psalm 147:3–11; Isaiah 26:3–9; Isaiah 61:3–6; Jeremiah 32:17–19; Lamentations
3:22–25; Matthew 6:34; Matthew 11:28–30; Romans 8:31, 35–39; 2 Corinthians 4:8–11;
Galatians 6:9, 10; Hebrews 2:17, 18; Hebrews 10:32, 33; 2 Peter 2:9

Heavenly Father, I put my hope in You. I will not walk by sight, but by faith.
I will trust in Your promises and find strength in Your faithfulness.

Don't Give Up

God's blessings in your life will not be delayed.
Trust in His perfect timing for every miracle you pray for.

Psalm 31:24

Impatience is our human nature. We tend to want to move ahead of God because He often seems to be taking too long. We feel more comfortable when He's working according to our schedule instead of His own. But rarely does our timing sync up with God's. He is working with perfection, orchestrating miracles to have the maximum effect on our faith. So don't get discouraged just because it seems like God isn't doing anything. Just because you can't see what He's doing doesn't mean He's doing nothing. He works in ways that are beyond our comprehension, and He often moves suddenly, without warning. So pray and wait patiently in faith, confident in expectation.

Psalm 31:24; Psalm 37:7; Psalm 40:1; Ecclesiastes 7:8, 9;
Lamentations 3:26; Romans 5:3–5; Romans 8:25;
Romans 15:4, 5; Galatians 5:22; Hebrews 6:12;
Hebrews 10:35–37; Hebrews 12:1; James 1:3–4

Lord God, upon You I patiently wait.
Strengthen my spirit to wait expectantly,
trusting in Your promises. Quiet my heart.

The Unsaved

Open your heart for God's love to flow through you freely, without judgment, so that the lost might be saved.

It's natural to have a passionate desire for those you love to be saved by Christ, just as you have been. The Spirit gives you the desire to lead others to Him, but you do not have the power to save them, so you shouldn't carry that burden. It is God at work in and through you that draws others to Him. Living out your faith is the greatest witness for His love, mercy, and grace. So don't try to overwhelm or force others into the arms of Jesus. We all have our journey of coming to Him, whether long or short, and we must allow God to work in the hearts of others in ways that will have the most powerful impact. Just trust, pray, and let God do what He does best—seek and save the lost.

Psalm 55:22; Proverbs 22:6; Isaiah 44:3;
Isaiah 50:10; Isaiah 56:1; Matthew 18:14;
John 16:7, 8; Acts 11:14; Acts 16:31; 2 Peter 3:9

Lord God, help me to open my heart for Your Spirit to work in and through me to reach others who are in need of Your love. Let my life be a living sacrifice to help save those who are lost and make them found.

Forgiving Others

*Pray that you will offer the same love, mercy,
and grace to others that God has freely given to you.*

We tend to beg God for mercy in our own lives, yet pray for justice in the lives of others. Our human nature wants vindication, even revenge, when we've been hurt deeply. When our pain seems inconsolable, we want those who have hurt us to suffer as well because we believe that their pain might somehow work for our gain. But it doesn't. When we've been hurt and our hearts are broken, it is God's love flowing through us that will comfort and mend us. Don't allow the bitterness within you to keep you from forgiving others, just as God has forgiven you. Don't allow your emotions to stand in the way of another person's salvation. And know that God's power works best in your weakness, so tell Him you need help when it comes to forgiving others.

Isaiah 43:18, 19; Matthew 5:10–12; Matthew 6:14, 15;
Matthew 18:21, 22; Mark 11:25; Luke 17:3; 2 Corinthians 2:14;
Philippians 3:13, 14; Colossians 3:13; Hebrews 10:30

*Heavenly Father, I need Your help when I need
to forgive others. Help me to trust in Your justice.
Let me be a light to others, even in my sufferings.*

For I am about TO DO SOMETHING New

Isaiah 43:19

Grace Never Runs Out

God's grace will always find you and keep you.

---

*D*on't for a second believe that God's grace runs out, that somehow you've expended His giving. God's love for you doesn't end. It doesn't have boundaries, and He'll never stop looking for ways to bless you in ways that will ultimately be for your good and His glory. So seek continually, knock, and He'll always open the door to you. Surrender your life daily, and expect His grace to meet you right where you are. All God wants is your faith, so just trust and rest, knowing that He is all you need.

Job 10:12; Proverbs 8:35;
1 Corinthians 15:10; 2 Corinthians 4:15;
Ephesians 1:5–7; Ephesians 2:4–8; Hebrews 4:16

*Heavenly Father, Your grace amazes me.
I am in awe of Your love that goes
beyond anything I deserve.*

Troubles and Trust

Don't allow your troubles to
trump your trust in God.

It's easy to become discouraged when we're struggling with situations in life that are challenging. We want to trust God, we want to believe what He's promised, but when nothing seems to be happening and when things seem to be getting worse, we get discouraged and lose hope. We place our hope in what we're experiencing instead of in God's promises. Far too often, we let go of our faith. So when we're depressed and losing hope, we've got to run to God . . . exposing our doubt to defeat the discouragement so we can find strength in all that He's promised us. God always keeps His promises, so we can trust them.

Psalm 27:1–3; Psalm 138:7; Isaiah 51:11;
John 14:1; Philippians 4:6, 7; 1 Peter 1:6–9

Lord, I tend to give in to doubt when my feelings challenge my faith. Draw me close to You; remind me of Your love for me. Help me to continue to believe and walk by faith.

THE *Lord* is my *Light* and *my* salvation so why should I be afraid? *Psalm 27:1*

Keep Asking

God has promised that you will receive whatever you ask for in prayer, so ask and keep asking until He answers.

here are promises that God has made to us that seem too good to be true. We contemplate His faithfulness through our humanness, as if He were a mere human. We want to believe Him, but we find it difficult. There's only one place to go when doubt tries to get the best of our faith—to our knees. Prayer turns our hearts to God; it's our faith in action. Nothing moves God's heart and hand like faith. Even though you may be filled with doubt, God's Spirit can sift through your heart and fill it with hope. You can have hope because God has made precious promises to you for every facet of your life. And He is faithful at all times and in all ways. All that you need to do is come to Him . . . and pray.

Psalm 91:15, 16; Psalm 145:18–20; Proverbs 15:29; Isaiah 65:24; Matthew 7:7, 8;
Matthew 18:19, 20; Mark 11:24, 25; John 16:23; Hebrews 4:16

Heavenly Father, thank You for the gift of prayer.
Thank You for listening to me and answering when I call to You.
Fill me with hope as I wait upon You to speak.

When You Feel Dismayed

When your heart is heavy, God promises to hold you.
Come to Him and allow Him to fill you with His joy.

There will be days when the heaviness of your heart will far outweigh your faith. And the fact that God loves you will seem insufficient to fill the emptiness you feel. But it's in that pit of darkness and despair that God will meet you. He will never leave you nor forsake you. Even through your doubt and little faith, He is there. And He's not there to just be present, but to be your ready help in your times of trouble. He knows what you're going through. You are not alone. He knows what each tear holds and He holds them for eternity. In your deepest sorrow, when you are disheartened, know that your darkest night will not overwhelm you. God is greater, His love is boundless, and His grace will cover, consume, and lift you up.

Nehemiah 8:10; Psalm 30:5; Psalm 34:17; Psalm 147:3; Isaiah 40:31; Isaiah 41:10; Isaiah 43:2; Isaiah 51:11; Isaiah 61:3; Luke 18:1; Romans 8:38, 39; 2 Corinthians 1:3, 4; Philippians 4:8; 1 Peter 4:12, 13; 1 Peter 5:6, 7

Lord God, thank You for never leaving me, for meeting me
in my emptiness and filling me with Your hope and peace. Help me
to lean on and rely upon You to strengthen my heart.

Isaiah 41:10

When Troubles Come

When troubles come, God has promised to be the refuge where gladness and joy will come upon you.

The tragedies of life often come suddenly, without warning, and they tend to press us on every side. But God has promised that they will not crush us. We may be bewildered, but we should not despair, for God is there at all times and in all ways. He is a ready help in times of trouble, and there is nothing that He cannot do. No matter what you are facing, there is no reason to be anxious and filled with worry. God's help is available to you through prayer. All that you need do is come to Him in faith. When you're tempted to fear, approach God's throne of grace with confidence, so that you might receive His mercy and find the grace to help you in your time of need.

Psalm 31:7; Psalm 121:1, 2; Psalm 138:7;
Isaiah 42:16; Isaiah 51:11; Nahum 1:7; Matthew 6:34;
John 14:1; Romans 8:28; 2 Corinthians 1:3, 4;
2 Corinthians 4:8, 9; Philippians 4:6, 7;
Hebrews 4:15, 16; 1 Peter 5:7

Heavenly Father, when I'm faced with the troubles of life, I am tempted to fear and draw back in my faith. I pray that Your Spirit will awaken mine and draw me near to You . . . my ready help in times of trouble.

All You Do and Say

*Let all that you do and say praise the Lord. He is your joy
and your salvation and worthy of your praise.*

We forget to praise. We are so easily captivated by all that is wrong in life, rather than by what is right. Yet God remains faithful even when our faith falters, so we should praise Him because when we fail, He never does. When we're struggling with a lack of joy in our lives, we should look to God, and we will find the joy that can be found in Him alone. Regardless of our circumstances, we can praise God . . . even when we don't feel like it. Even when there seems to be no reason why we should. We can praise Him for who He is and for His boundless love and grace that has saved us and continues to save us.

2 Samuel 22:4; Psalm 34:1–3; Psalm 47:1, 2, 6, 7;
Psalm 48:1; Psalm 50:23; Psalm 63:3–5; Psalm 71:5–8;
Psalm 92:1, 2, 4, 5; Psalm 96:4–8; Psalm 107:8; Psalm 147:1;
Isaiah 43:21; Acts 16:25; Ephesians 5:18–20;
Hebrews 13:14, 15; 1 Peter 2:9

*Lord God, fill me with Your Spirit,
and let all that I do and say bring praise
to Your name. Your joy is my strength.*

Discipleship

You have been called to follow Jesus,
to be a light in a dark world.

*L*ife can often seem to be without purpose. Daily responsibilities seem to yield nothing but emptiness. But you were never meant to live your life for the joys of this world. God has purposed you to live in His joy, bringing light to a dark world. It is through you that God can accomplish even greater things than that of the Resurrection. He has created you for a purpose, and in fulfilling those purposes for your life, you will be filled with the hope, peace, and joy you were meant to experience in this life. So set aside your will for your life and embrace God's will. Watch what He will do in and through you as you follow Him.

Matthew 28:18–20; Luke 5:27, 28; Luke 6:40; Luke 9:23–26; Luke 9:57–62; Luke 14:26; John 12:26; Acts 11:25, 26; Philippians 3:8, 9; Philippians 4:13; 2 Timothy 2:2; Hebrews 10:24, 29

Lord God, I surrender my life to You, offering up my life as a sacrifice to bring glory to Your name and lead others to Your boundless mercy and grace.

The Holy Spirit

*The Holy Spirit lives within you. He is your gift from God,
pouring out the love of God into your heart.*

We often feel as though we're living life on our own, and we struggle with our faith when life gets hard. We forget that God's Spirit lives within us, giving us all that we need—strength, joy, and hope amid all the uncertainties in life. There is nothing greater than our God and no greater gift than the Holy Spirit living within us. When we're filled with fear, the Spirit calms us. When we're struggling with doubt, the Spirit reminds us of God's promises to us. When we don't know what to pray, the Spirit intercedes on our behalf, calling upon God in ways we don't have the strength for. Each and every moment of your life should be filled with joy because you know that Almighty God is living within you.

Joel 2:28; Matthew 3:11; Luke 11:13; John 7:38, 39;
John 14:16–20; John 16:7–9, 14; Acts 1:4, 5, 7, 8; Acts 2:4;
Acts 2:38; Acts 4:31; Acts 8:14–17; Acts 10:44–47; Acts 19:1–6;
Romans 5:5; 1 Corinthians 6:19; Galatians 5:16, 17;
Ephesians 5:18–20

*Heavenly Father, thank You for the
Holy Spirit, who fills me and strengthens me
in Your joy. Open my heart to receive more
of Your grace and to walk in the Spirit.*

Let the Holy Spirit to guide your lives

Galatians 5:16

Healing Through Forgiveness

Forgive others as God has forgiven you,
and thereby be filled with His peace.

W e pray for justice upon others and beg for forgiveness for ourselves. Our human nature wants a price to be paid for our pain, yet the price has already been paid through the sacrifice of Christ— we're just not sure we want to share God's grace. But God requires us to forgive in the way that He has forgiven us. By surrendering our anger and bitterness to God, our hearts are freed to live in the joy we were meant to have. No matter what injustices you have suffered or are enduring, don't allow the pain to take any more away from your life than it already has. Open your heart to God and allow Him to do what only He can do: heal you from the inside.

Numbers 14:19–21; Isaiah 1:18; Isaiah 43:25–26;
Daniel 9:9; Micah 7:18–19; Matthew 6:14–15; Matthew 26:28;
Mark 11:25; Acts 3:19; Colossians 1:13–14; 1 John 1:9

Heavenly Father, help me to release my pain and
unforgiveness to You. Help me to offer others the
same grace You continually offer to me.

Focused on God Alone

God wants you to live according to His will and not your own,
because His ways are not only higher—they're also far better.

We tend to believe that we have life under control—until it isn't. And we often find ourselves with nowhere to look but up, which is where we should have been focused in the first place. When life doesn't meet our expectations and we're forced to run to God, we come to a place of hopeless surrender, realizing that God has designed our lives according to His plans and not our own. When we are living within His will, surrendered to Him and trusting in Him completely, we will be fulfilled in ways we thought impossible. Don't miss out on God's very best for your life . . . live for Him and within His promises, and your joy will last forever.

Joshua 1:8, 9; Nehemiah 9:9, 13, 20; Psalm 31:3, 5; Psalm 32:7–8; Psalm 37:23, 24; Psalm 48:14; Psalm 143:10; Proverbs 3:1, 5, 6, 11, 12; Proverbs 6:20, 22, 23; Isaiah 30:21; Isaiah 48:17; John 16:13, 14; Romans 8:14; Ephesians 5:17; Colossians 3:15–17; 1 Thessalonians 4:3, 4, 6; 1 Timothy 2:1, 3, 4; James 1:5, 6

Lord God, I surrender my will to Yours. All that I want in my life
is what You desire for me. Take my heart and make it Yours.

Saving Faith

Only Jesus saves, so surrender your heart
so that He might live in and through you.

You might be the only Bible people ever read. That truth is a heavy burden to accept, but your life is a witness to God's love, mercy, and grace that He can use to bring others to Himself. Your life can make a difference in someone else's. But the way in which you live can also turn people away from Him. Know that God isn't asking you to do anything on your own. Your obedience lies in your surrender. A heart that is open and willing to be used by God is one that is prepared to pray for those who are not saved and be the hands and feet of Jesus in their lives. It is God's power that saves; simply be the vessel for Him to do that through your daily surrender.

Psalm 55:23; Psalm 98:2, 3; Proverbs 22:6; Isaiah 44:3, 6; Isaiah 50:10; Isaiah 56:1; Matthew 18:12, 14; John 16:7–9; Acts 11:14; Acts 16:31; 1 Thessalonians 5:21–24; 1 Peter 3:1, 2; 2 Peter 3:9

Heavenly Father, let my life be a vessel for Your love and
grace to save those who are lost. I surrender all that I am for
the purposes of leading others to You through my faith.

for He who calls you is faithful

1 Thessalonians 5:24

God's Peace When Troubled

Whatever you're going through, God knows.
His love is unfailing—you need only put your hope in Him.

Whether you are aware of it or not, God's angels are encamped around you at all times. God is aware of every fear and all of the doubt that is threatening to overcome your faith. And He is your Deliverer. There is a greater miracle that God wants to work than merely calming the storms of your life. What He really wants to do is calm the storm *within* you. Troubles will come, but God wants you to be comforted at all times, at peace, knowing that He is with you and that there is nothing to fear. No matter what you are facing, you can have peace and be at rest because God is sovereign and His love for you is unfailing.

Psalm 25:16–18; Psalm 31:7; Psalm 33:17–22; Psalm 34:1–8;
Psalm 147:2, 3, 5, 6, 13, 14; John 14:27; 1 Peter 5:7–11; 1 John 4:4

Lord God, fill me with Your peace amid the troubles of my life.
Help me to rest in You, knowing that You will never fail me.

Encouraging Others

God has called you to encourage others through your faith, and He has promised that you will inherit countless blessings for doing so.

It may seem difficult to believe that you can encourage someone else when your life's circumstances leave you feeling hopeless. But in your time of helplessness, when you are being emptied and forced to rely on God more than you ever thought you would have to, the Spirit of God can flow through you more freely than ever. In your emptiness and despair, His power is more evident and effective. Whatever troubles you are going through, know that in your weakness, God will strengthen you to reach out to others with the love and grace He will pour into you.

Psalm 55:14; Proverbs 12:18; Proverbs 15:23;
Isaiah 35:1–4; Matthew 12:34, 36, 37; Romans 14:7–19;
Galatians 6:2; Galatians 6:10; Ephesians 4:29–32;
James 1:26; James 3:2–10; 1 Peter 3:9, 10

Heavenly Father, I want my life to be a living sacrifice to You, bringing Your love and hope to those around me who need You desperately.

Living in Truth

God does not lie, and neither should we. An honest heart is connected to God's, releasing His love and mercy into our lives.

It's easy to get lost in lies. When life gets hard, it seems easier to believe the lies than to believe what is true. We fail to trust God, and living a lie becomes a survival mechanism . . . but it's a short-term fix. Living within our lies may work for a time, but eventually they catch up with us and we awaken abruptly to reality. God has called us to a life of honesty; His truth sets us free from the lies that imprison us. So don't allow the temptation to lie in order to somehow control what you can't to drive you deeper into despair. Be determined to be free by living in truth.

2 Samuel 12:1–7; Psalm 119:43–45;
Proverbs 12:22; Proverbs 29:1; Jeremiah 31:29;
Matthew 7:1–5; Ephesians 4:21–25; Colossians 3:9, 10

*Lord God, help me to live in Your truth.
I need Your Spirit to examine my heart and
reveal any lies that keep me from living the
abundant life You intend for me.*

What Faith Does

God's timing is always perfect—
trust that He knows what's best for you.

$\mathcal{G}$od's answers to your prayers may not come in the ways you thought they would or in the timing you were expecting, but He will come with a perfect miracle beyond anything you can hope for or imagine. God hears your cries for help. But as you await His power, He wants you to rest in His presence and perfect peace. He wants you at His throne of grace, trusting that He's preparing answers to your prayers that go far beyond all you can dare to hope for or imagine. Don't miss out on what faith does . . . it changes everything.

Joshua 10:25; Job 6:8; Psalm 3:2–6; Psalm 147:11;
Jeremiah 29:11; 1 Corinthians 15:54–58

Heavenly Father, I thank You for always hearing me and
pouring out Your grace in the times I least deserve it. Help me to
trust in faith and remain calm and assured in your love for me.

Setting an Example

*A daily surrender of your life is the
greatest example of your faith in God.*

*D*on't be overwhelmed with living the Christian life. The life of faith is about trusting in God, surrendering our will to His, and allowing Him to live in and through us. It's a lot easier than we think. It's a matter of letting go of our desires so that God can use our lives to fulfill His greater purposes. And it's that surrendered life that shines bright, drawing others to Him. Just as when He looks at you, He sees Jesus, when others look at you, they also will see Jesus when if you lay down your life for the One who laid down His life for you.

Judges 13:4, 5, 7; Proverbs 31:25;
1 Timothy 5:4–6; Titus 2:2–5, 7

*Heavenly Father, take my life and let it be Yours.
Help me to surrender everything that keeps me from being
used fully by You to draw others to Your saving grace.*

Everlasting Joy

God has promised to bless you as you trust in His promises to you. Your joy comes from Him.

We look for joy in the temporary pleasures of life instead of searching for God, who brings us eternal joy, regardless of our ever-changing circumstances. And we need that kind of joy because life can turn on us without warning. Our life's expectations are often disappointed, and we need a peace and joy that enables us to take just one more step of faith. Yet we look in all the wrong places, seeking but never finding, because when life steals our joy, we fail to look to God. Don't miss out on the greatest blessings in your life. Trust God, and trust what He's promised, and then wait with patient expectation that your joy will be made complete.

Psalm 113:9; Psalm 118:24; Proverbs 23:25;
Proverbs 31:28–31; Luke 1:14, 44–49

Lord, I look to You to complete my joy. Help me to fully trust in Your promises to me, enabling me to walk in faith even amid the doubt.

Protection

God is your shelter, protector, and provider,
so there is nothing to fear.

*W*e are tempted to believe that since we cannot see God, He cannot see all that concerns us. But He knows everything. He is aware of all your fears, and He is able not only to protect you, but also to provide all that you need in this life. He may stretch your faith more than you like, and will probably ask you to wait longer than you think you can. But God knows what He's doing. He wants you to fully trust Him in ways you are not sure you can. So when you are filled with fear, look up and don't let life get you down. God is able to save you, and He will . . . He has promised to.

Genesis 7:7, 24; Exodus 2:3–6;
Exodus 21:22; Psalm 14:27; 2 Thessalonians 3:3

Heavenly Father, I am filled with fear
and I need You to reassure me that You will
protect me in every way. Help me to have
peace in this moment, knowing that
You are Almighty God.

Praying as a Family

***God has promised that if two or more of
you ask for anything in Jesus' name, it will be done.***

God loves to answer your prayers, and there's nothing He loves more than listening to the prayers of your family. He brought you all together for reasons that go far beyond anything you can imagine, but the very basic purpose is so that you might strengthen each other's faith, praying together and thereby bringing heaven to earth. When you are anxious, worried about what tomorrow holds, gather your family together and pray. There is nothing that God cannot do, and as you pray as a family, His power will draw you nearer not only to Him, but also to each other.

Psalm 37:4; Psalm 145:18, 19; Isaiah 56:4–7; Isaiah 65:24; Jeremiah 33:3;
Daniel 9:3–5, 17, 18; Matthew 18:19, 20; Matthew 21:22; 2 Corinthians 1:11–14;
Philippians 4:4–7; 1 Timothy 2:8; Hebrews 4:16; 1 John 3:22

*Lord God, we come before You together, as a family, to lay down our
lives before You. Strengthen our faith and fill us with Your love.*

The Return of Glory

Jesus is coming back.
Are you waiting for that blessed event?

We so easily lose hope, looking to what we see instead of what we don't. We forget that Jesus, King of kings and Lord of lords, is coming back. Suddenly, He will appear, and our joy will last forever. In a moment, we will not only see Him as He is, but we, too, will be like Him. Every sorrow will be turned to joy, and death will be no more. His second coming is a reason to rejoice, even now at this moment when it seems as though the world is falling apart. We can have hope when all hope seems gone because we know that Christ is returning.

Psalm 103:18, 19; Isaiah 51:11; Isaiah 65:17–19; Lamentations 3:24–26; Matthew 24:27–31;
Luke 21:25–28; Acts 1:11; Titus 2:13; 2 Peter 3:10–12; 1 John 3:1–3; 1 John 5:10–13; Revelation 21:4

Lord God, help me to live each day anticipating Your return,
living a life that is worthy of Your great love. Fill my spirit with
Your hope and the joys to come that will last forever.

The Lord is my INHERITANCE therefore I will Hope in HIM
Lamentations 3:24

Obedience

You will never regret being obedient to God.

When God commands us to do something, we often hesitate because it usually requires more faith than we have at the time. We reason things out ourselves instead of trusting in God's wisdom above our own. But when God commands us, it is for our good and His glory, and we should never second-guess God. Know that when God asks you to step out in faith and be obedient, it will usually require you to rely on Him more than you would like. But He will enable you to do everything He's asking you to do. He will strengthen you in every way to walk in the faith that He is asking of you. So step out in faith . . . God has promised that you won't regret it.

Genesis 7:7; Genesis 19:15; Genesis 19:26;
1 Kings 1:17; 1 Kings 17:13, 15; Luke 1:38;
Luke 17:32, 33; 1 Thessalonians 5:16; 1 Peter 3:6

Heavenly Father, I struggle and reason instead of trusting You. Strengthen my heart to know that my obedience brings about Your blessings.

God's Mercy Through Grace

God has come to help you;
His compassion for you is unfailing.

*P*art of God's faithfulness is His compassion. His love reaches into places we never expected, and his heart opens wider than we ever thought it could. No matter where we are or what we're going through, God knows, and His love is there. His grace consumes us when we're overwhelmed with sorrow, filled with pain, and desperate for hope. God's compassion never fails; He has promised that. So in your times of need, in the depths of despair, know that God is there and will help you in whatever way you need Him to.

Genesis 21:1–3; Genesis 29:31–34;
Genesis 30:24; 1 Samuel 2:21; Psalm 122:3;
Isaiah 49:15, 16; Lamentations 3:22–24;
Luke 1:41–45; Luke 2:6, 7; Luke 7:13–16

Lord, thank You for Your love and grace
that consume me. As I'm longing for someone to
care, I will continually trust that You are here
with me at all times and in all ways.

Prosperity

God will fill you when you empty yourself for Him and His purposes.

*T*here are no greater riches than those found in Christ, given to you by God. Yet we tend to find our pleasures in the physical prosperity of this world, and end up missing out on the fullness of God's greater blessings that await us through faith. If you're longing for more, to be prosperous in every way, seek God and allow Him to give you what you need. And trust in His timing. Sometimes God shows up to provide for you when you think He should, but more often, He's going to stretch your faith so that His presence and power are more dramatically revealed. Trust God to make your life flourish in all the ways you have always hoped for.

Exodus 3:22; 1 Kings 17:14–16; 2 Kings 4:2–7; Isaiah 40:31

Heavenly Father, help me to empty myself, allowing room to be filled by You so that I am available for Your purposes.

Promise after Promise

*God's promises are all you need to assure
you of the hope you long for.*

It is easy to lose hope and feel overwhelmed by the weight of the world. But God has assured you a future that is good—one filled with hope. It's up to you to trust in what He has promised you. Faith won't always be easy when you are faced with the unthinkable and dealing with the impossible, but God has given you promise after promise that He will be faithful to His Word. He will never forsake you, and He has promised that He is with you always. His love, mercy, and grace are assured, and that is all you need to know.

Ruth 2:13; 2 Samuel 12:24; 1 Kings 17:14;
Matthew 5:4; Romans 8:28

*Lord God, how I thank You that I can have hope because
of Your promises and the assurance of Your faithfulness.*

Power

Never underestimate the power of God,
and always call upon Him to do the impossible in your life.

*L*ife can bring us to "stuck" places, where there's no way out and the impossibilities outweigh our faith. But we forget that God is not only with us, He is also there to help us in every way we need Him to. Our prayers release His power and our faith opens His heart and His hand . . . so we need to pray that God's power will bring heaven to earth. Pray that God will work powerfully in your life and in the lives of others. Pray that His power will bring about good for His glory, and know that His power is able to save, at all times and in all ways.

Proverbs 31:17; Luke 1:41;
Acts 1:8; Romans 8:37

Heavenly Father, I trust in Your power
to save me at all times and in all ways.
Help me to look to You to be my
ready help in times of trouble.

The Sufficiency of Jesus

All you ever need is Jesus.

Don't miss out on the simplicity of faith and the sufficiency of Jesus. He is all you will ever need. He is your Shepherd, to lead and guide and rescue you when you're lost. It is because of your faith in Him that you will lack nothing. When you are weary, He refreshes your soul. When you are full of fear, He protects and comforts you. He watches over you when you are sleeping because He never sleeps . . . He is continually watching over your life. And His power is made perfect in your weakness. So it's okay to feel as though you're not able, because Jesus is. And He is all you need; your faith in Him makes *all things* possible.

Exodus 12:13; Psalm 23:1–4; Psalm 121:2, 3, 5, 7, 8;
Matthew 19:26; John 14:6; 2 Corinthians 3:4, 5;
2 Corinthians 12:9; Ephesians 2:13; Philippians 4:13;
Hebrews 4:14–16; Hebrews 9:14; Revelation 1:17, 18

Jesus, I need You. Help me to open my heart and surrender my soul to You each and every day.

Matthew 19:26

Protected by God

God promises that you can live in safety and be at ease because He will protect you. You can rest because God never does.

There will be situations in life where you will be consumed with fear. The reality of a fallen world can fall upon you suddenly and cause you to doubt God's sovereignty. But you must trust. You must depend upon the promises God has made to you. They are countless, and He is faithful. When you are fearful, know that God is always with you and promised NEVER to leave you nor forsake you. In the midst of chaos, peace will come from standing firm in your faith and trusting that God is who He says He is. Rest in God alone.

Psalm 4:8; Psalm 27:1–5; Psalm 34:7; Psalm 91:3–7;
Psalm 121:5–8; Proverbs 1:33; Isaiah 43:2; Isaiah 54:10, 13, 17;
Isaiah 59:19; Matthew 10:29–31; John 10:11

Lord God, so often I am filled with fear when I look at my circumstances. Help me to look only to You and trust You completely. Help me to have peace.

Victory

If you trust in God, there is always victory;
you need only stand firm in your faith.

It may seem like your circumstances are bigger than God, but they're not. There is nothing too difficult for Him. Nothing. Whatever battles you are facing, you need only stand still, in faith, because the battle belongs to the Lord. Pray, obey, and wait for the victory that God will give you. Don't make faith harder than it is. Don't allow doubt and despair to get the best of you. Believe God, even when what you see discourages you from doing so. God is not only a current help in times of trouble; He's Almighty God—and though defeat may seem imminent, His victory is promised and sure. So praise Him in this moment, knowing that you are in His grace.

Joshua 1:9; Nehemiah 8:10; Psalm 23:2–6; Psalm 24:1–10; Psalm 25:1, 2; Psalm 28:8; Psalm 34:17–19; Psalm 37:5–9; Psalm 40:1–17; Psalm 41:1–3; Psalm 47:1–9; Psalm 48:1; Psalm 60:11, 12; Psalm 118:24, 25; Psalm 121:5–8; Psalm 122:1; Ephesians 5:19, 20; Philippians 4:12–14; 1 Peter 1:7–9

Heavenly Father, encourage my faith, in this moment,
to believe that victory is Yours in every battle that I face.

THE Lord himself WATCHES over YOU

Psalm 121:5

Judging

*Always offer to others the grace
that's been given to you by God.*

Colossians 3:12, 13

CLOTHE yourselves with Kindness HUMiLiTY gentleness and PATIENCE

It is easy to pray for justice when we've been wronged, yet pray for mercy when we're the ones who have done wrong to others. We fail to forget the forgiveness that God has offered us when we are suffering pain due to the sin committed against us. But God's love and grace are enough. If you surrender your heart, He will fill it with His own. When you are tempted to judge others, ask God to allow you to see them through His eyes and to help you love them with His heart.

Matthew 7:3, 5; John 5:22;
1 Corinthians 4:5; Colossians 3:12, 13

*Lord God, fill my heart with Your love
and help me to see others through Your eyes.
I pray that Your mercy and grace will
consume me and draw others to You.*

Pride

Let God be the one to lift you up.

We want God to work the way we do, but He doesn't. He says that whoever will be first will be the last. God asks us to humble ourselves because if we don't, He will do it for us. The key to our faith is realizing that God is God and we are not. It is fully surrendering *our* power to make way for *God's* . . . and there is no greater power. God can do far more than you can hope for or imagine, so let faith work in the way it's supposed to, and simply trust that God is who He says He is and that He will do what He says He will do.

Proverbs 27:1, 2; Matthew 18:2–4;
Luke 18:11–14

Heavenly Father, examine my heart and show me the ways in which I must more fully surrender to all that You are.

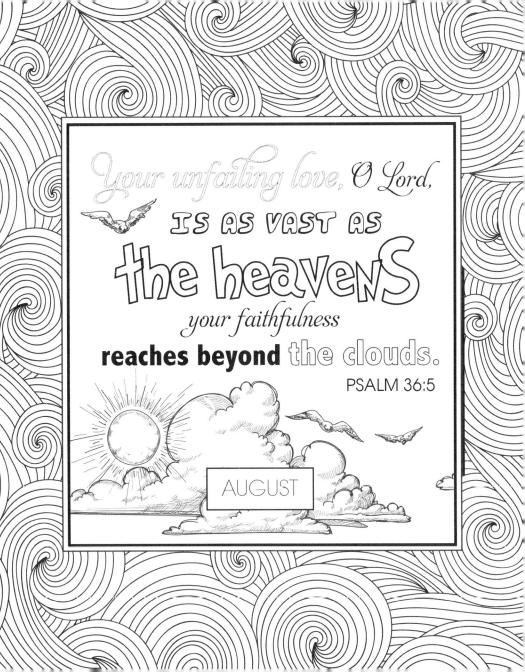

Your unfailing love, O Lord,

IS AS VAST AS

the heavens

your faithfulness

reaches beyond the clouds.

PSALM 36:5

AUGUST

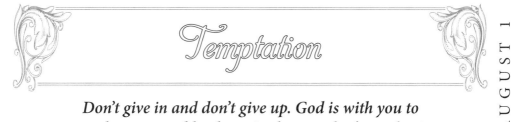

Temptation

Don't give in and don't give up. God is with you to strengthen you and lead you in the way that's everlasting.

Trials will come, and so will temptations. Our fallen world lures us to long for what is temporary—what we see—instead of what is eternal. We must always keep our eyes on God. It's not easy, but if we stay connected to God and seek Him at all times, He will keep us from falling. He will keep us from the sin that threatens to overtake us. We can find strength in His Word when we're struggling with the temptations of the world. His Word will keep us firm in the foundation of our faith. So let nothing move you . . . God is with you.

James 1:2–4; James 1:12; 2 Peter 2:9

Lord God, help me to always resist the temptations of this world and find my satisfaction in You alone.

In the Deepest Gloom

**God has promised to bring light
to the deepest gloom.**

If God has promised to bring us out of the deepest gloom, then we shouldn't be surprised when we find ourselves in the depths of it. As if life were not difficult enough, the darkness of depression falls upon us, and we are driven deeper into despair by the guilt of where we find ourselves . . . empty, without joy, and supposed to be filled with faith. But it's right where you are that God wants to meet you. Now, when you're certain that you are drowning so deep down that no one can save you, God will reach down and rescue you. Trust him.

Psalm 30:5; Psalm 34:17; Psalm 130:5; Psalm 147:3;
Isaiah 41:10; Isaiah 61:3; 2 Corinthians 1:3, 4;
Philippians 4:8; 1 Peter 4:12, 13

*Lord God, save me from the depths of despair.
Help me to focus on You and not on my feelings.
In this moment, I run to You.*

Loneliness

You are never alone. God has promised that He is always with you.

*T*here is nothing more emptying than feeling alone. Life can get hard, and our feelings can easily overwhelm our faith. It is in these moments, when you're certain you've been abandoned and you need help, but there is none, that you must run to God and be consumed by His Word. His voice, speaking through His promises, will assure you that you are not alone. His voice will comfort you and give you peace. Though the world may forsake you, He never will. God's love for you will never fail, so run to Him so that His grace can embrace you.

Deuteronomy 4:31; Deuteronomy 31:6;
Deuteronomy 33:27; 1 Samuel 12:22; Psalm 27:10;
Psalm 46:1; Psalm 147:3; Isaiah 41:10; Isaiah 54:10;
Matthew 28:20; John 14:1, 18; 1 Peter 5:7

*Heavenly Father, consume me with
Your presence and embrace me with Your love.
I need to know that I am not alone and
that You are with me.*

Wrestling with Faith

*You can rest and have peace because
God has promised to meet all of your needs.*

We would spend a lot less time worrying if we focused more on trusting—trusting God and His promises to us. We want to believe, but so often we doubt, and we wrestle with our faith more than we should. We can so easily find ourselves spiraling out of control, overwhelmed by our circumstances and overcome by the emotions that result from feeling like life is falling apart. Sometimes worry gets the best of us. Life gets hard. Yet through it all, God is inviting us to trust Him more. By stretching our faith, we can win over the worry by keeping our eyes on Him.

Psalm 4:8; Proverbs 3:24; Isaiah 26:3; Matthew 6:25–32;
Romans 8:6; Philippians 4:19; Colossians 3:15; Hebrews 4:3, 9; 1 Peter 5:7

*Heavenly Father, I so easily become consumed with worry.
Help me to know that life is not falling apart but falling into place as
You have promised to care for me in every way I need You to.*

Bewildered by God

***God has everything under control,
even when it seems like He doesn't.***

*A*s if life isn't confusing enough, we are told to trust in a God we cannot see and seldom can hear. We're told to trust in His Word and depend upon His faithfulness, but our doubt gets in the way. So we try to figure things out, try to make sense of God, and we only find ourselves more confused and our faith failing further. In the moments when we just don't have the strength to take another step of faith, we must do so anyway. We cannot ever allow ourselves to walk by sight, because it's in walking by faith that God works miracles. Don't try to make sense of it all; just trust and obey.

Psalm 18:30; Psalm 34:19; Psalm 55:22; Psalm 138:8; Isaiah 26:3; Isaiah 55:8, 9; Jeremiah 32:40; Jeremiah 33:3; Romans 8:28; Romans 8:35–37; 1 Corinthians 10:13; Hebrews 10:23; Hebrews 13:5

*Lord God, help me not to lean upon my own understanding
but to simply, completely, trust You at all times and in all ways.*

YOU will KEEP in PERFECT peace all who trust in you — Isaiah 26:3

Choosing Your Words

**The power of life and death is in your words.
Choose carefully.**

*W*e often believe that life is out of control and that we are at the mercy of it all. But we're not. God has told us that we hold the power of life and death in our words. What we speak impacts our lives more than we realize; God has given us a measure of control. Each and every word we speak has the power to bring about trouble or triumph in our lives, and we must choose between them. We must speak what God speaks, think as He thinks. And we do that by meditating on His Word day and night. Don't miss out on God's very best in your life; speak the words that God speaks.

1 Chronicles 16:9; Job 37:3, 4; Proverbs 13:3;
Proverbs 16:24; Proverbs 18:21; Proverbs 21:23;
Proverbs 24:28; Matthew 12:36; Luke 6:45;
Ephesians 4:29, 31, 32; 1 Timothy 6:20, 21; Titus 3:9;
1 Peter 1:15; 1 Peter 2:23; 1 Peter 3:10

*Lord God, I pray that Your Spirit
will draw me to Your Words. Give me the
wisdom to choose my words wisely.*

Comfort in Affliction

God's Word will bring healing to your heart and soul and comfort you in your affliction.

This fallen world brings with it pain and sorrows that only God can comfort, yet we often fail to come to Him when we're hurting. We're not sure that our faith will be enough for the miracle we so desperately need. When we're weary, we don't want to wait. And we are certain that if we are depending on God, we might have to wait longer than we think we can. But it's through the stretching pain of faith that God's power works best. He shines through our weakness. Know that God wastes nothing and that whatever you're going through, God can and will use it for good. Run to His arms, rest in His embrace, and be consumed by His grace.

Psalm 23:4; Psalm 48:14; Psalm 49:15;
Psalm 77:10–14; Isaiah 26:3, 4; Jeremiah 17:14;
Romans 12:19; 2 Corinthians 4:15, 18; 2 Corinthians 5:1;
James 5:14–15; 1 Peter 2:24

Heavenly Father, I need You to comfort me, to strengthen my heart and fill me with faith. Lord, help me to rest in Your peace.

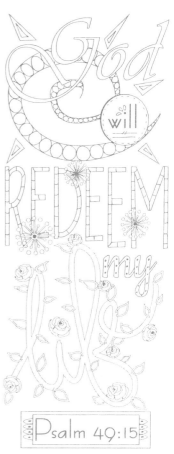

God will REDEEM my life

Psalm 49:15

God Will Make You Holy

Jesus is all you need to live a godly life.

*T*here's no need to ask yourself to do and be more than God is asking of you. You can stop striving to be holy, because only He is holy. All you need is Jesus. It is in surrendering your life to Him and allowing Him to live in and through you that you are holy. So don't wear yourself out trying . . . it's about trusting. God's mighty power in you will transform your life and give you a new heart, one that is filled with His love, mercy, and grace. He will enable you to live the life He's called you to live . . . just remember to surrender daily.

Proverbs 4:23; Romans 3:22–24; Romans 4:5;
Romans 10:10; 1 Corinthians 1:30; 2 Corinthians 5:21;
Galatians 3:6, 7; Titus 3:4; 1 Peter 1:15, 16

*Heavenly Father, I long to be
holy as You are holy. Fill me with Your
Spirit and cleanse me so that I might
fulfill Your purposes for my life.*

A Multitude of Sins

*Turn to God when you have sinned and allow Him to forgive
and heal you completely . . . in all the ways you need to be.*

It's easy to feel trapped in sin. It seems like there's no way out, and certainly no place to hide. The consequences of sin can chain you like nothing else can, causing you to feel as though things will never get better and that God will never forgive you. But He will. And things will get better. You need only turn to Him, allowing His love and mercy to pour over you. You may not escape the consequences of sin, but God will forgive you and strengthen you to endure. His love covers a multitude of sins . . . allow Him to cover yours.

Psalm 32:1; Psalm 103:12; Isaiah 1:18; Isaiah 43:25;
Isaiah 55:7; Mark 11:25; 2 Corinthians 5:17; Ephesians 1:7, 8;
Colossians 2:13; Colossians 3:13; Hebrews 8:12; 1 John 1:9; 1 John 2:1

*Lord God, I repent of my sins, surrendering my heart to You completely,
so that I might be transformed in the ways You need me to be.*

Disappointment

**God has promised that if you trust in Him, goodness
and mercy will follow you all the days of your life.**

*L*ife may not always go according to your
plans, but you can be sure that it will always
go according to God's . . . and His plans are to give
you a future and hope. The only disappointment we
experience in life is when things don't turn out the
way we thought they would. But that doesn't mean
that all hope is gone. God is able to do the impossible.
He's able to work miracles that go far beyond anything
you can hope for or imagine. So hope, imagine, and
pray, and don't give up until God shows up.

Psalm 37:17–19; Psalm 37:39, 40; Psalm 119:165–169;
Isaiah 25:8, 9; Isaiah 26:3, 4; Isaiah 55:8, 9, 12;
Isaiah 57:19–21; 2 Corinthians 4:6, 8, 9

*Heavenly Father, help me to walk by faith.
I want to trust You more, so draw me near
to You and strengthen my spirit.*

Life Through the Word

*God's Word will provide all the wisdom you need
to live the victorious life God intends for you.*

We are constantly seeking and rarely finding. Our souls will remain lost and confused if we rely on wisdom coming from any other source than "The Source," God Himself. He has graced us with His Word and the power that it holds, but we rarely rely on it in all the ways that we should. Whatever you're dealing with, God has something to say about it. He has given you His Word so that you can know you are never alone and that He Himself, God Almighty, is always there to lead and guide you in the way that you should go. All you need is God and His Word; seek Him and you will find!

Nehemiah 8:10; Psalm 18:1–3;
Psalm 119:28; Proverbs 8:14; Ephesians 3:16, 17;
Ephesians 6:10, 13, 14; Colossians 1:11, 12

*Lord God, speak to me through Your Word. Lead
and guide me in Your paths of righteousness.
Turn my eyes from worthless things and
give me life through Your Word.*

Be strong IN THE Lord and in HIS Mighty Power
EPHESIANS 6:10

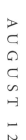

The Battle

***Though you have an enemy of your soul,
you have a God who is greater and assures you of the victory.***

There will be times when you feel the world is against you, and it may very well be . . . because you have an enemy. But God is guarding your soul. God remains in control, even though the battle is raging and it seems that all hope is gone. God is always sovereign, and He is your strength in your weakness. Even when you're in the darkest valleys, there is nothing to fear; God is with you always and has assured you victory through every battle.

Psalm 16:8; Psalm 55:22; Proverbs 18:10; Isaiah 26:3;
Isaiah 41:10; John 14:27; John 16:33; 2 Timothy 1:7

*Lord God, strengthen my faith in every battle. Turn my
eyes from worthless things and give me life through Your Word.
Fill me with Your peace that surpasses all understanding.*

God's Faithfulness

God is faithful even when you aren't.

We compare our faith to God's faithfulness and determine that since our faith often falls short, so will God's faithfulness. But God is faithful forever. His love, mercy, and grace do not change according to our circumstances, nor are they drowned out by our doubt. God is God and He never changes. He never will. So though doubt may get the best of you, it will never get the best of God. He is true to His Word and He will accomplish all that He desires to. You can thus find strength in knowing that if you continue to trust, even though you have doubts, God will show up. He *will* answer your prayers . . . it's just a matter of time, so wait expectantly. He is full of surprises.

Genesis 9:16, 17; Deuteronomy 7:8–10; Psalm 36:5; Psalm 89:1, 2;
Psalm 119:64, 65; Isaiah 54:9, 10; 1 Corinthians 1:9; 2 Timothy 2:13

*Heavenly Father, I thank You for being faithful even when
I'm not. Help me to stand firm in my faith and not to allow
doubt to discourage me from resting in Your faithfulness.*

God will BLESS you in everything
Deuteronomy 15:10

Make Every Day Count

*There is no greater joy
than a life surrendered to God.*

Isaiah 65:18

We all struggle to know what our purpose on earth is. We look to God and get a glimpse from time to time. Sometimes it's easy to see the ways in which God uses our lives; at other times, it seems as though there is little purpose at all. The daily struggle can seem overwhelming, and our faith can be easily overcome when we're not living for God alone. So each and every day, pray and ask God to help you live the day for Him. Ask Him to help you be sensitive to His direction for your life, and ask Him to fill you with His love, mercy, and grace so that you might lead others to Him. Then your joy—and your purpose—will be made complete.

Psalm 90:12; Proverbs 5:21; Proverbs 10:4, 5;
Proverbs 13:20; Proverbs 23:4, 5; Proverbs 25:11;
Ecclesiastes 8:5–7; Ecclesiastes 10:18; Isaiah 65:18

*Lord God, each and every day, I want
to live for You alone. Take my life and let it
be all that You've designed it to be. Help me
to surrender my will to Yours.*

One Way

There's only one way . . . Jesus.

What would Jesus do? is not just a cliché question; it's a question that should be asked in everything we do and say because Jesus is the only way. We struggle to live our lives in the way we think we should and yet be obedient to the ways in which God is calling us to live. And we give up so easily because living the way God wants us to seems like a setup for complete failure. But we fail to truly understand what God is asking us to do. He is simply asking us to surrender our hearts and allow Jesus to live in and through us. Faith is much simpler than we make it out to be. We have just got to keep our eyes on Jesus.

Mark 10:43–45; John 13:14, 15;
John 13:34; Romans 15:5–7; Ephesians 5:1, 2;
Philippians 2:5–8; Colossians 3:12, 13; Hebrews 12:2, 3;
1 Peter 2:21; 1 John 2:6; 1 John 3:16

Heavenly Father, help me in my struggle.
Help me to surrender my heart, and grant me
the strength to keep my eyes on Jesus.

Anxiety

The question is, Whom do you trust?

When we're filled with doubt and overcome with despair, we are not trusting God. And we don't want to hear that because that means we're lacking faith, and we're not sure we have the strength to have any more faith than we've got at this moment. But it's at those moments, when our faith doesn't seem to be working that we must run to God and know that He is there to help us in every way that we need it. Listen, you can rest. You can have peace. You don't need to worry; God is sovereign . . . just trust Him.

Psalm 91:1–2; Psalm 119:43; Proverbs 3:24; Isaiah 26:3; Matthew 6:25–34;
John 14:1; John 14:27; Romans 8:6; Philippians 4:6, 7; Philippians 4:8;
Philippians 4:19; Colossians 3:15; Hebrews 4:3, 9; 1 Peter 5:6, 7

*Lord God, bring peace to my soul. Strengthen my spirit
to trust You more than I think I can.*

Feeling Abandoned

God's unfailing love for you can never be shaken.

*Y*ou might feel alone, but you are not. God has promised to be with you always. And you need to trust that right now, at this moment, in your doubt. If God has made a promise to you, then you can count on Him to be true to His Word. That faithfulness might not work in the timing you think it should, but He will fulfill every promise He has made to you. So there's nothing to fear. God's love for you never changes. And His power and presence are always present in your life, regardless of how you feel. Right now, make the decision to trust that God is your refuge and strength and know that He loves you unconditionally. He is with you always.

Deuteronomy 4:31; Deuteronomy 30:6; Deuteronomy 33:27;
1 Samuel 12:22; Psalm 27:10; Psalm 46:1; Psalm 147:3; Isaiah 41:10;
Isaiah 54:10; Matthew 28:19, 20; John 14:1; John 14:18;
Romans 8:35–39; Hebrews 13:5; 1 Peter 5:6, 7

Heavenly Father, help me to trust You beyond my feelings.
Help me to know that You are with me even when it feels like You're not.

Sadness

Even Jesus wept.

⸻※◈◈◈⸻

here will be times when we are sad beyond understanding and, often, for reasons that we are not sure of. Yet God is there, with us, in it and through it. Whatever is causing you to feel sadness in your heart is sovereignly controlled by God. And as hard as that is to hear, also know that in His sovereignty, He can wholly heal your heart and bring joy from your tears. So weep, and let God bottle each one of your tears. Then open your heart to be embraced by God's love and grace. He has promised to turn your sadness to joy.

Psalm 37:17–19; Psalm 37:39, 40;
Psalm 119:165–169; Isaiah 25:8, 9; Isaiah 26:3, 4;
Isaiah 55:8, 9, 12; Isaiah 57:19–21; John 14:27;
Romans 5:1, 2; Romans 8:7–9; Romans 14:17–19;
Romans 15:13; 2 Corinthians 4:6, 8, 9; Philippians 4:6, 7

*Lord God, I turn to You to change my
sadness to joy. I trust in Your grace and find
peace in knowing You hold my heart and
that the joys to come will last forever.*

Counting on God's Blessings

*You may not be able to count God's blessings,
but you can count on them.*

God has promised that if you seek Him, you will lack nothing. In what ways are you lacking? God can give you all you need and more, so trust Him in this, and wait with expectant faith as you pray. Know that He knows what you need, but He wants to see your faith in Him; He wants you to seek, knock, and find. It's not a game, it is faith, and God's purpose is that you would know Him better. Don't for a second believe that He can't meet your financial needs. God can do anything. So let nothing get in your way of asking God to help you, and then expect Him to.

Deuteronomy 8:7–14, 18; Deuteronomy 28:11–13;
Joshua 1:8; Job 41:11; Psalm 24:1; Psalm 34:10; Psalm 37:4;
Proverbs 14:23; Ecclesiastes 2:26; Malachi 3:10–12;
Matthew 6:31–33; Matthew 10:8; Luke 6:38; 1 Corinthians 16:2;
2 Corinthians 9:6–8; Philippians 4:12–13; 1 Timothy 6:9, 10

*Heavenly Father, I am at a loss of what
to do. I feel as though I am drowning in despair
and there is no one to save me. I look to You.
I need your presence. I pray for You to
pour out Your grace upon me.*

Take delight in the Lord and he will give you your Heart's desires

PSALM 37:4

261

AUGUST 20

Foundation of Faith

Stand firm in God's Word
and nothing will shake you.

he world is ever changing, and it is easy to be shaken when the world around you seems to be hopeless and you are feeling helpless. But you can have peace in the storms of life, and your faith can remain unshaken if you're trusting in what God's Word has assured you. The Bible is God's voice, Him speaking to you, assuring you through His promises that He is with you and that there is nothing to fear. It is through His Word that He leads and guides you, taking you from glory to glory. So when you don't know what to do, when you are filled with doubt and consumed with fear, run to the Bible and listen to God's voice.

Deuteronomy 33:27; 1 Kings 8:56; Psalm 40:2, 3; Psalm 46:1; Psalm 119:89;
Proverbs 4:20–22; Proverbs 18:10; Isaiah 40:8; Ezekiel 12:24, 25; Matthew 5:14–18;
Matthew 24:35; Romans 8:28, 31; 2 Thessalonians 3:3; 1 Peter 1:23–25; Jude 24, 25

Lord God, help me to stay focused upon Your Word.
Speak to me and help me to trust in You more.

A Humble Heart

Let everything within you praise the Lord.

We tend to praise God for what He does instead of simply who He is. Praise has its purpose, and it is not about satisfying God's ego—it is about the powerful change that occurs within our hearts when we lift God up above everything in our lives. Praise brings us to a point of realizing that God is God and we are not. A humble heart is necessary for praise, and that strengthens our faith. So at times in life when you're not sure what to do, simply take that moment to praise God just for who He is. You'll find that when you do, God will make His presence known to you and, often, show His grace in your life.

2 Samuel 22:4; Psalm 34:1–3; Psalm 47:1, 2, 6, 7; Psalm 48:1; Psalm 50:23;
Psalm 63:3–5; Psalm 71:5–8; Psalm 92:1, 2, 4, 5; Psalm 96:4–8; Psalm 107:8; Psalm 147:1;
Isaiah 43:21; Acts 16:25; Ephesians 5:18–20; Hebrews 13:14, 15; 1 Peter 2:9

Heavenly Father, I praise Your mighty name. I lift You up
above all in my life and worship You in awe and adoration.

A Godly Life

Obedience opens the door to blessings.

I have Hidden up with your WORD in my Heart

PSALM 119:11

It's often difficult to determine which way to go when we are facing life's challenges. We have questions, and we don't seem to get answers to them. But we forget that God has given us His Word as our instruction book for life. God leads and guides us through His Word, and He only calls us to be obedient. He doesn't ask us to walk out our faith in our own strength; He commands us to surrender and do it in His. Jesus is all we need for a godly life. Through Him, we can do all things. So listen to God and do what He says, and the blessings of that obedience are sure to follow . . . He has promised they will.

Deuteronomy 11:26–28; 1 Samuel 15:22; 1 Kings 3:14;
Psalm 119:11; Psalm 143:10; Isaiah 48:17, 18;
Jeremiah 7:23; John 14:15, 21; Acts 5:29;
Ephesians 6:1–3; Colossians 3:20, 22–24;
1 Peter 2:13–21; 1 John 2:2–6

_Lord God, grant me the spirit of surrender
that trusts in You and obeys Your Word.
Transform my heart with Your own._

God's Plans for You

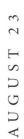

God's plans for your life
are far better than your own.

We like to make our plans, set our expectations, and then demand of God to follow and fulfill them. But a life of faith is all about surrender. It's about trusting God not only to use your life for His purposes but also to give you the desires of your heart, giving you the hope and joy you're intended to have. So don't allow your ways to get in the way of God's. Trust Him and His plans for your life. He can do more than you can hope for. He can accomplish far more than you can. So let Him be who He is . . . Lord of all.

Joshua 1:8, 9; Nehemiah 9:9, 13, 20;
Psalm 31:3, 5; Psalm 32:8; Psalm 37:23–24; Psalm 48:14;
Psalm 119:105, 106; Psalm 143:10; Proverbs 3:1, 5, 6, 11, 12;
Proverbs 6:20, 22, 23; Proverbs 16:3; Isaiah 30:21; Isaiah 48:17;
Isaiah 58:11; John 16:13, 14; Romans 8:14; Romans 12:2;
Ephesians 5:17; Colossians 1:3, 9, 10; Colossians 3:15–17;
1 Thessalonians 4:3, 4, 6; 1 Thessalonians 5:16–18;
1 Timothy 2:1, 3, 4; James 1:5, 6

Lord God, bring my heart to a place of surrender
to Your will and Your ways. Help me to trust You
with the details of my life and rest in knowing
that Your plans for me are for good.

Growing in the Spirit

The Spirit will strengthen you with all power according to His glorious might so that you may have great endurance and patience.

We so often overlook the spiritual world and spiritual forces because we're constantly consumed by our physical world. But we are spiritual beings living in a physical world. And the Holy Spirit is the One who leads and guides us through this life. It is thus vital that we stay completely connected with God, relying on Him in every way and depending on His Spirit to lead us into righteousness. If we continually seek God, being filled with His Spirit, our faith will be able to endure through any of life's circumstances. Ask God to continually fill you with the Spirit so that you might live a life that is worthy of Him.

Psalm 92:13; 2 Corinthians 3:18; Ephesians 3:14–19; Ephesians 4:14–16;
Philippians 1:6, 9, 10; Colossians 1:9–11; Colossians 3:16; 1 Timothy 4:15;
2 Timothy 2:15; Hebrews 6:1; 1 Peter 1:25; 1 Peter 2:2, 3; 2 Peter 3:18

Heavenly Father, fill me with Your Spirit. Overwhelm me with all that You are so that I am not overcome by the world.

God Is Listening

God hears you from heaven.

We underestimate the power of prayer because we so easily doubt the power of God in the face of our impossible situations. The truth is that not only does prayer change things; it also changes us. It turns our focus from ourselves and our circumstances to God. And that's where our focus should be . . . at all times and in all things. Don't wear yourself out trying to make happen what only God can. When you don't know what to do, pray. And then expect God to answer because He has promised that He will.

2 Chronicles 7:14; Psalm 4:1; Psalm 17:1; Matthew 7:7, 8;
Matthew 18:19; Matthew 21:22; Ephesians 6:18; Philippians 4:6, 7;
1 Thessalonians 5:16–18; 1 Peter 3:12

Lord God, I come to You in prayer, relying on You
for all that I need. I pray that You will give me the
strength to believe beyond all doubt.

Victory over Sin

Whoever you are and whatever you've done,
God's grace is enough to cover every sin.

We judge sins as much as we judge others. We often feel as though we sin in ways that God simply cannot forgive, because that's the way we work. But God's ways are higher and better. He offers forgiveness to all who come to Him. He simply asks for a surrendered heart and the desire to be obedient to Him, bringing about victory over sin. You are set free through confessing your sins and surrendering your heart to God. Don't allow anything to get between you and God. Whoever you are, wherever you are, and whatever you've done, God's love and grace is enough . . . *run to Him.*

Psalm 69:5; Isaiah 1:16–19; 1 Corinthians 15:55–58;
2 Corinthians 4:1–6; 2 Corinthians 5:17–21;
Galatians 3:10, 11; Galatians 5:1; Ephesians 6:10–18;
1 John 1:5–10; 1 John 3:5–7

Heavenly Father, examine my heart and
know me. Show me the sin that is within me
and help me to repent. I pray that You
will revive and refresh my soul.

Reach Out to Those in Need

You are God's hands and feet.

W hen you are struggling to have the needs of your life met, it seems illogical that God would ask you to help others in need. But God doesn't think the way we do; He operates from a place of sovereignty. He knows that He will meet your needs. He wants you to learn to trust Him. And often, when you have a need, He will ask you to meet that specific need in someone else's life. Be determined to bless someone who needs your blessing, and God has assured you that His goodness and mercy will follow you all the days of your life.

Leviticus 19:9, 10; Psalm 9:18, 19; Psalm 82:3, 4;
Psalm 146:5–10; Proverbs 21:13; Isaiah 58:7–11;
Matthew 25:34–40; Hebrews 13:1, 2; James 2:15–17;
1 Peter 4:8–10; 1 John 3:17–19

Lord God, replace my heart with Your own and help me to be sensitive to the needs of others, to be Your hands and feet and offer Your love to those who need it.

Resting in God

**God will never ask you to wait for *nothing* . . .
He's always up to *something*.**

We tend to look at our waiting times as wasted time. But God doesn't make us wait on nothing. God is working in our waiting times. He's drawing us closer to Himself, challenging our faith in ways that will ultimately strengthen it, and bringing us to a place of peace that isn't controlled by what we have or don't have. If you're struggling in your faith over something you need God to do and He just isn't doing it right now, know that you are right where God wants you. Be determined to rest in who He is and start praying for His promises. Let God grow your patience, because when your endurance is fully developed, you will be perfect and complete, needing *nothing*.

2 Chronicles 5:13; Psalm 27:14; Psalm 37:7–9; Ecclesiastes 7:8;
Romans 15:3–5; Philippians 2:1–4; 1 Thessalonians 5:14; 2 Timothy 2:24; 1 John 5:1–3

*Heavenly Father, I struggle to be patient with Your timing.
Help me to rest in Your faithfulness and find strength in the hope
You have given me through Your promises.*

His faithful love endures forever

2 CHRONICLES 5:13

Comfort in Troubled Times

In times of trouble,
do one thing: turn to God.

$\mathcal{M}$oments of emptiness will come upon you quickly when you're suddenly facing circumstances that seem impossible even for God. And when all hope seems gone, depression and despair can descend in ways that consume you. But even then, when you're sure you just can't go on, God is there to heal your heart and help the hurt. His Spirit brings comfort even when it seems as though everything is falling apart. Just turn to Him, pour out what's left of your heart, and wait for his embrace of grace.

Psalm 25:16–18; Psalm 31:7; Psalm 33:17–22; Psalm 34:1–8;
Psalm 147:2, 3, 5, 6, 13, 14; John 14:27; Romans 14:7; 1 Peter 5:7–11

Heavenly Father, I need You.
My heart is breaking, and all hope seems gone.

From Glory to Glory

God will guide you continually from glory to glory.

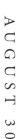

We were never meant to venture through this life alone. God has promised to be with us always because He wants us to recognize that we need Him always. God wants to guide us in our thoughts, words, and deeds because reliance upon Him for guidance throughout our ever-changing lives is the key to a successful, righteous life. Don't be fearful when you're not sure which direction to take. God is there to help you at every turn. All that you need to do is turn to His Word, seek Him, and pray until His direction becomes clear and the path is sure.

Psalm 143:10, 11; John 7:38, 39; John 14:16, 17;
John 16:7, 13; 1 Corinthians 2:10–16; 2 Corinthians 3:17, 18;
Galatians 5:16–26; 1 John 4:13

*Lord God, open my heart and mind to
Your guidance. Grant me clear vision for
the ways in which You are leading me, and
strengthen me for the journey of faith.*

Satisfaction

If you're empty, God will fill you to overflowing.

We find ourselves dissatisfied when life's circumstances aren't meeting our expectations. And when life doesn't go according to our plan, we look to God and hope He has a better plan for us. And He does. Always. But in our emptiness, we need to realize that God is doing something. He's allowing us to be emptied so that we can be fully filled by Him. With less of us, there can be more of Him. So allow yourself to be emptied; don't give up or give in. If you're not satisfied with life, turn to God and allow Him to satisfy you in ways that only He can.

Job 11:18; Psalm 22:26; Psalm 37:4, 5;
Psalm 63:5, 6, 8; Psalm 103:5; Psalm 107:5, 9;
Psalm 145:15–17; Isaiah 55:2; Isaiah 58:10, 11;
Jeremiah 31:14; Joel 2:18, 19, 26; Matthew 5:6;
John 4:13, 14; John 6:35; Romans 8:32

*Lord, life often leaves me empty and alone.
I want so much from life to be happy, but I know
I simply need more of You. Empty me so that I
can be filled with all that You are.*

But those who
TRUST
in the Lord
will find new strength.
They will soar high on
wings like eagles.

SEPTEMBER

ISAIAH 40:31

Self-doubt

Whatever you can't do, God can.

We rely too much on ourselves and not enough on God, the One who does the impossible. We try to reason through life's problems even though we're commanded not to, mostly because we want to be in control—even though we're really not. So when we start doubting ourselves, we should recognize it as the Spirit awakening our souls to place our hope in God. Don't allow life to get you so down that you don't look to God. He has promised to do the impossible, which is far more than you can do. All He asks is that you trust Him.

Psalm 30:5; Psalm 55:22, 23; Psalm 106:3;
Psalm 119:165; Psalm 147:3; Proverbs 3:5, 6;
Proverbs 15:4; Proverbs 21:23; Proverbs 29:18; Isaiah 41:10;
Isaiah 43:2; Isaiah 50:7; Luke 6:31; Romans 8:38, 39;
1 Corinthians 14:33; 2 Corinthians 1:3, 4; Ephesians 4:29;
Ephesians 5:1–4; Philippians 4:6–8; 2 Timothy 1:7;
James 3:16–18; 1 Peter 2:6

*Heavenly Father, awaken my soul to all that You
are. Help me to humble myself and realize that
You are in control at all times and in all ways.*

275

Grief

God heals—let Him heal you.

When sorrows come, we instantly feel alone. Even if we are surrounded by those who love us, we feel abandoned by God's grace in our pain. It seems like nothing comforts us or eases the emptiness that comes with our loss. But we have a Savior who has been there. He knows our pain, and He shares in whatever you're going through at this moment because He is in you and you are in Him. Shed as many tears as necessary, but do so at the throne of God so that He might bottle each one and comfort you in ways that only He can.

Psalm 23:4; Psalm 119:41, 50; Isaiah 41:10; Isaiah 43:2, 3;
Isaiah 49:13; Isaiah 51:11; Isaiah 61:1–3; Matthew 5:4;
1 Corinthians 15:55–57; 2 Corinthians 1:3–5;
2 Corinthians 5:8–10; 1 Thessalonians 4:13, 14;
2 Thessalonians 2:16, 17; Hebrews 4:14–16;
1 Peter 5:7; Revelation 21:4

*Lord God, my heart is breaking. I am empty
beyond understanding, and although I know You
can help me, I wrestle with doubt in the midst of
my faith. Strengthen my heart and heal me with
Your amazing grace.*

Nothing Is Going Right

Trust God . . . no matter what.

When your life is falling apart, trust God. When your heart is breaking beyond anything you believe can be mended, trust God. When you want to give up, don't. God is a ready help in times of trouble. And if He has promised us that troubles will come, we shouldn't be surprised when we experience them. Trials of life don't mean that God isn't in control. In fact, they provide opportunities for miracles to show us that He really is. So when nothing seems to be going right, just stand firm and trust God . . . no matter what.

Psalm 27:14; Psalm 33:20; Psalm 62:5; Psalm 130:5; Psalm 145:15, 16; Isaiah 25:9; Isaiah 40:31; Habakkuk 2:3; Romans 13:13, 14; Ephesians 5:8–11; Ephesians 5:15; Hebrews 3:14; Hebrews 10:23; 1 John 2:28

Heavenly Father, I need to know that You are still in control, even when it seems like my life isn't. Help me to have faith through my doubts.

Turning to the Promises

God has promised you that
every promise will be fulfilled.

We tend to give up on God right before the miracle. In times of trouble, we are to stand firm in our faith, but we seldom do. Doubt and despair take over quicker than we can respond to them. Often our faith fails, but God's faithfulness does not. When we're consumed with doubt, there's one thing we must do: turn to the promises of God. Whatever you're going through, God has made a promise that will strengthen your faith through it. So don't give up on God, because He will never give up on you. Have faith until the miracle happens—until God shows up and demonstrates His presence.

Genesis 9:16, 17; Genesis 28:15; Deuteronomy 7:8, 9;
Joshua 23:14; 1 Kings 8:56–58; Psalm 36:5; Psalm 89:1, 2, 19, 34;
Psalm 119:64, 65; Psalm 121:3, 7, 8; Isaiah 54:9, 10; 1 Corinthians 1:9;
1 Corinthians 10:13; 1 Thessalonians 5:23, 24; 2 Timothy 2:13, 19; 2 Peter 3:9

Lord God, I am determined to trust You, regardless of what I see before me.
I know You are above all things, faithful and full of grace.

Each Day

Live today for God alone.

We must begin each new day in the mercy and grace of God, knowing that He gave us life for purposes that go beyond what we can fully comprehend. Our lives of faith require discernment and obedience. But life gets hard, and we can get caught up in the way the world is moving us instead of the ways in which God wants us to move. Start your day in prayer. Don't let your feet hit the ground before you talk to God about how He'd like you to be His hands and feet. Even if your day doesn't go according to your plans, if you're being led by God, you can be sure it will go according to His plans and that He will take you from glory to glory.

Psalm 37:23; Psalm 90:12; Proverbs 4:20–26; Proverbs 5:21; Proverbs 10:4, 5; Proverbs 12:1; Proverbs 12:24; Proverbs 13:20; Proverbs 17:17; Proverbs 23:4, 5; Proverbs 25:11; Ecclesiastes 3:9–14; Ecclesiastes 8:5–7; Ecclesiastes 10:18; Acts 1:7

Heavenly Father, guide me into Your perfect will today and every day. Let nothing distract me from all that You intend for me to accomplish for Your glory.

The Hope of Glory

Hope is never gone.

There is a hope that goes beyond our circumstances and into eternity. It's a hope that never leaves us. It's the hope of glory, based on the truth of God's promise that there is salvation for all who put their faith in Jesus. The circumstances of your life may cause you to feel as though hope is gone, but we don't walk by sight. Faith lifts our eyes when life gets us down, knowing that in the end there will be a joy that's everlasting. There will be a day when all sorrow is turned to joy and there will be no more tears. But until that day, we hope in the promises God has made to us.

Psalm 147:7–13; Romans 6:23;
Romans 8:14–18, 24, 25; Galatians 2:16, 20;
Ephesians 2:4–7; Colossians 1:5, 6;
1 Thessalonians 5:8–11; 2 Timothy 4:7, 8;
1 Peter 3:9; 1 John 2:24, 25

I have fought the GOOD FIGHT
I HAVE finished the race

2 Timothy 4:7

Lord God, turn my eyes from the circumstances that cause me to feel as though all hope is gone. Lift my eyes to Jesus, my eternal hope.

Blessedness

You are highly favored . . .
God is with you.

*D*on't get caught up in what's wrong in life—be focused on what is right. There might not be much that's right, but God is with you, and that's enough. If you are relying on God's promises, you are aware that even through the pain, there is purpose. The part we miss about faith is that if we need a blessing, we need to bless others. God intends us to be a *part* of His grand plan, not merely to be spectators. And what you'll discover through being His hands and feet is that His heart will open wide for all the blessings you'll ever need.

Genesis 17:16, 17; Matthew 1:16–23;
Luke 1:28–30, 42; Luke 11:27

*Heavenly Father, help me to trust
that You will bless me in the ways I need.
Drive my spirit to focus upon the needs of
others, showing them the love and
grace that I trust in.*

As Good as Done

God promises to take care of your every need.
Just trust in His promises to you and rest in faith.

*W*orry tends to get the best of us. It consumes our souls in ways that cause us to doubt our faith and question God. The challenges we face make us uncertain that God is there for us, when in fact they are opportunities for Him to demonstrate His presence. God wants you to learn to rest in what He has promised and find peace even when you see no reason to believe. Hoping in God is about trusting Him completely, believing that the miracle is not only being orchestrated but is as good as done. Now is the time to find contentment in simply who God is. If you do that, He will never fail to show you all He can do . . . and *that* is far beyond anything you can hope for or imagine.

Matthew 6:31–34; 1 Timothy 6:6–8; Hebrews 13:5, 6

Lord God, help me to rest in faith, to trust in the promises
You have made to me, and to cast out the doubt that so disturbs me.

Children

Children are a blessing,
a gift from God to be cherished.

*G*od is overjoyed to have us as His children and to bless us with the great joy of experiencing the children of this world. But with the blessing comes great responsibility. We are to lead children to Him, being an example of Jesus in every way. We must see them as precious souls, given to us by God to make the world a better place. It is in fully receiving God's love and grace that we can love children in the way that He loves us, and there is great joy in seeing these precious lives love God as we do.

Genesis 4:1; Genesis 30:1, 2;
Psalm 127:3; Isaiah 54:13

Heavenly Father, help me to lead children to You.
Let my life be an example that is worthy of You,
so that these precious lives might see You in me.

Justice

**God may present Himself at the last minute,
but He will make Himself known to us.**

*A*ll too often, life just doesn't seem fair. We struggle with our faith in God because our souls demand justice for the wrongs committed against us, and too many wrongs are not made right. God stretches our faith in Him much more than we like, and often we are forced to sit by and watch His mercy and forgiveness when we feel there should be condemnation and punishment. But God's justice is different from ours. It works out of His love. He rules from a different perspective, an eternal one. We must be careful not to demand mercy for our sins and justice for the sins of others. We must simply trust God and His ways, even when we don't understand them.

Genesis 30:6; 1 Kings 3:25–27

*Lord God, sometimes I don't understand
why justice is not always seen in this life,
but help me to trust You and not lean
on my own understanding.*

Set Free Through Truth

The truth sets you free and enables you to have the faith that leads to God's greatest blessings in your life.

When we are not living a life full of truth, we are missing out on God's very best in our lives. We can live a lie and maybe get away with it for a time, but doing so fetters us in ways that we cannot imagine. God requires us to walk in truth because He is truth. If we are walking in faith and walking with God, there is no other way to live than in the truth. And His Word is truth. If we're committed to seeking God and allowing Him to fill us with His truth, we will find His mercy and goodness following us all the days of our lives.

Psalm 103:17; John 8:32;
John 8:36; John 16:13; 3 John 4

*Heavenly Father, fill me with truth.
Help me to distinguish the lies of the enemy
and the world. I want to live a life that is free,
full of faith, and trusting only in You.*

PSALM 103:17

Being Christ-centered

*Fix your eyes on Jesus—
the perfecter of your faith.*

It's easy to lose faith when your focus is on your problems and not on Jesus. And troubles have a way of doing just that. We struggle to deal with our physical world in a spiritual way. We so easily forget that God is sovereign over even the smallest things in our lives. The key to overcoming every obstacle is simply to remain focused on Jesus. When you focus on Him, you are able to call upon His power through your faith. That power is available to you in all that you are facing. So keep your eyes on Jesus, let nothing move you, and watch how He calls you to "walk upon the water."

Psalm 34:4; Psalm 63:1, 2, 5, 7; Psalm 71:1, 5, 8; Psalm 104:33, 34;
Psalm 113:3; Acts 17:28; Romans 8:1, 2; Romans 13:14; Galatians 2:20;
Colossians 3:16; Titus 2:12, 13; Hebrews 12:2; 1 John 2:28

*Lord God, help me to keep my eyes on Jesus and to trust and
not be afraid. Perfect my faith according to Your Word.*

Bitterness

*Give to others the grace
that you have been given.*

W e so easily surrender to our emotions. We are hurt, we endure ongoing injustice, and bitterness sets in. We remain bitter, never recovering from it. When we're struggling with the raging emotions within ourselves, we need to urgently ask for God's help in addressing the things that are keeping us from being filled with His love, mercy, and grace. Bitterness is poison to our souls until God cleanses us of it. So pray, even when you don't feel like it, and ask God to refresh your soul. Ask Him to fill your heart with all that is within His.

Ephesians 4:31; Hebrews 12:15; James 3:14, 15

*Heavenly Father, I am often overcome by my
emotions, feeling bitter and angry. Refresh my soul
and cleanse me of anything that is not of You.*

When in Doubt

Don't be confused; God is in control.

*I*t's easy to fall into doubt when we are trying to figure God out. We expect Him to work in the ways we want Him to and in the timing we think He should, but God's ways go far beyond our own. We simply need to rest in His sovereignty. Even when we don't understand, even when life is confusing and full of chaos, we can be certain that God is still God and is still on His throne. So don't give in to confusion. Don't try to reason what you simply can't. Your faith in God is what will give you the peace that surpasses all understanding.

Deuteronomy 3:27; Isaiah 26:3;
Isaiah 55:8, 9; 1 Corinthians 14:33

*Lord God, the ways of the world
confuse me, so help me to trust in Your ways.
Grant me peace when I don't understand
what You are doing, knowing that Your
good purposes always prevail.*

His everlasting arms are UNDER you

Deuteronomy 33:27

Weakness

In your weakness,
Christ's power will rest on you.

*L*ife can bring us down as we quickly become aware that we aren't able to accomplish all that we wish to do. Yet, for some reason, we continue to struggle within ourselves, trying to do what only God can. You may be weak and weary, but God is not. He is your ready help in times of trouble and He has promised that His power works best in your weakness. So let God fight your battles for you. He's promised that He will, and the victory will be His. All you need to do is rest and trust.

Psalm 121:2, 3; Matthew 11:28–30;
2 Corinthians 12:9

Heavenly Father, there are times
when I feel weak and weary, tired of the
daily struggle. I ask that You strengthen
me according to Your Word.

Marriage

God's love will hold you together.

Marriage is a blessing, but it can come with burdens that are unexpected and heavy to bear. The bond made in marriage is one that God holds together when both individuals are trusting in God and walking in faith. But the challenges and temptations of life can threaten that commitment. God has promised that He will make a way of escape when you are tempted. Be determined to keep your marriage under God's care. Be dedicated to praying for one another and for the love that you have for one another, and trust God to protect what He has brought together.

1 Corinthians 7:10–17;
2 Corinthians 6:14–17; Hebrews 13:4

Lord God, I pray that You will protect this marriage,
strengthening us to uphold the commitment we
have made to each other and to You.

Perfect Peace

Through every storm of life,
God will give you peace.

eace doesn't come easy. Life is hard. But God is there through it all. And He offers a peace that goes far beyond your feelings. The peace that God invites you to rest in is a peace that isn't shaken by the circumstances of your life. His peace gives you a calm within your soul throughout the storm. It's a peace that is unchanging and never failing. All you need to do is seek God. Open your heart and allow Him to flood it with His peace, and then rest because You are being held by Almighty God.

Psalm 37:11; Psalm 37:37; Psalm 119:165; Isaiah 26:3; Isaiah 26:12;
Isaiah 55:12; Isaiah 57:2; John 14:27; Romans 8:6; Romans 14:17–19; Romans 15:13;
2 Corinthians 13:11; Philippians 4:6, 7; 2 Thessalonians 3:16

Heavenly Father, I pray that You will fill me
with Your peace. Help me to rest in You at all times.

Financial Worries

God has promised to meet all of your needs.
There's nothing that He cannot do.

*W*e tend to feel out of control when life is. But what we must never forget is that God is always in control and there is nothing that He cannot do. If you trust Him, believing His promise that He can work miracles in your life, you will see God manifesting Himself in ways you never thought He could or would. He has supernatural power beyond your understanding, so don't reason yourself out of a miracle. Just keep your eyes on God, let nothing move you, and rest in the peace God gives you to continue to trust Him even when you're not sure you can.

Deuteronomy 28:11–13; Psalm 23:1;
Psalm 34:10; Psalm 37:25; Proverbs 4:11;
Matthew 6:31–33; Matthew 10:8; Luke 6:38;
1 Corinthians 16:2; Philippians 4:19; 3 John 2

Lord God, I pray that You will grant me
peace to believe that You will help me in my
desperate places. Fill me with faith to believe
in Your promise to meet my needs.

Reading God's Word

*Set your heart upon God's Word and
be filled with the Spirit and life.*

God's Word is more than just His voice—it's who He is. His Word holds the power to transform your life in the ways you need it to. So fill your heart with it and count on His faithfulness. Meditate on His Word in times of trouble and in moments of joy. When trials bring confusion, God's Word will support your faith and assure you of His faithfulness. Whatever you do, hope in God and trust in His Word.

Psalm 33:6; Psalm 119:11, 16; Psalm 119:29, 30; Psalm 119:89, 90; Psalm 119:103–105;
Isaiah 40:8; Matthew 4:4; Luke 21:33; John 6:63; John 8:31, 32; John 15:3;
Hebrews 4:12; 1 Peter 1:23–25; 1 Peter 2:2, 3

*Heavenly Father, open my heart to receive Your Word.
Turn my eyes from worthless things and give me life through
Your Word. In You alone I put my hope and trust.*

Broken and Blessed

Know that God heals all things, so come to Him and allow His unfailing love to heal your brokenness in all the ways you need Him to.

God knows your pain; He holds your tears. Know that the pain and sorrows that you are experiencing will be transformed into unthinkable joy, in the blink of an eye, if you place your hope in God. Often He will allow you to be broken so that you can be blessed. His ways are higher, so don't try to understand it all; just be determined to trust that whatever God is doing is for good, and find peace in His promises.

Psalm 34:18; Psalm 51:8, 17;
Psalm 147:3; Isaiah 61:1

I cry out for Your comfort and mercy as my heart is broken and my soul is desperate for Your love. Help me to rest in Your promises, expecting Your healing and restoration.

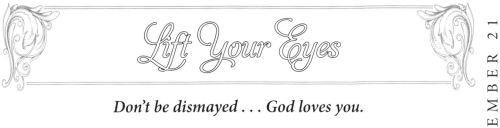

Lift Your Eyes

Don't be dismayed . . . God loves you.

There's one thing you need to know when you're feeling down: God loves you. You may not feel His love in this moment, you might not even feel as though He exists, but He's promised to be with you, and He loves you right there where you are. God is faithful to His Word. If He has promised to comfort you in your affliction, He will. If He's promised to be your ready help in times of trouble, He is. His Word does not return void. So when you're feeling depressed, unable to lift your eyes, let God lift your heart with His promises, and He will be all the strength you need.

Nehemiah 8:10; Psalm 30:5; Isaiah 40:31;
Isaiah 41:10; Isaiah 43:2; Isaiah 61:3; Luke 18:1;
Romans 8:38, 39; 2 Corinthians 1:3, 4; Philippians 4:8;
1 Peter 4:12, 13; 1 Peter 5:6, 7

The Joy of the Lord is your Strength

Nehemiah 8:10

Lord God, I am filled with darkness, unable to see a way out, and I need You. Fill me with Your Spirit and strengthen me through Your promises.

Clearing the Confusion

God is not a God of confusion. Seek Him and you will find Him, and He will lead and guide you.

*L*ife can bring about situations that cause us to instantly be filled with fear and confusion. We expect things to happen one way, only to find them taking a very different direction. And when we don't understand, when we cannot make sense of it all, we fall into fear . . . giving way to despair. But God is with us. There is nothing that surprises Him or catches Him off guard. We must never forget His sovereignty over this world and our lives. And we must remember to trust Him, even when we're not sure we can. When you don't know what to do, run to Him and listen to His voice. He will guide you along the paths of righteousness.

Psalm 32:8; Proverbs 3:5, 6; Isaiah 30:21;
Isaiah 50:7; 1 Corinthians 14:33; Philippians 4:6, 7;
2 Timothy 1:7; James 1:5; James 3:16–18

Heavenly Father, there is so much I don't understand, and it's often hard to trust in what I don't see, rather than in what I do. Help me, my Deliverer, the One who carries me and guards my mind with peace.

This is the WAY YOU SHOULD Go

Isaiah 30:21

Overcoming the Overwhelming

Be determined to persevere and receive God's promises.

*D*on't be surprised when you find yourself overwhelmed. Be determined, instead, to be overwhelmed by God and not by your circumstances. It's about your focus and perspective; and when you are absorbed with the promises of God, you can view your life's situations through His eyes instead of your own. Our problems may look too big for us, but they are never too big for God. So when life is just too much, run to Him and ask Him to do what you simply cannot. Your faith in Him will flood your soul with a peace that surpasses all understanding.

Psalm 27:14; Psalm 37:7, 8, 16; Psalm 40:1;
Lamentations 3:25, 26; Romans 5:3–5; 1 Thessalonians 5:14;
Hebrews 10:35, 36; James 1:2–4; James 5:7, 8

Lord God, life gets so overwhelming. Fill me with Your peace. Help me to trust in You in greater ways and to find rest for my soul.

Resting in Hope

Be strong, take heart,
and put your hope in God.

Your faith will overcome your fear if you truly trust that God is who He says He is. He is your protector and defender, the keeper of your soul. He's commanded you not to fear, so don't. Don't allow the enemy to seize control of your thoughts and make you fall into fear. Don't fear either the unknowns or what you know. Don't walk by sight . . . be determined to stay focused on God and walk by faith. Trust that God will never fail you. Fear cannot exist in the presence of faith. Rest, be at peace, because God has promised that He is with you always, and He has commanded you to trust and not be afraid.

Psalm 23:4; Psalm 31:24; Psalm 56:11; Psalm 91:1, 2, 4, 5;
Psalm 91:10, 11, 14; Proverbs 4:11; Romans 8:29; 2 Timothy 1:7; 1 John 4:18

Heavenly Father, help me to trust that You will
protect me. Help me to be obedient and not be afraid,
knowing that You, God Almighty, are with me always.

Rejection

God loves you and accepts you as His child,
and that is all that matters.

It's easy to get caught up in pleasing people instead of God. But the world demands things of us that God does not. God loves you unconditionally. There is nothing that can separate you from His love. His grace is always waiting for you, and He is always ready to forgive. Though others may judge you, God sees your heart, and your relationship with Him is the only thing that really matters. So even though others may reject you, God never will. Accept His love for you, and you will find the peace and joy your soul longs for.

1 Samuel 16:7; Psalm 1:1–3; Psalm 37:5–7;
Matthew 5:10–12; John 6:37; Colossians 3:12–14; 1 Peter 4:16

Lord God, thank You for loving me just as I am. Help me to live
each day only to please You. Help me to see myself as You see me.

Surrendering Anger

Let God handle all that angers you;
He's promised you He will.

There is righteous anger over injustice and sin, and then there's the anger that causes us to live contrary to the way God has commanded us. If situations in your life cause you to be filled with anger, bring it to God. He promises that if there is justice to be served, He will take care of it; there's no need for you to take over His throne. Simply do what is right in the eyes of God, and leave the rest to Him. If you surrender your struggle, God will calm your soul and give you the peace that He wants you to live in.

Psalm 37:8; Proverbs 14:16, 17;
Proverbs 14:29; Proverbs 15:1; Proverbs 16:32;
Proverbs 25:21, 22; Ecclesiastes 7:9; Matthew 5:22–24;
Romans 12:19; Ephesians 4:26, 31, 32;
Colossians 3:8; Hebrews 10:30; James 1:19, 20

Heavenly Father, I surrender my anger so
that You can work in the ways that You need to.
I pray that You will calm my soul and renew my
spirit with Your love, mercy, and grace.

Healing Faith

Faith heals . . . God has promised it does.

In our fallen world, there is sickness and disease, but God is a God of miracles. And that's all we need to know. When we are ill, or praying for someone who is, we must have faith that God can and will heal. We can't always understand His ways. Sometimes He doesn't heal in the way we want Him to or in the timing we expect, but He may use illness to work out a healing in our souls. Our faith, through illness, sometimes works greater miracles than the actual physical healing. So be determined to trust God through it all. Wait in faith and watch what He will do.

Psalm 107:20; Proverbs 4:20–22; Isaiah 53:3; Jeremiah 17:14; Jeremiah 30:17;
Matthew 8:8; Matthew 9:35; Luke 6:19; James 5:14, 15; 1 Peter 2:24; 3 John 2

Lord God, I pray for healing. Only a miracle from Your hand will do.
Help me to trust and wait in faith.

Your Ultimate Strength

Let your strength come from God and all that He's promised you.

We forget that God is God and can do anything. Life leaves us weary, and we struggle with faith far more than we should. The promises of God in the Bible hold power over everything and anything we're facing. But we seldom recognize that God's Word is all we need. Every battle should be fought upon our knees, praying God's promises to us and anticipating His miracles in our lives. What promise are you praying for and expecting God to fulfill?

Psalm 56:1; Acts 20:32; Acts 26:16–18;
1 Corinthians 2:9; Galatians 3:29; Ephesians 1:11–14;
Ephesians 3:6; Colossians 3:23, 24

*Heavenly Father, strengthen me
through Your promises. Help me to trust that
You are all I need and that even when my
faith fails, You are still faithful.*

The Body of Christ

You are the body of Christ, His church.
You are His hands and feet.

God has designed us to participate in His story. He has called us to live a life in Christ so that we might experience His glory. Jesus went around doing good, and we are now His body, sent to do His work in the world. Our greatest joy will come from being filled with the Spirit and living the life God has called us to. So seek God's will for your life, be ready to do whatever He calls you to do, and live completely for the One who died for you.

Psalm 133:1; Romans 12:4–8; Ephesians 1:10, 22, 23;
Ephesians 5:29, 30; Colossians 1:13, 18; Colossians 2:8–10; Hebrews 10:25

Lord God, lead and guide me in the
paths of righteousness. Empower me to live a
life that is worthy of You, drawing others to You.

The Reward of Obedience

Give and you will receive.

*O*ur prayers tend to be focused on the receiving side of life, and we overlook God's principles for generosity. God tells us to give freely, and He will take care of our needs. But when we're struggling with our needs, it's hard to find the faith to give what we don't really have. Yet God reminds us not to depend on our own understanding. His greatest blessings in our lives will come when we step out in faith and trust Him even when we're not sure we can. Give your prayer, your love, your time, whatever you have, and watch what God does with your obedience.

Proverbs 11:24, 25; Matthew 6:19–21;
Matthew 6:33; Luke 16:10; 2 Corinthians 5:9, 10;
2 Corinthians 9:6–8; Galatians 6:10;
Colossians 3:23, 24; Hebrews 4:13; 1 Peter 4:10, 11

*Heavenly Father, help me to be obedient
to Your Word. Guide me in the ways that I
can give, and help me to trust that You
will bless all that concerns me.*

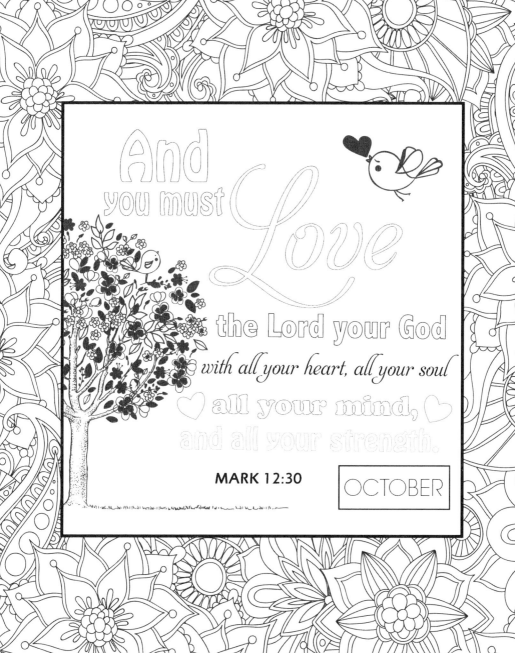

And
you must *Love*
the Lord your God
with all your heart, all your soul
all your mind,
and all your strength.

MARK 12:30

OCTOBER

Surrender to God's Love

You can never love unless you receive God's love.

Jeremiah 31:3

Our love is far different from God's. Our love holds expectations and makes demands when it shouldn't. God's love is unconditional, freely forgiving, and never lacking. The love you long for is not of this world. Your soul longs for what only the Spirit can give, so seek God's love and surrender to it. Be filled with His peace and joy as His love permeates your soul and enables you to love others in the ways He loves you . . . then your joy will be made complete.

Jeremiah 31:3; Mark 12:30, 31; John 3:16;
John 14:21; John 15:12–14, 17; Romans 5:8;
Romans 8:37–39; 1 Corinthians 13:1–8, 13;
1 John 4:7, 8, 10–12, 16, 19–21

*Lord God, help me to receive Your love
and grace so that I might love others and
fulfill Your purposes for my life. Help me to
love in the ways You love me, freely,
forgiving, and never lacking.*

Victory in Every Battle

Be strong in God and His power.

Your battles in life will be many, but God is with you, so there is nothing to fear. You will grow weak and weary, but God never does . . . so find your strength in Him. When you are faced with the trials and tribulations of this life, don't surrender to anything or anyone but God. He will fight your battles for you; you need only stand still in faith. Don't give in to the temptation to believe that you have to fight your battles on your own. God has promised that if you trust in Him, He will give you the victory. All He wants is your faith.

Deuteronomy 18:10–14;
2 Corinthians 10:3–5; Ephesians 6:10–18

Heavenly Father, strengthen me according
to Your Word. Give me the faith to rest in You and
trust You for the victory in every battle that I face in life.

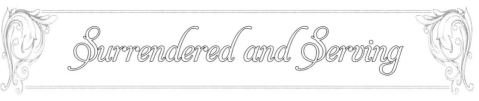

Surrendered and Serving

God has given you His Spirit
to fulfill His good purposes.

We fail to realize just how much our lives impact the world. Our faith in God can change the course of history in our lives and in the lives of others. It comes down to our discernment and obedience. God is always speaking to us, always providing a path that works all things out for good and His glory. But we must choose to surrender each day to whatever His will is. Surrender each and every day to God's purposes for you; you will never regret doing so.

Daniel 12:3; Matthew 5:14–16; Mark 16:15–20; John 4:13, 14;
John 13:34, 35; John 14:12; Acts 17:30; Romans 10:14; Romans 12:2; 1 John 5:3–5

*Lord God, I surrender my will to Yours. Help me to live a life
that is worthy of You, bringing Your love, mercy, and grace into the world.*

Trust in Jesus

*When you're struggling in life,
turn to Jesus . . . always.*

*S*o often we are absorbed by our problems instead of by Jesus. We put our trust in people and situations instead of in God. Our faith wavers when we're just not certain that God can do all things in the impossible situation we're facing. It simply doesn't seem possible that He can reveal Himself in the ways we need Him to. But Jesus walked the earth to show that all things are possible. All that you need do is trust in Him.

Psalm 103:2–4; Matthew 21:22;
Mark 10:24; John 14:13; John 15:7; John 16:23, 24;
Romans 8:31, 32, 37; 2 Corinthians 3:5; 2 Corinthians 9:8;
2 Corinthians 12:9; Ephesians 1:3; Ephesians 1:19, 20;
Philippians 4:12, 13, 19; 2 Peter 1:3, 4

*Jesus, I come to You . . .
fill me with faith. Help me to trust
that whatever I need, I have in You.*

Fully Trusting

Don't try to understand God;
just decide to trust Him.

Our faith wavers when we're constantly trying to figure God out. That's something we simply cannot do. His perspective and power go far beyond anything we can comprehend. And that makes faith hard because we like to trust in what we can know through our senses. But greater things, mighty miracles, come from faith . . . not from any other source. And the only way we can have faith in situations that demand it is to find hope in the promises that God has made to us. Whatever you're facing, seek God's Word in it. Listen for His voice and then rest in faith. You don't have to know it all; you just need to know the One who does.

Psalm 18:30; Psalm 34:19; Psalm 55:23; Psalm 138:8; Isaiah 41:10;
Isaiah 55:8, 9; Jeremiah 32:40; Jeremiah 33:3; Hosea 6:1–3; Romans 8:28, 31, 35–37;
1 Corinthians 10:13; Hebrews 10:23; 1 Peter 4:12, 13

Heavenly Father, I often don't understand Your ways, and that causes my faith to falter. Help me to trust You more fully and find strength in Your promises.

Identity

*Stay focused on God's thoughts about you, and
don't allow your feelings to determine who you are.*

We are so easily influenced by the world. We tend to listen to others more than we listen to God, and our thoughts about ourselves can easily become distorted, driving us to act in ways that are contrary to who we know we are in God. It's vital that we stay connected to God through His Word and through prayer so we don't lose sight of God's will for us. Set your eyes upon Him . . . seek Him always, and don't just listen to what He says; believe it with all your heart.

Psalm 31:5; Psalm 55:22, 23;
Psalm 106:3; Psalm 119:165; Psalm 147:3;
Proverbs 3:5, 6; Proverbs 15:4; Proverbs 21:23;
Proverbs 29:18; Isaiah 41:10; Isaiah 43:2; Isaiah 50:7;
Luke 6:31; Romans 8:38, 39; 1 Corinthians 14:33;
2 Corinthians 1:3, 4; Ephesians 4:29; Ephesians 5:1–4;
Philippians 4:6–8; James 3:16–18; 1 Peter 2:6

*Lord God, help me to stay focused on You.
I pray that You will transform my thoughts and
my life to be fully what is pleasing to You.*

Be filled with the Spirit.

W e so easily forget that the Spirit of God lives within us. And all His power resides within us as well. When we submit to Him, we allow the Spirit to work in and through us. We can hinder the Spirit or we can allow Him to radiate through our souls—the choice is ours. God has assured us that a life filled with the Spirit brings about His glory, and it is a gift that keeps us full of faith and secure in His peace. All you need to do is simply receive what God has given and reap what He has promised.

Matthew 3:11; John 7:38, 39;
John 14:16–20; Acts 1:4, 5, 7, 8; Acts 2:4;
Acts 2:38; Acts 4:31; Acts 8:14–17; Acts 10:44–47;
Acts 19:1–6; Romans 5:5; 1 Corinthians 6:19;
Galatians 5:16, 17; Ephesians 5:18–20

*Heavenly Father, I thank You for
Your Spirit, who fills me with Your
presence and power. Help me to live a
surrendered life, filled by You.*

Made to Serve

Love God with all your heart and soul.

God has promised that when we live a surrendered life, He will bless us. We were made to serve God, to allow His Spirit to live in and through us in order to accomplish His purposes. Living for Him is what will fill us with the joy that is everlasting. Daily seek God's will for your life. Look for ways in which you can be a witness for His love, mercy, and grace, and watch the ways in which He blesses you.

Exodus 23:25; Deuteronomy 10:12, 13;
Deuteronomy 11:13–15; Deuteronomy 13:4;
Joshua 22:5; Joshua 24:15; 1 Samuel 12:20–22;
1 Chronicles 28:9; Psalm 100:1, 2; Ecclesiastes 11:9;
Matthew 4:10, 11; Matthew 6:24; Romans 7:6;
Romans 12:1, 2; Romans 12:10, 11, 13; 1 John 2:17

*Lord God, I long to serve You,
to live a life that brings glory to Your name.
Fill me with Your Spirit so that I might
fulfill Your purposes for my life.*

But anyone who does what pleases GOD will live forever

1 John 2:17

Healing Through Love

Pray for those who hurt you.

*I*t's hard to forgive. We allow our feelings to get in the way of our forgiveness because we feel that revenge is the only remedy when we've been hurt. But God has assured us that it is through His love, through forgiving, that our souls are set free. We cannot hold on to what God wants us to let go of. If He has commanded us to forgive, we must do so freely, without hesitation. And when this seems too difficult, we can rely on Jesus, through whom we can do all things . . . even the impossible.

Isaiah 43:18, 25; Matthew 5:10–12; Matthew 5:44; Matthew 6:14, 15;
Matthew 18:21, 22; Mark 11:26; Luke 17:3, 4; Ephesians 4:31, 32; Philippians 3:13, 14;
Colossians 3:13; Hebrews 10:30; 1 Peter 2:19–23; 1 Peter 3:9, 10; 1 Peter 4:12–14

*Lord God, I pray that Your heart will flood
mine and enable me to love and forgive in the ways
You have loved and forgiven me.*

Overcoming Obstacles

Hold on and stand firm in your faith.
There is nothing God cannot do.

*I*t may look like "the end," but it's not. Don't be deceived . . . walk by faith. Your prayers may not be answered, but God is not finished. You may very well be in the center of God's will even as you face the most challenging circumstances of your life. It is only another opportunity to trust God. Your obstacles give you the chance to see God's power and presence in your life . . . expect Him to show up in ways you have never imagined.

Psalm 27:1; Isaiah 41:13; Romans 5:3–5;
Philippians 4:13; Hebrews 10:36; James 1:2–4; 1 Peter 5:7

Lord God, help me to stand firm in my faith, trusting that
You can do the impossible and that there is nothing for me to fear.
I pray that You will strengthen my heart to walk by faith alone.

The Challenge of Faith

You will be tempted, but God will strengthen you to stand firm against whatever temptations you face.

We can be assured that we will be tempted in life, in more ways than we ever thought possible. But God is with us. He is our ready help in times of trouble, and His Spirit is in us to help us stand firm in our faith against whatever temptations we face. We must be ready by being grounded firmly in our faith, being focused on God's Word, and having a constant relationship with Him through prayer . . . then we'll be ready for anything.

Psalm 119:11; Proverbs 28:13; Romans 6:14;
1 Corinthians 10:12, 13; Ephesians 6:10, 11;
Hebrews 2:18; Hebrews 4:14–16; James 1:2, 3, 12–14;
James 4:7; 1 Peter 1:6, 7; 1 Peter 5:8, 9; 2 Peter 2:9;
1 John 1.9, 1 John 4.4, Jude 24, 25

Lord God, strengthen my spirit when I'm tempted. Help me to stand firmly in my faith and not waver in obedience to Your Word.

Singleness

*Trust in God's plans for your life even
when you don't understand them.*

God's plans for each of us are different, and we should work to make our expectations the same as God's. He may have a plan for us to live our lives with someone through marriage, or He may want to bring about our joy through being single, living wholly for Him. Whatever God's desire is for you, trust that His plans are for your good and His glory. Don't be moved by the expectations of the world. Place your trust in God, pray your heart out to Him, and then trust Him to bless you in powerful ways through His great love for you.

Psalm 18:32; Psalm 37:4; Proverbs 3:5–7; Hosea 2:19; Romans 7:4;
1 Corinthians 7:8, 9, 17; 1 Corinthians 7:28; 1 Corinthians 7:32, 33, 35–37;
Galatians 6:4; Hebrews 13:4; 2 Peter 1:5–8

*Heavenly Father, help me to trust in Your plans for my life,
to find joy in an intimate relationship with You. Fill me with Your love
and peace, which do not change according to my circumstances.*

Lifting God Up

Worship before the miracle.

Often we get the order of God's ways confused. We worship after we see the miracle, but we should worship before it happens. That's faith. Faith believes before it sees. It's our faith that opens God's heart and hand. Now, when nothing is happening, is when we should thank Him and believe that He will answer our prayers in His way, in His perfect timing. And we can walk forward in faith, full of hope, by clinging to His promises and trusting in His faithfulness.

Deuteronomy 8:18, 19; Psalm 95:3–7; Psalm 96:4, 8, 9;
Psalm 99:5, 9; John 4:24; Philippians 3:1, 3; Hebrews 12:2, 3;
1 John 2:17; Revelation 14:7; Revelation 22:8, 9

*Lord God, thank You for always hearing my prayers.
I lift You up in every circumstance in my life and ask
that You strengthen my faith as I wait upon You.*

Determined to Obey

Obey God so that all will go well with you.

We have a hard time obeying God when we can't make sense of His ways. We want to go our own way, believing that we know better than God, but God's ways are not only higher . . . they're also better. He knows our lives from beginning to end. He knows what robs us of our joy and what fill us with it. He knows what we need even before we do. And His desire is that we might walk in His will so that we might reap the blessings of faith. Don't allow the world's worries to keep you from focusing on God and His perfect ways. Keep your eyes upon Him when you don't know what to do, and He will show you the way.

Leviticus 18:4; Deuteronomy 4:29–31; Deuteronomy 5:29; Psalm 18:28, 30; Psalm 19:7, 8; Psalm 119:100, 101; Luke 4:4; Romans 15:4; Hebrews 4:12; James 4:8; 1 Peter 2:2

Heavenly Father, help me to walk obediently in Your will, not questioning You or wavering in my faith. Make my paths straight.

Integrity

God weighs you on honest scales.

We often work endlessly and tirelessly trying to please people. We are desperate to be accepted, appreciated, and deemed successful, but those efforts often also mean compromising our integrity. God has set before us a path of righteousness. Not one to be traveled on our own, but one in which we are relying completely on Him to fill us with His Spirit and guide our hearts and minds. Having integrity, walking in faith as God has commanded, is not always easy. There are temptations to go our own way or follow the way of others, but God is our strength, and His Word is our guide. Focus on pleasing God alone.

Job 27:1–6; Job 31:5, 6;
Psalm 1:1–6; Psalm 7:8; Psalm 112:5–7;
Psalm 119:1–8; Proverbs 11:1–3; Proverbs 12:17–19;
Proverbs 15:33; Proverbs 20:7

*Lord God, help me to have integrity
in my daily life. Whatever I do or say,
let it be representative of You.*

Sharing Your Faith

Let your light shine before others,
bringing glory to God.

*J*esus is the light within you that shines brightly in this dark world. You may not see how your life impacts the world, but God assures you that if He is in you and you are in Him, you are working greater miracles than you will ever know. Each and every day that God gives you life is a blessing to the world. You are wonderfully made by God Almighty to fulfill His greater purposes. And there is no greater joy than living the life of faith, bringing glory to God and faith to those around you. Let your light shine.

Daniel 12:3; Matthew 5:16; Matthew 10:32, 33;
Matthew 28:19, 20; Mark 16:15, 16; Luke 4:18;
Luke 12:8, 9; Luke 15:7; Luke 19:10; John 3:16, 17;
John 12:26; Philippians 2:9–11; 2 Peter 3:9;
1 John 5:12; Revelation 3:20

Heavenly Father, fill me with all that
You are and make my light shine brightly to
the world around me. I pray that all I do and
say brings glory to Your name.

Serving the Church

Pray for those who are bringing the love of God into the world.

$\mathcal{G}$od has special purposes for each of us, and some have the responsibility—and also burden—of leading others into deeper faith. And we're to carry one another's burdens in whatever way we can. Ask God to show you how you can help your church and your pastor. Listen carefully to what He might have you do, and be ready to follow His directions. You will find God enabling you to do all He's calling you to do, and you'll be a greater blessing, even if just in praying, than you will ever know.

Psalm 15:1, 2; Psalm 133:1; Romans 12:4, 5; 1 Corinthians 12:12–28;
Ephesians 4:11, 12; Colossians 2:10–19; 2 Timothy 2:12; Hebrews 13:7, 17; 1 Peter 5:5

Lord, lead me in the ways You might have me help and encourage my pastor. Help me to be a blessing to my church in whatever ways You see fit to use my gifts.

Comforting Others

OCTOBER 18

*The love of God within you can bring
comfort to those who are hurting.*

God never asks you to do something without His help. The power of His Spirit within you can comfort others even in the midst of your own hurting. Don't rely on your own strength; lean on God and allow Him to move powerfully in and through you. His love brings comfort and healing, replacing all pain and sorrow with His love and grace.

2 Samuel 22:5–7; Psalm 103:17;
Isaiah 40:11; Isaiah 41:10, 15, 16; Isaiah 49:13–16;
Matthew 10:29–31; Romans 15:1–4; 2 Corinthians 1:3–5;
1 Thessalonians 5:11, 14, 15

*Heavenly Father, help me to be
a comfort to those who are hurting.
Use my life to show others Your love
and lead them to Your grace.*

BUT·THE Love of the Lord remains forever *Psalm 103:17*

323

Anchor of Hope

Life brings about circumstances that threaten your faith. But God is able to do the impossible, and His promises are your anchor of hope.

*L*ife is hard. And there are circumstances that arise that will cause you to question your faith in ways you have never imagined. But even in your doubt, God is there to encourage your faith through the hope of His promises. His love and provision for you are unshakable, eternal. And God alone is where your hope must reside. You may not be able to control your circumstances, but God can. And He's the God of miracles. So trust Him, even when it's hard to . . . and pray without ceasing.

Proverbs 24:14; Jeremiah 29:11; Zephaniah 3:17;
Romans 8:24–25; Romans 15:13; 1 Corinthians 15:19;
2 Corinthians 4:16–18; Titus 3:7

*Heavenly Father, help me to trust You more,
to be more firm in my faith through Your promises.
Fill my spirit with Yours so that I will find
my joy in You alone as I hope in You.*

From the Inside Out

Clothe yourself in the Lord Jesus Christ.

---

*G*od found you where you are, but He doesn't want you to stay there. His goal is to grow you into the likeness of Christ, filling you with His Spirit while pervading you with His grace. But you must choose to daily surrender and open your heart to Him. It's your willing spirit that will yield to His. God transforms you from the inside out through the process of sanctification—emptying you so that you can be filled with all of Him. Don't miss out on the blessings that come from walking with God and growing in Him. Let your life be a moment-by-moment surrender to Him and His purposes for your life.

Psalm 86:11, 12; Psalm 119:33–35; Psalm 119:105–109; Proverbs 23:12; Luke 18:10–14;
Romans 8:4–6; Romans 13:11–14; 1 Timothy 6:12; 1 John 2:3–6

Lord God, take my life and let it be all that You intend it to be.
Grow my faith and strengthen me for whatever is required
for me to become all You have created me to be.

Asking for Forgiveness

OCTOBER 21

Confess and you will find mercy waiting.

It's not easy to confess sin. It makes us realize how far we fall short of the glory of God and how deeply we have failed God and ourselves, and we'd rather not feel the guilt and shame that go along with that. But the only way out, the only way to be free, is to confess and repent. *You* do the confessing part, and *God's Spirit* will help you with the repenting part. You are not alone, and God will never turn you away. He's always waiting for you to come to Him and receive His love, mercy, and grace. Don't wait one more moment to lay your heart openly and honestly before Him.

Proverbs 28:13; Proverbs 29:33; Matthew 6:14, 15;
Mark 11:25, 26; Luke 17:3, 4; Romans 12:17–19;
Ephesians 4:1–3; Ephesians 4:31, 32; Colossians 3:13

Heavenly Father, I open my heart to You, confessing my sins that I am aware of and asking You to show me those that I am not. Cleanse me, make me new, and fill me with Your Spirit.

When No One Will Listen

God always hears you.

Matthew 7:7

KEEP on asking and you will RECEIVE WHAT YOU ASK

You may feel alone, but you're not. You may not think anyone cares or is listening to you, but God does and is. God is always with you, always ready to listen, and more importantly, He promises to answer when you call to Him. So pray, believing that God hears you, and wait patiently for His voice. Don't hesitate to come to Him, and don't keep anything from Him. He can handle your anger, your hurt, and everything in between. He is your God and He loves you.

2 Chronicles 7:14; Psalm 4:1; Psalm 17:1;
Matthew 7:7, 8; Matthew 18:19; Luke 11:9;
Romans 12:12; Ephesians 6:13–18; Colossians 4:2;
1 Thessalonians 5:16–18; Hebrews 4:16; 1 Peter 3:12

*Lord God, I am so thankful that You
are with me always. Thank You for always
listening to my voice and comforting my heart
when I need to know that You are there,
even when no one else is.*

327

Putting God First

Submit yourself to God
at all times and in all ways.

*L*ife gets busy and we try our best to fit God into it, but often we fail miserably. It takes a conscious, diligent effort to put God first in life. Our faith can so easily get drowned out by the troubles in our lives and the worries of the world. Each and every day, make it a priority to talk to God, to pray your way through the day and rely on Him in ways you're not sure you can. Be determined to draw near to Him continually, and make your relationship with Almighty God your life's first priority.

Deuteronomy 31:6; Joshua 1:8, 9;
Psalm 18:1–3; Isaiah 40:31; Proverbs 2:10–12;
Daniel 6:19–22; James 4:7, 8; 1 Peter 5:6, 7

Heavenly Father, my desire is that You will be first in my life. Strengthen me to focus upon my faith and not give in to the troubles of life and the worries of the world.

Facing Changes in Life

Wherever God takes you,
He will be with you.

*L*ife brings with it many changes, and change can be hard. But if you're trusting in God to help you through the tough parts, the times when you are overwhelmed and unsure if you're walking in His will, He will be sure to strengthen and encourage you to fulfill His purposes for your life. When you're facing difficulties in your job, know that there is nothing that God can't help you with. His resources go far beyond your own, and His supernatural power can work greater miracles than you can even ask for. So seek God in all that you do and know that He will help you in every way you need Him to.

Psalm 146:3–5; Proverbs 18:10;
Proverbs 23:4, 5; Ecclesiastes 2:18–20, 26;
Ecclesiastes 3:9–13; Matthew 6:25–34;
1 Corinthians 3:11–15; 1 Timothy 5:18

*Lord God, I'm overwhelmed with
the changes in my life. Strengthen me
through Your Spirit and enable and equip
me to fulfill Your will for my life.*

Worry and Doubt

God has promised to carry your burdens, so let Him.

We tend to carry burdens we were never meant to carry. And when we do, our souls suffer. When we're trying to manage our lives instead of allowing God to, we can find ourselves overwhelmed and cast into a state of despair. We've got to keep grounded in God's Word, where He assures us of His help and His faithfulness. Don't allow doubt to get the best of you. There's no need to worry . . . God's got everything under control, even if you don't.

Deuteronomy 7:8, 9; Psalm 4:8; Psalm 36:5;
Psalm 68:19; Psalm 128:1–6; Psalm 145:15–21;
Proverbs 23:24–26; Isaiah 26:3; Isaiah 32:17; Isaiah 44:3

Heavenly Father, I am tempted to worry and give in to doubt.
Life is overwhelming, and I need You to strengthen me and fill me with faith.

Led by God

God goes before you; just follow Him.

W

e weren't meant to go through life alone—we were created for God and to walk with Him, to be in an intimate relationship with Him so that we might experience the fullness of life. But all too often we get impatient and we move ahead of God, finding ourselves traveling paths we were never meant to take. Know that at each and every turn in life, however big or small the decision might be, God wants to guide you into His perfect will. When you're not sure what to do, pray, and then wait for His direction. His ways are always perfect. Don't settle for less.

Psalm 59:16; Proverbs 6:22, 23; Isaiah 40:28–31; Isaiah 41:10; Isaiah 43:18, 19; Isaiah 45:2, 3;
Isaiah 45:12, 13; Isaiah 54:10; Isaiah 55:10, 11; Luke 19:10; 2 Corinthians 5:7; 1 John 2:1

Lord God, I need You to guide me into Your perfect will.
Help me to always seek You and not move ahead of Your perfect
plans for my life but wait patiently upon Your direction.

Anticipating Christ's Return

You can look forward to eternal joy.

ife can keep us focused on our problems instead of on our faith. And when it seems as though our world is falling apart and there's nothing to look forward to, our faith tells us that we can anticipate, with joy, the return of Christ. So don't let today's worries consume you and keep you from experiencing the joy you were meant to live in today. Be assured that God has promised you a future and a hope . . . and eternal happiness upon Christ's return.

Isaiah 51:11; Isaiah 65:17–19;
Matthew 24:27–31; Luke 21:25–28; John 14:1–3;
Acts 1:11; Titus 2:13; 2 Peter 3:10–12; 1 John 3:1–3;
1 John 5:10–13; Revelation 21:4

*Heavenly Father, fill me with the joys
to come that will last forever. Keep my eyes
upward, focused on Your promises and filled
with the hope that Christ will return
and take me into glory.*

Completely Dependent

Allow God to do, in and through you,
what you are not able to do.

We were meant to feel inadequate and unable to fulfill, on our own, God's purposes for our lives. We were designed to need God in every way. Our flesh fights for independence, but God created us to be completely dependent upon Him. So don't try to live this life on your own and in your own strength. You can do all things only through Christ, who will give you all the strength you need.

2 Chronicles 16:9; Psalm 37:18; Psalm 131:1–3; Isaiah 44:22; Isaiah 50:7; Matthew 11:28–30;
1 Corinthians 15:10, 11; 2 Corinthians 3:5; 2 Corinthians 6:18; 2 Peter 1:4–8

Lord God, help me to lay down my pride and my will and lean on and depend upon You completely. In my weakness, I trust in You to be my strength.

OCTOBER 29

Embraced by Grace

Though your sins are like scarlet,
God will make them whiter than snow.

Whoever you are or whatever you've done, God's grace is enough to forgive, and His love is able to cover a multitude of sins. You don't need to fix yourself or your life; God can do that in better ways than you ever can. All He wants is for you to come to Him and receive His love and grace. He will enable you to overcome every sin that separates you from Him. So lay down your pride and allow God to rid you of guilt and shame. Be embraced by the grace that gives you victory over every sin.

Psalm 51:10; Psalm 69:5;
Proverbs 4:11; Isaiah 1:16–19; 2 Corinthians 4:1–6;
2 Corinthians 5:17–21; Galatians 2:20; Galatians 3:10, 11;
Galatians 5:1; 1 John 1:5–10; 1 John 3:5–7

Heavenly Father, thank You for Your
mercy that invites me to Your throne of grace.
Help me to surrender my soul to You and to be
cleansed and renewed in Your Spirit.

create in me a Clean Heart O God

Psalm 51:10

Putting Pride Aside

*Don't allow your pride to keep you
from God's very best in your life.*

With all the sins to fall into, it is pride that can quickly separate us from God and send our lives spiraling out of control. Pride keeps us from allowing God to be God. When *we* take control of our lives instead of permitting God to be who He is, we rob ourselves of the blessings that come from faith. Don't allow your pride to keep you from continually humbling your heart before God. He wants you living a life that is abundant, full of grace, and under His control.

Psalm 138:6; Proverbs 16:18–20; Proverbs 22:4;
Proverbs 29:23; Matthew 20:26, 27; Luke 18:11–14; 2 Corinthians 10:17, 18;
Ephesians 4:1; Colossians 3:12; James 4:7, 10; 1 Peter 5:5, 6

*Lord God, I humble myself before You.
I surrender my soul to You, for You are God and I am not.*

Nothing to Fear

**There is nothing to fear when
God has promised to be your protector.**

*J*t's easy to be consumed with fear when the world around us is filled with chaos. Everything seems out of control, and all hope seems gone. But when we're trusting in Almighty God, the One who holds the universe in motion, the One who spoke it into existence, we can have peace because we know that regardless of how things appear, God is still in control. And if God is in control, there is no reason to fear because there's nothing He can't do. God has promised to protect you, to be a ready help in times of trouble. You are secure because God is always sovereign.

Psalm 23:6; Isaiah 40:26; John 6:27; John 6:37; John 10:27–30;
Romans 8:35, 38, 39; 2 Corinthians 1:22; Ephesians 1:13, 14; Ephesians 4:30; Philippians 1:6;
2 Thessalonians 3:3; Hebrews 6:11, 12, 18–20; 1 Peter 1:3–5; Jude 24, 25

*Heavenly Father, I come to You for protection.
Help me not to fear and to trust in Your sovereignty and love.*

He will cover you with his *feathers.*
HE WILL SHELTER YOU
with his wings.
HIS FAITHFUL PROMISES
are your armor & protection.

PSALM 91:4

NOVEMBER

Far from God

You can run, but you can't hide . . .
God is everywhere you are.

Sometimes we find ourselves walking down paths we never expected to travel. We can't even remember consciously deciding to go one way or another because life moves so furiously fast. We have to make a constant effort to slow life down, to be present in the moment, and to seek God continually. Don't allow the ways of the world to lead you in directions that are contrary to God's will for you. If you can't see Him, if you can't hear Him, seek Him with all that you are.

Deuteronomy 4:2, 6, 9; Deuteronomy 8:5, 6, 11, 19;
Psalm 44:20, 21; Proverbs 10:9, 11; Proverbs 28:18;
Jeremiah 6:16; Hosea 14:2, 4, 9; Malachi 3:7; Romans 12:2;
Hebrews 3:12, 13; Hebrews 5:11, 12; Hebrews 12:15;
2 Peter 2:20, 21; 1 John 1:9, 10; Revelation 2:4, 5, 7;
Revelation 3:2, 15, 16, 19

Lord God, draw me closer to You. Strengthen
my spirit to stay on the narrow path so that
I might live a life that is pleasing to You.

He KNOWS the SECRETS of EVERY Heart

PSALM 44:21

Our Guide for Life

*You can find the answers
to life in one place: the Bible.*

We're always looking for answers, yet searching for them in all the wrong places. We have questions for God, but we fail to truly seek Him for the answers. Sometimes the answers He provides us with aren't what we were hoping for. But God sees all. He knows our lives from beginning to end. He knows what is best for us, even when His ways are difficult to understand. God wants you walking in His victory in every area of your life, but in order to do so, every step of faith must be guided through His Word.

Joshua 1:8; Psalm 19:8–11; Psalm 23:3; Psalm 32:8; Psalm 37:23, 24; Psalm 119:9, 11;
Psalm 119:24; Psalm 119:105; Proverbs 5:20–23; Proverbs 6:22, 23;
Isaiah 30:21; Luke 1:73–75; John 8:31, 32; 2 Timothy 3:16, 17; 2 Peter 1:4

*Heavenly Father, create a spirit within me that stays completely focused on
Your Word so that I might live the life that is for my good and Your glory.*

Instruct Your Children

Live the life of faith to which God has called you,
and your children will follow.

Children learn by example—whether good or bad—and parents have an enormous responsibility to care for them not only physically, but also spiritually. This is a challenge, because we all make mistakes, and sometimes our children are watching. The greatest example we can set is to confess, repent, and receive forgiveness from God. Be quick to talk to your children about their struggles and the fact that God is their guide, with them at all times and always ready to help. Show them by your example how to obey God's Word in all that you say and do.

Psalm 71:16–18; Psalm 78:1–8;
Proverbs 1:5–9; Proverbs 4:1–4; Proverbs 4:20–22;
Proverbs 8:32–35; 1 Corinthians 4:14–21;
2 Timothy 3:16; Hebrews 4:12; James 1:22;
1 Peter 1:24, 25; 1 Peter 2:1, 2

Lord God, help me to be an example
to my children, to show them Your love
and mercy, and assure them of Your
constant presence and provision.

Kindness

Allow the love of God to
fill you until you overflow.

*B*eing kind may not always come easily. The troubles in our lives seem to permeate our souls and keep us from allowing the Spirit to work in and through us in the ways He is supposed to. So each and every moment of our lives, we need to ask God to empty us of ourselves so that we might freely give to others the love He gives to us. God's desire is that you will be used by Him, so open your heart to His love for you so that you will overflow with all that He is and be a blessing to others.

Genesis 27:26; Genesis 50:19–21;
Joshua 2:12–14; Ruth 1:8; Proverbs 8:20–22;
Proverbs 10:12; Proverbs 25:28; Matthew 7:9–11;
Mark 10:43–45; Romans 12:21; Romans 15:1;
Ephesians 4:31, 32; 1 Thessalonians 2:10–12

Heavenly Father, take my life and let it be Yours.
Open my eyes to the ways in which I can show
others the continual kindness You show to me.

Tested Faith

*Never forget that God is for you
and faithful to His Word.*

Trusting God can be difficult when life is falling apart. It isn't easy when everything you see before you seems to indicate that God is not doing His job. You pray, but it seems as if God either isn't listening or has decided not to answer, and that makes you doubt Him. Don't be surprised when your faith is tested. It's tested so that it can grow, so that you will learn to trust God more. It's in those moments that you must seek God's promises and then pray until God fulfills them. Trust God, even when it's hard.

Job 23:1–12; Job 37:21–24; Psalm 20:7–9;
Psalm 86:7–10; Psalm 107:19, 20; Psalm 121:4–8; Proverbs 30:5;
John 14:1; Romans 11:33–36; 1 Thessalonians 3:7, 8

*Lord God, strengthen my faith to trust You even
when it's hard. Help me to believe that You hear me and will
answer my prayers according to Your perfect will.*

Don't let YOUR Hearts BE troubled trust in GOD AND trust also in ME

JOHN 14:1

Disciplining Your Children

Lead your children to God and
live out your faith before them.

We need God's help in every area of our lives, in our parenting most of all. If we are connected to God, in an intimate relationship with Him, He is ready to help when we're uncertain how to handle the difficult situations that arise in parenting. Children will inevitably try to go their own way, but as parents, we have a responsibility to raise them in the ways of God. We know that God's ways are best, but our children have to learn this, just as we did. So when it comes to disciplining them, we must discipline them as God disciplines us . . . with love, mercy, and grace.

1 Samuel 15:22, 23; Psalm 86:15, 16; Psalm 89:30–34; Psalm 103:13–17; Psalm 106:6–8;
Psalm 106:43–45; Proverbs 10:1; Proverbs 13:1; Proverbs 20:11; Proverbs 22:15; Isaiah 1:19, 20;
Ephesians 6:1, 4; Hebrews 5:8; Hebrews 13:17; 1 Peter 5:5, 6

Heavenly Father, help me to raise my children in the ways
You desire me to. Help me to discipline them in the ways
You discipline me . . . through love, mercy, and grace.

Comfort in Loss

***God will comfort you in
your pain and sorrow . . . let Him.***

PSALM 145:13

One of the greatest sorrows we experience in life is the loss of a loved one. We want the life we share with the ones we love to last forever, and it will, but only when we are joined together in heaven . . . and some of us just get there sooner than others. When you experience loss, know that God will heal your heart and comfort you. He wants you to be filled with joy knowing that one day you will see your loved ones again. And until then, He wants you to gain a better perspective on the treasure of the life you've been given. God is ready to hold your tears and heal your heart . . . let Him.

Psalm 145:13, 14; Psalm 147:3–5; Ecclesiastes 3:1–8;
1 Corinthians 15:16–26; 1 Thessalonians 4:13–16

*Lord God, my heart hurts and
I need You to comfort me in ways that
I'm not even sure I can be comforted. I need
You to fill me with Your peace as I trust in
You to bring beauty from my ashes.*

The Influence of the World

Don't worry; just pray.

*T*here comes a point in life when you realize there's little you can do to protect your children from the ways of the world. No matter what you do, they are still subjected to the sinful world around them. But they are never beyond the protection and care of God. You must trust Him to be with them, lead them, and guide them when you can't. He is with them always, so pray that they will have open hearts to discern God's voice when He speaks to them. When you don't know what to do . . . pray and trust God to care for your children in the ways that you cannot.

Proverbs 6:5–11; Proverbs 6:20–23; Proverbs 22:6;
Proverbs 28:7; Isaiah 55:11–13; Matthew 7:15–17; Mark 8:34–36;
Romans 12:1, 2; 1 Corinthians 7:14; 1 Corinthians 10:13;
2 Corinthians 6:14–18; Ephesians 5:6–12

*Heavenly Father, I pray that You will
protect my children and strengthen their faith
to walk the straight and narrow path You
desire them to follow. Open their hearts
so that they might know Yours.*

345

Tithing

Give and it will be given to you.

od wants to bless you in all the ways you want Him to, and He is able to do that in every way that is within His perfect will for your life. But what He wants is for you to experience the joy that comes from giving, so He asks you to give even when you don't think you have anything to give. Give what you have. And if you give all you have, know that God has promised to take care of you and provide for you in all the ways you need Him to. Trust Him with your giving . . . then miracles will begin to happen in your own life.

Deuteronomy 16:16, 17; Psalm 92:12; Psalm 96:7–9; Proverbs 3:9, 10; Malachi 3:8–12;
Luke 6:38; 1 Corinthians 16:1, 2; 2 Corinthians 9:6–12

Heavenly Father, show me the ways in which You want me to give in order to honor You as my God. Open my heart and help me to trust You in the ways You are asking me to give.

Loving Your Spouse

*Your spouse is a gift from God,
one to be treasured.*

One of the greatest blessings you can be given is a spouse who loves the Lord and loves you. If you are given that blessing, remember all the ways in which God has loved you to bless you in such a way. Then readily pour out God's love and grace upon your spouse. Never allow them to forget that they are loved and treasured, not only by God, but also by you. Lift them up above all others, even when they fall short of your expectations. Cover them with God's love and your own, and continually thank God for His grace in giving you the blessing of a spouse.

Genesis 2:18, 21–25; Psalm 103:5;
Proverbs 5:18, 19; Proverbs 18:22; Proverbs 19:14;
Ecclesiastes 9:9; Song of Solomon 4:10–16;
Song of Solomon 8:7; Matthew 19:4–6; Mark 10:6–9;
1 Corinthians 7:2–6; Hebrews 13:4

*Lord God, thank You for loving me enough
to bless me with my spouse. Help me to love
him/her in all the ways You desire me to, and
to treasure him/her in the ways that You do.*

While You're Waiting

While you're waiting . . . worship.

*W*e get caught up in worrying during our waiting, and we forget to worship. We forget that worship turns our eyes from our troubles and focuses our hearts on God. When we shift our focus, and we're trusting in God's faithfulness, our faith is strengthened in ways that enable us to rest in His peace as we wait upon Him to answer our prayers. Don't allow the worries of the world to keep you from worshipping. Be determined to praise God for all He's done and all He has yet to do.

Deuteronomy 26:7, 10; 2 Samuel 22:47;
Psalm 71:22–24; Psalm 95:6, 7; Psalm 99:9; Proverbs 3:27;
Isaiah 40:18, 21, 22; Isaiah 42:12; Isaiah 43:21;
Isaiah 58:14; Matthew 4:10; John 4:21–24;
Acts 17:22, 23, 28–30; Colossians 3:16

*Lord God, I praise You for all that You are.
Thank You for Your love, faithfulness,
and prevailing peace. Help me to trust
You and keep my eyes on You.*

may God the Rock of my salvation be EXALTED

2 Samuel 22:47

God Is in Control

God has promised to watch over all those who love Him.

*I*t's easy to be fearful. We live in a fallen world. We see tragedies unfolding around us and cannot help but worry about those who are closest to us, those whom we love. But worry can keep us from experiencing the joy we were meant to live in. And even though there are things that are out of our control, they are never out of God's. So when you're filled with fear, worried about those you love, cast your burdens upon God . . . the One who is with you always and working miracles beyond anything you can hope for or imagine.

Deuteronomy 7:8, 9; Ruth 2:4–12;
Psalm 4:8; Psalm 36:5; Psalm 68:19;
Psalm 128:1–6; Psalm 145:15–21; Proverbs 23:24–26;
Isaiah 26:3; Isaiah 32:17; Isaiah 44:3

*Heavenly Father, I need You to
fill me with peace and strengthen
my faith to trust that You are watching
over those I love so dearly.*

Relationship Struggles

Pray that God will bring love and understanding into your relationship.

*L*ife is hard, and people are difficult. Often our relationships with those we love the most are the most difficult. Because we love them, we have higher expectations of them and desire more from the relationship. But we're all just human. We make mistakes and we don't always think clearly. And at times when our faith is soaring, our spouses could be struggling. We can't go through our relationships without God, so make sure that you always pray for your spouse: for their heart to be open and for them to understand everything they need to. And then trust God to work in spiritual ways that will make your relationship stronger.

Genesis 2:18, 20–25; Proverbs 25:11, 15; Proverbs 27:8;
Ecclesiastes 4:9–11; Matthew 5:46–48; Romans 12:9, 10; Romans 13:8–10;
Romans 14:7; 1 Corinthians 11:11, 12 ; 1 Corinthians 13:1–13; 1 Peter 3:7–11

Lord God, I pray for my spouse's heart to be open to Yours and that our relationship will grow even stronger when life is difficult. Help us to always stay focused on You.

An Open Heart

**God is compassionate toward you so that you
can show His compassion and love to others.**

$\mathcal{S}$howing compassion to others isn't for their benefit alone; it does something powerful within our spirits as well. When we're compassionate, we open our lives for God to move in miraculous ways, and there is no greater joy than being used by God. So open your heart and your hands, and be willing for God to use you in whatever way He sees fit to reach a hurting world. You can be the one who leads someone to Jesus and saves their soul through your compassion.

Genesis 24:67; Exodus 2:6–10; Proverbs 31:20;
Isaiah 49:15; Isaiah 66:13; Matthew 9:36

*Heavenly Father, use my life to show the compassion to others
that You continually show to me. Let my life lead others to You so
that they might fully know Your love, mercy, and grace.*

When He saw the crowds he HAD compassion on them because they were CONFUSED and Helpless Matthew 9:36

Greater Blessings

God has promised that great faith
brings about greater blessings.

We look at life's challenges as situations from which we need rescuing instead of working to get through them. God has greater purposes for our faith than just providing an escape route. Faith is a journey, not a destination, so we shouldn't expect to stop needing to have faith. Faith will always be hard, yet God will strengthen us to believe in His faithfulness. We have to trust God and His promises even when it doesn't appear that He is going to show His presence. When you need a miracle, focus on your faith and keep your eyes on God.

Exodus 2:3; Ruth 2:12;
Psalm 31:14, 15; Matthew 15:28

Lord God, fill me with faith. I want to trust You,
but I often struggle to. I pray that the Spirit will
keep me focused upon Your faithfulness.

Godliness

*Continually surrender to all that God
wants to do in and through your life.*

We often struggle to live a life that is worthy of God. After all, He's God—perfect and unfailing. But God doesn't expect us to be perfect; He just wants us to surrender. It's about letting go of our desires for our lives and allowing Him to do with us as He wills. Godliness is simply surrender. If you're saved through Christ, then He is living within you, enabling you to walk in His will even if you're not sure you want to. His Spirit within you is all you'll ever need to live a godly life. So, don't *try* harder; just *trust* God more.

Proverbs 31:10–12; Proverbs 31:30;
Luke 1:41; 1 Timothy 2:10; 1 Timothy 4:7

*Lord God, help me to surrender my
will to Yours. Search my heart and know me
and show me the way that is everlasting. Help
me to yield my spirit to Yours and to live a
life that is worthy of Your great love.*

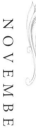

Fruitfulness

**Gods' desire is that you will bear much fruit
as you live for Him and He lives in you.**

*G*od has told us that faith without works is dead. And dead faith doesn't yield the abundant life we were made to live. God living in us yields the fruit that produces those things that draw others to Him. It is not a burdensome task. All God wants is for us to open our hearts and allow His Spirit to move in us. It is the Spirit, alive and working in us, who will help us to fulfill God's purposes for our lives and yield the fruit we were meant to bear.

Genesis 21:1–3; Genesis 30:24; 1 Samuel 2:21;
Psalm 17:8; Psalm 122:3; Luke 1:41–45; Luke 2:6, 7

*Heavenly Father, I long to be fruitful in order
to bring You glory. Help me to discern Your will
for my life each day and to bring honor to Your name.*

Favor

*You cannot earn **God's grace**, so don't try.*
His love gives us what we don't deserve.

God's grace isn't called "amazing" without reason. Deep within, we know that we don't deserve God's love, yet He loves us unconditionally anyway. He doesn't see us as we are, but as we were created to be in Christ. So right where you are, whoever you are, God meets you and embraces you with His grace, drawing you in and sanctifying you through His love. Don't hesitate to run to Him when you realize you've misplaced your faith in life. He's always waiting, and forgiveness is continually offered. His discipline may be necessary, but you can trust in His promise that when you turn to Him, His favor lasts a lifetime.

Genesis 17:19; 1 Samuel 2:26; Luke 1:15, 16; Luke 1:30

Lord God, thank You for Your amazing grace. I pray that I will be living proof of Your unconditional love that is mighty to save.

Respect

We are all created by God, and we must look at others through His eyes rather than our own.

We cannot allow ourselves to judge others in the way our flesh so naturally desires. It's easy to fall into the ways of the world, deeming ourselves better than others and holding ourselves in lofty places. But we are all created by God, and all of us need to bow before His throne of grace. Know that others will see God in you if you lift others up. Treat others in the way you yourself want to be treated but, even more so, in the ways that God has treated you . . . with love, mercy, and grace.

Leviticus 19:3; Proverbs 1:8, 9;
Proverbs 6:20–22; Proverbs 20:20

*Lord, help me to quickly lift others up.
I want others to see You in me in all I say
and do. Fill me with Your Spirit, so that I
might live the life You've called me to.*

Resurrection

There is no greater power than the power of God.

L ife is filled with impossibilities, and only God can work miracles. We pray, but often without faith. We tend to believe that God's miracles aren't for us, that we don't deserve to be blessed in the ways that we're asking to be. We forget God's grace . . . and we forget the power of God. When you're praying for God to answer prayers, to do the impossible in your life, remember that God brings the dead to life. So when things are falling apart in your life, they might in fact just be falling into place as you trust in the power of God to save you in every way you need Him to.

2 Kings 4:32–37;
Psalm 126:4; Luke 7:11–17

Heavenly Father, I thank You for
Your presence and the grace that allows me
to pray for Your power to perform the miracles
in my life that I so desperately need.

Fulfillment

***God can fill you until you overflow,
but only if you empty yourself.***

*I*n order to live a life of faith, we have to empty ourselves of our expectations of life. We have to surrender to the knowledge that God created us with purpose, on purpose, and has a detailed plan that will be for our good and His glory. We're constantly searching for happiness and desperate to find joy, but true happiness and joy can only come from God. So seek Him, and you will find Him, and your joy will be made complete.

1 Kings 1:28–30;
Psalm 18:28; Psalm 128:3

*Heavenly Father, empty me so that I
can be filled with You. I long to live in the
joy and peace You desire me to. Help me to
set aside my hopes and desires and
trust in Your plan for my life.*

Committed to Love

God's desire is that you will love one
another in the same way He loves you.

The commitment of marriage is often undervalued. We live in a world that is full of temporary pleasures that easily take us off track from God's plans for our lives. And when they do, when we put ourselves first instead of God, the consequences destroy the blessing God has given us. If God has blessed you with someone to love and cherish, make sure that you do just that. If you place God first, then your spouse, and yourself last, you have the priorities right. Lift God up and praise Him for the blessing He has given you in your marriage.

Genesis 2:24; Genesis 29:18; 1 Samuel 1:8; 1 Samuel 1:18; Proverbs 31:23

Lord God, strengthen me to resist temptation and the
ways of this world. Help me to cherish my marriage and love
my spouse in the ways that You have commanded me to.

No Matter What

God has promised that
His blessings are upon you.

*O*ur faith fails when we're faced with more than we can handle in life. When we're struggling and feel abandoned by God, alone and afraid, it's difficult to have faith even the size of a mustard seed. But in those moments, when all hope seems gone, we must simply surrender to Him with a humble heart, full of praise, even if we don't know what we're praying for or if God is even listening. At His throne of grace, there is hope, there is peace, and there are promises that will enable you to trust God . . . no matter what.

Psalm 3:1–8; Psalm 11:1–7; Psalm 18:28–35; Psalm 125:1–5; Psalm 126:1–6; Matthew 5:3–12

Heavenly Father, my faith grows weak and weary as I face
what I'm not sure I can handle. I need You to fill me with Your
strength to keep trusting in all that You've promised me.

VICTORY COMES FROM you O LORD PSALM 3:8

Overcoming Addiction

God will give you the victory.

*D*on't allow anything to separate you from God, especially temporary pleasures that leave long-term consequences that you cannot live with. If you're relying on anything other than God, run to Him. Lay out your heart, surrender your sins, and allow God to do what only He can do—fill you with His Spirit so that He can transform your life in the way it needs to be, through His power. Only God can save you. Only He can fill you with strength to face your battles and win the victory. God's grace is enough. He is all you need . . . run to Him and don't look back.

Proverbs 20:1; John 8:32; Galatians 5:1

Lord God, I need You to help me.
I need Your power to help me in overcoming
the addictions that are keeping me from You.
I need Your grace to consume me.

Faith over Feelings

*Entrust your anger to the
One who judges justly.*

*A*nger can get the best of us. When we feel as though we've been wronged, our human instinct is to demand that justice be served. But when our spirit is filled with anger, we don't think clearly. We say and do things we shouldn't, and above all, we fail to obey God. When your feelings start to dominate your faith, pray immediately that God will take your burden from you and give you peace in surrendering all that is stealing your joy. Give it all to God, whatever is raging within you, and know that He will never fail you.

Ephesians 4:26, 27; 1 Thessalonians 5:9; 1 Peter 2:23

*Heavenly Father, help me to release my anger
into Your hands. I want to live full of peace and
joy and trust in You to handle what I cannot.*

A Troubled Heart

Don't let your heart be troubled.

W e don't want to hear that we're in control of our worries. It's easier to simply succumb to them and surrender to hopelessness. Our true fear is that hope will disappoint, and we don't want to lose what faith we have left. God has commanded us not to worry, not to allow our hearts to be troubled, but we don't feel as though we have the strength to do what He's asking us to do. It's in that moment that we find ourselves in a place of surrender, letting go, because we have no choice. Obeying God and not worrying means one thing: trusting God more.

Psalm 46:1, 2; John 14:27; Philippians 4:5–8

*Lord God, help me to surrender all that
causes me to worry into Your hands. Strengthen my
faith to trust that You can do all things and that
You are my ready help in times of trouble.*

Believe in the Hope of Glory

Though life may not be fulfilling in the ways you expect it to be,
have faith that God will fill you in the ways you need to be.

Remember that we brought nothing into this world and will take nothing out. All that is given to us is a gift from God, and the joys to come will last forever. In God's promises, we can be content and satisfied because He is the hope of glory. So although you may not *feel* satisfied with your life, you can *decide* to trust in God's promises to you and rejoice in the hope that He's promised.

Proverbs 27:20; 1 Timothy 6:6–8; Hebrews 13:5, 6

Heavenly Father, help me to be content in the joys to come that will
last forever. Fill my spirit with praise and thanksgiving for Your many
blessings, those that I am aware of and those that I am not.

Backsliding

*You are not perfect, so don't hold yourself
to that standard . . . God doesn't.*

Sometimes we ask of ourselves more than God is asking of us. We're not perfect. In fact, God has said that not even one of us is good. Without His Spirit, without the work of Jesus, we fall far short of the glory of God. So when you're walking in faith and suddenly find yourself off the path of righteousness, know that God can restore your soul. All you need to do is turn to Him. Wherever you are, whatever you've done . . . His grace is there to meet you and renew a steadfast spirit within you.

Psalm 51:10–12; Proverbs 28:13; John 6:37

*Heavenly Father, I know that I often
fall short of Your glory, and I need Your
grace to save me. I turn to You in this
moment, asking that You will restore
my soul and refresh my spirit.*

Insecurity

You are wonderfully made by God Almighty, and you are loved by Him.

God will enable and equip you to do all that He's purposed you to do. All that you need to do is rely on Him and trust in His supernatural power to provide the resources and strength you need. Focus on God instead of on your shortcomings. Know that God uses those who are humble and are willing to be used by Him. Christ in you enables you to do all things. If life is overwhelming, know that that's the way it's supposed to be . . . you were made to rely on God at every moment of your life and know that you are not competent in yourself. Your competence comes from God, so trust Him and watch the miracles He will do in and through you.

Psalm 91:3–7; Proverbs 30:5;
2 Corinthians 3:4, 5; 2 Thessalonians 3:3

*Lord God, help me live surrendered to You.
I can't walk through this life alone. Help me to
rely on Your wisdom and power so that my life
will achieve all that You have purposed it to.*

EVERY WORD OF GOD proves true

PROVERBS 30:5

Nothing Is Impossible

If someone is sick, you should pray.

We underestimate the power of prayer because we question the power of God. We forget that God has told us that our weapon against worry is prayer. Prayer may not seem like it's doing much because God isn't answering how or when we think He should, but that doesn't mean our prayers aren't heard or that God isn't working. God's power raises the dead. It gives life. So when we or someone we know is ill, there's one thing to do: pray. If God has promised that He never changes, then neither does His power. And that means He can work a miracle . . . suddenly . . . without warning. So don't stop praying.

Psalm 23:2–4; Psalm 43:5; James 5:14

Heavenly Father, help me to truly believe that Your miracle-working power is at work today, in the ways that I need it to be.

He *comforts* us in all our troubles SO THAT WE CAN Comfort *others.*

2 CORINTHIANS 1:4

DECEMBER

Lust

*Keep your eyes upon God and your
heart surrendered to Him in all ways.*

e live in a fallen world where temptations surround us and evil is ready to steal our faith, peace, and joy. We must stay alert, conscious of our thoughts and yielded to the Spirit so that He can control our actions. Don't be surprised when your flesh is tempted, but be ready for the battle and immediately call out to God in those moments. The Spirit will strengthen you to walk the straight and narrow path. God will flood your soul with His Word and He will keep you from stumbling. Whatever tries to overtake you in this world . . . God is greater still.

Proverbs 6:25, 26; Matthew 18:8, 9; 2 Peter 2:9

*Lord God, keep my eyes upon You and my heart pure. When I am tempted,
help me to turn to You and walk away from the sins of the world.*

Never Alone

God has promised He will come to you.

Whatever your circumstances, whatever is causing you to feel lonely at this moment . . . God is greater than what makes you question His love and presence in your life. You may not feel Him near, you may not know He's there, so you must seek Him with all that you are—even the empty parts. Bring it all to Him, and allow Him to heal your heart and flood your soul with peace in the truth that He is with you always. Never will He forsake you. He is here with you at this moment and every moment thereafter until you see Him face to face. That's His promise to you.

Psalm 27:10; Psalm 147:3; John 14:18

_Heavenly Father, I am empty and lonely,
and I feel as though all hope is gone. I need You. I need
Your love and Your presence, and most of all, Your grace._

Held by God

You might be pressed on every side, persecuted, and struck down, but God is with you; you are not abandoned and will never be destroyed.

We so easily allow our feelings and circumstances to get the best of us. We give in to the emotions that tell us we're suffering in ways that we shouldn't be suffering, and we blame God and get distracted from God's promises to us. We forget that this world will soon fade away, but God never will. We fail to have the faith that sees beyond our troubles, and we give in to our worries. But God is with us in our moments of suffering. It is in our weakness that His power is most strongly seen. So in your suffering, know that He is with you. Know that He will never leave you. Know that His promises will carry you through. You can and will endure in His strength, not your own.

2 Corinthians 4:8–10;
Hebrews 5:8, 9; 1 Peter 4:19

*Lord God, help me to endure,
to keep my eyes on the Cross, knowing
that victory is sure, and that peace and
joy are coming, as I trust in You.*

Held and Healed

God's promises will preserve your life.

*L*ife can take us into deep, dark pits from which we are sure we will never find a way out. But wherever we are, God is able to save us. Pray that God will help you to believe, even when you're suffering unthinkable pain. When you're feeling alone, when nothing seems to comfort you, know that God can and will. God is greater than anything you're facing. Let Him hold and heal your heart.

Psalm 23:4; Psalm 119:50;
Isaiah 41:10; Isaiah 49:13; Jeremiah 32:27;
Matthew 5:4; 1 Corinthians 15:55–57;
2 Corinthians 1:3, 4; 1 Thessalonians 4:13, 14;
1 Peter 3:12, 13; 1 Peter 5:7; Revelation 21:4

Heavenly Father, I need Your presence in my life when I feel as though my suffering is too much to endure. Heal my heart according to Your Word and fill me with the peace and joy that You've promised I have in You.

Assured of Hope

Let God's love for you wash over your disappointment.
He has promised that He has good plans for you.

When we find ourselves in a place of discontentment, disappointed with the life we've lived and uncertain of the life ahead, we simply need to step into God's grace and not look back. We tend to hold on to what's gone wrong instead of what's gone right, and we take our eyes off God. We've got to let go of what holds us back from walking forward in faith, trusting that although the world may fail us, God never does.

Psalm 91:1, 2; Psalm 145:14–16;
Isaiah 26:3, 4; Matthew 6:31–34;
Romans 8:6; Romans 8:28; 1 Corinthians 9:27;
Philippians 4:6, 7, 11–13; 1 Timothy 6:6–8;
Hebrews 13:5, 6

Lord God, I feel as though my life isn't working out the way I hoped it would. I pray that You will help me to surrender my plans for Yours, knowing that in You I have promises that bring my soul peace, joy, and contentment in Your love.

Jesus Is Your Companion

*Jesus is with you at all times and in all ways,
in your joys and in your sufferings. He is always there.*

*P*eople in your life will fail you. At one moment they are there, the next they're not, so don't place your hope and trust in people. God is faithful even when they are not. God's gift of love for you, the sacrifice of His Son Jesus, is the gift of mercy that you will need throughout your life. And He is there with you, in your joy and in your suffering. Through it all, He is with you to assure you that the life of faith leads to victory.

Psalm 18:35; Psalm 27:10; Proverbs 18:24; Isaiah 54:10; John 14:18;
John 15:14–16; Hebrews 13:5; James 4:8

*Thank You, Jesus, for sacrificing Yourself
so that I might live a life filled with hope and peace.*

Beyond the Walls

As the body of Christ,
we're to bring heaven to earth.

*C*hurch is not about four walls; it's about breaking out of them. Jesus went around doing good, and so must we if we are to be obedient to God and live a life that brings light into a dark world. God has purposed you, in some gifted way, to share your faith and draw others to Him. If you're not sure where your purpose in His body on earth lies, seek Him, and don't stop seeking. Listen for God's voice, seek His direction, and then follow Him wherever He leads you.

1 Kings 8:56; Psalm 36:5; Psalm 89:1, 2, 33, 34;
Psalm 121:3, 4; Matthew 16:15–18; Ephesians 1:10, 22, 23;
Ephesians 2:20–22; Ephesians 3:15, 21; Colossians 1:13, 18; 1 Timothy 4:13

Lord God, I want to live the life You created me to live. My desire is that You will use my life to bring light to a dark world and draw others to You.

Saved and Loved

Jesus gave His life to give you yours.

———✦———

We get confused when God tells us we are "free." When God saves us, breaking the chains of sin and delivering us into victory, we assume that we're then able to live the life we want to. But that's not the freedom God has released us into. He's freed us from *ourselves* and from the sin of the world so that we might live in Him. He has delivered us to live a life of faith, grounded in Him, so that we might reap the abundant blessings He intends for us. We must daily surrender our souls and cast aside our will to embrace God's will. We must rid ourselves of pride and yield our souls to the One who saved us . . . and continues to do so.

Psalm 23:3; Proverbs 15:33; Proverbs 16:18–20; Proverbs 28:25, 26;
Jeremiah 13:15–17; Matthew 11:29, 30; Matthew 18:2–4; Matthew 20:26, 27;
2 Corinthians 4:7; James 4:6, 7, 10; 1 Peter 5:5, 6

Heavenly Father, thank You for saving me from myself. Help me to continually yield my soul to You and to obey Your every command.

Witnessing Effectively

Let God do what you cannot.
The life of faith is a life surrendered.

We feel overwhelmed by the command to bring our faith into the world and witness to others. We doubt our abilities and question God's understanding of them. But we were never meant to live out our faith in our own strength. Our lives are to be continually surrendered and yielded to God's mighty power. It's our relationship with Christ and the Spirit working within us that works miracles in and through us. We're able to draw others to God only through His grace that is alive within us. So surrender and keep surrendering, and your faith will rise to do all that God has called you to do.

Psalm 104:33; Proverbs 11:30;
Matthew 5:14–16; Luke 11:33; Luke 12:8, 9;
Luke 21:14, 15; John 14:31; Ephesians 6:18–20;
2 Timothy 1:8–10; 1 Peter 3:8–11, 15

Lord God, I surrender my life to You.
Help me to be discerning of Your voice and to be
obedient in every way You're asking me to be.

The Struggle with Life

*Jesus set an example that we
should do as He has done for us.*

We struggle with life, unsure of what we should do, what we should say, and everything in between. Often we seek advice from people and places that we shouldn't. Jesus is all we need to live a life of faith that is filled with the grace and glory of God. So when you're just not sure which direction to take, or what to say or do, look to Jesus, dig deep into God's Word, and you will find the wisdom and power you need to live the abundant life you were meant to.

Mark 10:43–45; John 13:14, 15; John 13:34; Romans 15:7; Ephesians 5:1, 2;
Philippians 2:5–11; Colossians 3:13; Hebrews 12:3; 1 Peter 2:21; 1 John 2:6; 1 John 3:16

Heavenly Father, thank You for giving me Jesus so that I don't have to question how to live my life. Thank You for the peace I can have in keeping my eyes on Him, knowing that His way leads to victory in all things.

Never Alone

God's love for you is unfailing.

Isaiah 54:10

The world might fail you, but God never will. Everyone may abandon you, but God won't. When you're feeling all alone, know that it is just a feeling—not reality. God has promised that He is with you always, and nothing is going to change that. Whether you are sitting in the midst of sin that causes you to feel alone, or are uncertain as to why exactly you're feeling that way, God's love pierces through the darkness. If you need Him, tell Him so . . . and know that His grace will be sufficient to love you in all the ways you need to be loved.

Deuteronomy 4:31; Deuteronomy 31:6;
Deuteronomy 33:27; 1 Samuel 12:22;
Psalm 147:3; Isaiah 54:10; Matthew 28:20;
John 14:1; John 14:18; Romans 8:35–39

*Lord God, in this moment,
when I'm feeling so alone, I need to
know that I am not. I need Your presence
and Your power; I need You to make
Yourself known to me and embrace
me with Your love.*

Unfailing Love

God's love for you is unfailing.

Whoever you are and whatever you've done, God's grace is waiting for you. God has promised to rid you of your guilt and shame over sin. All you need do is come to Him. We all fall short of the glory of God and must find our way to Jesus in order to be saved. Guilt should drive you to God, not away from Him. So when you're feeling ashamed, as if no one could love you for what you have done, know that God loves you unconditionally and is ready to embrace you with His grace.

Psalm 32:5; Psalm 103:10, 12;
John 3:17, 18; John 5:24; John 8:10, 11;
Romans 8:1; Hebrews 8:12;
Hebrews 10:22; 1 John 1:9

*Heavenly Father, I need Your grace,
for I have fallen short of Your glory and
need Your forgiveness to set me free from
the guilt that keeps me from experiencing
the fullness of Your joy.*

Continually Faithful

You can trust God because of all He has promised and the continual proof He gives of His faithfulness.

The Bible wasn't given to us merely for good moral reading and instruction; it was given to us so that we might know God. He wants us to know Him so that we can come to Him, be saved, and be able to live intimately with Him throughout our lives. We don't have to question, we don't have to doubt who He is and all that He does, because His Word holds the promises that assure us of His love. So when doubt tries to defeat you, run to God and run to His Word. His Spirit will flood your soul with the truth that He is Almighty God and that there is no God but Him.

Psalm 18:30–32; Isaiah 55:10, 11; Mark 11:22–25; Romans 4:19–21;
Romans 10:17; 1 Thessalonians 5:23, 24; 2 Peter 3:9

*Lord God, reveal Yourself to me in all the ways You want to.
I want more of You and less of me. Fill me with Your truth
and strengthen my faith according to Your Word.*

Filled to the Full

You are filled with the fullness of God.

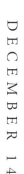

Faith takes you beyond your expectations for yourself or the expectations others have for you. God has created you, and that makes you important because you're living for something greater than yourself—you've been given life by God for God. So although the world may not see your worth, God does, and if you'll trust in Him, humbling yourself before Him and recognizing Him as Lord of your life, He will lift you up.

2 Samuel 22:3; Isaiah 40:31; John 14:12; Romans 8:26, 27; Ephesians 3:18, 19;
Ephesians 4:22, 23; Philippians 1:6; Hebrews 10:35, 36; 1 John 3:20

Heavenly Father, thank You for loving me and
giving me life so that I might accomplish Your purposes.

The Bible

Keep God's Word locked tight within your heart.

⟡

*G*od commands us to keep the Bible and all that is within it upon our lips, meditating on it day and night, so that we will be careful to do everything that is written within it. He assures us that in doing so, we will be prosperous and successful. God's Truth is joy to our hearts; His commands yield blessings. In keeping His way, there is great reward. God's voice is clear and His command simple: live according to His Word; live in His truth.

Joshua 1:8; Psalm 19:8–11; Psalm 32:8; Psalm 119:9, 11, 24;
Psalm 119:105; Proverbs 6:20–23; John 8:31, 32; 2 Timothy 3:16, 17

Lord God, fill me with Your truth. My desire is that I will clearly see the path of righteousness and be filled with the Spirit to have the strength to follow it.

Beyond What You See

Have faith, and nothing is impossible.

When we're struggling through life, unsure of where we've been and where we're headed, feeling as if everything is out of control, we have one place to go: the throne of God. He holds all the answers and His hand performs all the miracles. He tells us that all we need is faith, but when we're faced with impossibilities, faith isn't easy. It takes moving beyond what we see and know and trusting in the One who sees beyond all that we are able to see. When you don't know what to do, have faith in God, and He will make the impossible possible . . . then your faith will know no bounds.

Matthew 9:28, 29; Matthew 17:20;
Mark 9:23, 24; Romans 10:17; Romans 12:3;
2 Corinthians 5:7; Hebrews 11:6; Hebrews 12:1, 2

*Heavenly Father, I need You to give
me a measure of faith that believes in You
above and beyond the impossibilities that I'm
facing in my life. Help my unbelief!*

Anything
is
Possible
IF
@
PERSON
believes

Mark 9: 23

Praising God Even More

Praise God as long as you live.

---

*P*raising God has power. You may not see that power manifested in the ways you desire or in the timing you want, but God's power permeates through impossibilities behind the scenes of your life. God is working even when you can't see what He's doing. He asks us, thus, to live in faith, praising Him before the miracles. Our praise opens God's heart wide and fills ours even more.

2 Samuel 22:4; Psalm 34:1–3;
Psalm 47:1, 2, 6, 7; Psalm 48:1; Psalm 50:23;
Psalm 63:3–5; Psalm 71:5–8; Psalm 92:1, 2, 4, 5;
Psalm 107:8; Psalm 147:1; Isaiah 43:21; Acts 16:25;
Hebrews 13:14, 15; 1 Peter 2:9

*Lord God, I praise Your mighty name
and lift You up in my life above all things.
I pray that the Spirit within me will move
me to praise You more and more.*

Patient Expectation

God has promised to satisfy you.

$\mathcal{G}$od is with you and wants you to have deep joy. Life may bring disappointments, but He wants your faith to take you beyond what you see. He wants you trusting in Him for the joys to come that will last forever. He knows your heart's desires. He knows all that you're struggling with and all the prayers that you so desperately need answered, and He has promised to give you a future and a hope. He just needs you to believe in what He's promised you. Rest in His faithfulness and wait with patient expectation for His promises to be fulfilled in your life, because He is faithful to His Word.

Psalm 34:10; Psalm 37:3; Psalm 63:1–5; Psalm 103:1–5; Psalm 107:9; Proverbs 12:14; Isaiah 12:2, 3; Isaiah 44:3; Isaiah 55:2; Jeremiah 31:14; Joel 2:26; Matthew 5:6; 2 Corinthians 9:8; Philippians 4:12, 13

Heavenly Father, even though life isn't filled with the blessings I had hoped it would be at this moment, I have faith in You and the promises You have made to me. And that is all I need to know, so I will be content and rest in You.

Secured Victory

Find your rest in the shadow of the Almighty.

If God is for you, who dare be against you? You have the power of God on your side, and there is nothing greater. The question you must face in your fear is: Where is your faith? Are you trusting in what you see, relying on what you know, instead of completely trusting in God's truth? God has commanded you not to fear, and there is nothing that can overcome you when God is fighting your battles for you. So take up the armor of God, lay down your weapons of the world, and let God do what only He can do . . . give you rest while He secures the victory.

Psalm 23:4, 5; Psalm 27:1, 3; Psalm 31:24; Psalm 56:11;
Psalm 91:1, 2, 4–7, 10, 11; Proverbs 3:25, 26; Isaiah 40:31; Isaiah 54:14;
John 14:27; Romans 8:15, 16; 1 Timothy 1:7; Hebrews 13:6, 8; 1 John 4:18

Lord God, help me not to fear, as You have commanded.
Help me not to allow the situations of my life to determine my faith.
Help me to be at peace and to rest in You and Your power.

Simply Believing

God is faithful. Trust in every one
of His promises to you.

Our faith is rarely going to match up with our feelings. Most often, we're going to have to press past our emotions and simply believe God. Everything we see before us may indicate that God isn't going to reveal His presence, but He will, because He is faithful. There's not one of His promises to you that He won't fulfill. There's nothing He cannot or will not do for you, simply because of His love for you. So decide to count on God, not count Him out. He is faithful, even when we're not.

Genesis 9:16, 17; Genesis 28:15;
Deuteronomy 7:8, 9; Joshua 23:14; 1 Kings 8:56–58;
Psalm 36:5; Psalm 89:1, 2, 19, 34; Psalm 119:64, 65;
Psalm 121:3, 7, 8; Isaiah 54:9, 10; 1 Corinthians 1:9;
1 Corinthians 10:13; 1 Thessalonians 5:23, 24;
2 Timothy 2:13, 19; 2 Peter 3:9

Heavenly Father, I'm so tempted to
walk by sight, instead of by faith, and I
need You to strengthen me. Thank You for
being faithful, even when I'm not.

Love Is Greater than Pain

*When you choose to forgive,
you're setting yourself free.*

When we've been wronged, anger and hurt is our first response. God asks us to forgive, but often we're just not sure we can do that. Forgiveness seems like we're letting the other person off the hook when they deserve to pay for the way they made us suffer. But forgiveness isn't about letting the other person off the hook. God's justice remains whether we forgive or not . . . it's about setting *ourselves* free from the burden of unforgiveness. God's love is greater than your pain, so trust Him to handle your injustices by forgiving and allowing Him to do what only He can: heal your heart.

Psalm 103:7–13; Matthew 6:14, 15;
Matthew 18:21, 22; Mark 11:25, 26;
Luke 6:35–37; Luke 17:3, 4; 2 Peter 2:9

*Lord God, I pray that You will enable me to
forgive in the ways You've commanded me to.
I pray that You will fill me with Your love so
that others might know Your amazing grace.*

Live for God; Love Others

Live for God and you'll share your faith.

W hat you need to know when it comes to sharing your faith is that all you really need to do is live for God. We get wrapped up in doing and saying the right things, but God can bring good out of our mistakes. When others see our failures, they can also see us turning to God for grace. When they see us confessing our sins, they see God's forgiveness in ways that are inexplicable. God wants you to live for Him, and He will display your faith to others in ways you cannot imagine. Just stay connected to God, and He will do the rest.

Proverbs 11:24, 25; Daniel 12:3; Luke 6:38; John 4:7, 8; John 14:12, 13;
Romans 10:8–11; Galatians 6:9, 10; Ephesians 4:12–15; 1 Timothy 2:3, 4; James 5:19, 20

*Lord God, use my life's circumstances to display my
faith in You. Help me to live surrendered to Your will, helping
to lead those who are lost to Your throne of grace.*

Letting Peace Reign

*Don't allow anger to rob you
of your joy . . . because it will.*

We face many frustrations in life, most of which we have very little control over. But what we can control is the way we respond to all that life brings. We can get angry and bitter, or we can decide to stand firm in our faith and let peace reign. It may be difficult to believe this is a choice, but it is. God is there to help us in those moments when we're not sure we can let go of all we're holding on to. So when you're angry, pray. And if you can't seem to find peace, keep praying. Ask God to fill your spirit with His so that you can enjoy the life He's given you.

Psalm 133:1–3; Proverbs 14:29; Proverbs 15:17–18;
Proverbs 16:32; Proverbs 17:14; 1 Corinthians 1:10; 1 Corinthians 14:33;
Ephesians 4:26; Colossians 4:6; James 1:19, 20

*Heavenly Father, I often get angry and need Your help to let go of
all that I hold on to. I want to respond to my circumstances with the
knowledge that You are sovereign and that I can cast my burdens on You.*

1 Corinthians 14:33

FOR God is not a GOD OF DiSorder BUT OF peace

The Best Is Yet to Come

The best is yet to come,
so live in joy, and hope in faith.

*W*e become consumed with the troubles of the day, which steals our joy. We fail to embrace the hope God has given us in knowing that there is glory ahead for all eternity. Too often, we overlook all that God has promised us when it comes to eternal life. We forget the price that was paid, we forget the hows and whys, and we forget that God has given us something that cannot be taken away from us—eternal life with Him. We can rejoice right now, in this moment, that one day we will see God face to face and will live in the continual joy and peace that we were meant to. No more tears, no more pain and sorrow . . . only joy everlasting.

Psalm 22:26; Psalm 23:6; Psalm 37:18; Psalm 49:15;
John 3:16–18; John 4:13, 14; John 5:24; John 6:27;
John 6:46, 47, 50, 51; John 10:27, 28; John 11:25, 26;
1 Corinthians 15:54–57; 1 John 5:11, 12; 1 John 5:20

Heavenly Father, thank You for the gift
of eternal life. Thank You for having loved me
before I loved You. I pray that You will help me
live in the joy of today and trust in Your
promises for all my tomorrows.

Determined Faith

You might not understand God, but you don't need to . . .
you just have to trust in who He is and all that He has promised you.

More often than not, God isn't going to make sense. He works in our lives in supernatural ways, ways that are beyond our understanding. And that's where faith comes in. Its purpose is to get us past understanding to trust. Because if we can't see God, we're going to have to trust Him—we have no choice. But God has given us a gift to support and strengthen our faith: His Word. In it, God has made countless promises to you. Are you praying them? Do you believe in God's faithfulness to fulfill them? Trust God and rely on His faithfulness, even when you don't understand.

Joshua 1:9; Psalm 18:30–32, 36; Isaiah 46:10, 11;
Isaiah 54:10; Isaiah 55:3, 6, 10, 11; Mark 11:22–25;
Luke 12:29–31; Romans 4:19–21; Romans 10:17;
1 Thessalonians 5:23–24; 1 Peter 4:12–14; 2 Peter 3:9

Lord God, thank You for Your countless
promises. What joy I have in knowing that You
love me unconditionally and that I can have faith
for the future because of Your promised hope!

When You Feel Inferior

God has made you, and what
He thinks of you is all that matters.

We get wrapped up in what people think of us. We allow them to judge us when they aren't in a position to. God is our Creator, the One who judges justly . . . and we need to live to please Him instead of earthly people. Each and every day, we must focus upon God and His purposes for our lives. It is vital that we stay connected to Him, so that we can live the life we're intended to, bringing glory to His name. The only thing that matters is that your heart is right with God. People judge on outward appearances, but God looks at your heart.

Psalm 103:2, 3; Proverbs 3:25, 26; Isaiah 40:31; Isaiah 43:2; Zechariah 4:6; John 14:12;
Romans 8:26, 27; Ephesians 3:11, 12, 17–19; Ephesians 4:22, 23; Philippians 1:6;
Philippians 4:13; Hebrews 10:35, 36; Hebrews 13:6; 1 John 3:21; 1 John 5:14, 15

Lord God, thank You for loving me for who I am and transforming me into all
that You desire me to be. Keep my heart focused upon You and Your purposes
for my life, knowing that I am fully, unconditionally loved by You.

THE LORD is your SECURITY

Proverbs 3:26

Grace Wins

Love is all you need—God's love.

W e can only love others because we're loved by God. But sometimes we can't quite believe that we are loved by Him. For some reason, we think that God changes with our attitudes and behaviors, even though He's promised us that nothing can change His love for us. God's love is not a feeling. It doesn't come and go with emotions; it is the same forever and ever . . . unchanging. In order to fully love others, we must wholly experience the love of God. We must realize that even though we're not worthy of His love, He's decided to love us anyway. And we must receive His grace and not refuse the gift.

Jeremiah 31:3; Mark 12:3–31; John 3:16; John 13:34, 35;
John 14:21; John 15:9, 10, 12–14, 17; John 16:27; Romans 5:8; Romans 8:37–39;
1 Corinthians 13:1–8, 13; 1 John 4:7, 8; 1 John 4:10–12; 1 John 4:16, 19, 21

*Heavenly Father, sometimes I don't know why You would choose to love me,
but I am so thankful that You do. Help me to receive Your love so that I
might know the fullness of it and be able to love others fully in return.*

The Truth About Trust

***If you don't think you can trust God,
tell Him so.***

*S*ometimes it's hard to trust God, and He knows it. We can't hide our hearts from Him. So when you're filled with feelings of doubt, struggling with your faith and frustrated with God, go to Him, pray, and then trust Him beyond all doubt. Know that when you're walking with God, He is going to test your faith to make you cleave to Him. So don't be surprised when your faith is tested; just know that God is drawing you closer to Him . . . He loves you that much.

2 Samuel 22:2, 3; Job 13:15, 16;
Job 23:1, 2; Psalm 4:3–5; Psalm 16:1, 2;
Psalm 86:7–10; Psalm 107:19, 20; Psalm 121:4–8;
Proverbs 3:5, 6; Romans 11:33–36

*Lord God, there are times when
I don't know if I can trust You, and that
causes me to feel guilty. Help me to cleave
to You and push past my doubt.*

Your Source of Power

*When you're weak and weary, uncertain
and full of doubt, turn to God and His Word.*

You may not know which direction to take in life, you may not understand what your future holds, but God does. So when in doubt, run to Him. When we're moving fast and furiously through life, we forget that God's Word is not only our instruction book for life, but it also holds power beyond anything we can imagine. The Bible is the very voice of God. And when God speaks, miracles happen. So listen to His voice, do what He says, and your life will start to transform in powerful ways.

Nehemiah 8:10; Psalm 18:1–3; Psalm 27:1, 2; Psalm 119:28; Proverbs 8:14;
Isaiah 30:15; Isaiah 40:29–31; Isaiah 41:10; Daniel 10:17, 19; Ephesians 3:16, 17;
Ephesians 6:10, 13, 14; Philippians 4:13; Colossians 1:11, 12

*Heavenly Father, move the spirit within me to think
as You do and speak as You do. Help me to always look to
Your Word as the authority and power in my life.*

Faith in Action

Don't give up just because you feel like giving in.

⟶◦◦◦◦◦⟵

Our faith so easily rides upon our feelings because we let it. We forget that our faith is grounded in God's Word, not the circumstances of our lives. They change . . . God never does. Life is hard, and God knows we doubt, but when we do, we need to be conscious of our thoughts, ready to test them against God's. And if our thoughts don't match up with God's, we must redirect them according to His Word. A life of faith requires action, meditating on God's Word and actively and wholeheartedly trusting in it.

Matthew 9:20–22; Matthew 11:22–24; Matthew 17:20; Mark 9:23, 24;
Romans 1:17; Romans 10:17; Romans 12:3; 2 Corinthians 5:7; Hebrews 11:3, 6;
Hebrews 12:1, 2; James 5:14, 15; 1 Peter 1:7–9; 1 John 5:3–5

Lord, life sometimes seems so overwhelming; overwhelm me with Yourself.
Fill me with faith and help me to trust You more, just because of who You are.

When You Feel Forsaken

God's love for you is unchanging, full of mercy and grace.

PSALM 55:22

There may be times in your life when you feel like God has forsaken you. Difficult times leave your faith feeble, and you wonder if God has deserted you . . . but He has not. He allows you to go through difficult times for a reason, in His love and sovereignty, and He never takes His eyes off you. He is aware of every detail, and if He's allowing trials in your life He does so for purposes which you many never understand in this life. Here are the truths you must hold onto when you're falling apart and your heart is in pieces: God loves you, He is with you always, and He will never abandon you. Never.

1 Samuel 16:7; 1 Chronicles 28:9;
Psalm 1:1–3; Psalm 34:18; Psalm 37:5–7;
Psalm 55:22; Matthew 5:10–12; John 6:37;
Romans 8:37; Colossians 3:12–14;
1 Peter 4:16

Heavenly Father, hold my faith together. Life leaves me weak and weary, tired of fighting, and I need Your help in surrendering to Your will. I need You to hold me and give me hope.